A MASTERCLASS IN DRAWING & PAINTING

LANDSCAPES

SKY, SEA, LAKES, TOWN & COUNTRYSIDE

A MASTERCLASS IN DRAWING & PAINTING

LANDSCAPES

SKY, SEA, LAKES, TOWN & COUNTRYSIDE

Learn to produce beautiful compositions in oils, acrylics, gouache, water paints, pencils and charcoal
With expert step-by-step tutorials and over 30 projects shown in more than 800 photographs

SARAH HOGGETT & ABIGAIL EDGAR

LORENZ BOOKS

This edition is published by Lorenz Books,
an imprint of Anness Publishing Ltd,
Blaby Road, Wigston, Leicestershire LE18 4SE,
info@anness.com

www.lorenzbooks.com; www.annesspublishing.com

If you like the images in this book and would like to investigate using them for publishing, promotions or advertising, please visit our website www.practicalpictures.com for more information.

A CIP catalogue record for this book is available from the British Library.

Publisher: Joanna Lorenz
Editorial Director: Helen Sudell
Project Editor: Rosie Gordon
Designer: Nigel Partridge
Photographer: Martin Norris
Production Controller: Wendy Lawson

PUBLISHER'S NOTE

Although the advice and information in this book are believed to be accurate and true at the time of going to press, neither the authors nor the publisher can accept any legal responsibility or liability for any errors or omissions that may have been made nor for any inaccuracies nor for any loss, harm or injury that comes about from following instructions or advice in this book.

Parts of this book were previously published in *The Practical Encyclopedia of Drawing*, *The Practical Encyclopedia of Watercolour*, *The Practical Encyclopedia of Acrylics, Oils and Gouache*, and *How to Paint and Draw*.

ACKNOWLEDGEMENTS

The authors and publishers are grateful to the following for permission to reproduce paintings and sketches: Gerry Baptist: page 76 (bottom left); Joan Elliot Bates: page 72 (top); Mike Bernard: page 76 (bottom right); Oliver Bevan: page 73 (bottom right); Madge Bright: page 39 (top); Pip Carpenter: pages 39 (bottom), 162 (top); James Crittendon: page 75 (bottom); Patrick Cullen: page 72 (bottom left and right); David Curtis: pages 77 (top), 164 (top); Doug Dawson: page 74 (bottom); Paul Dyson: page 165 (top); Timothy Easton: page 43 (bottom), 164 (bottom), 167 (bottom); Abigail Edgar: pages 40 (all), 41 (bottom left and right), 42, 46 (bottom left and right), 47 (all), 48 (left, centre and top right), 50 (top), 52 (top), 54 (top), 60 (top), 62 (all), 64 (top), 66 (all), 122–123, 168–169; Trudy Friend: pages 41 (top), 43 (top), 46 (top); David Gould: page 77 (bottom); Wendy Jelbert: pages 36 (right), 48 (bottom right), 56 (top), 58 (top), 98–99, 170–171; Ronald Jesty: pages 163 (top), 165 (bottom); Maureen Jordan: page 76 (top); Geoff Marsters: page 37 (right); Juliette Palmer: page 75 (top); Karen Raney: page 73 (top right), 74 (top), 166 (bottom); Ian Sidaway: pages 32 (top right, bottom left), 33 (top and bottom), 36 (left), 37 (top and bottom left), 162 (bottom); Jackie Simmonds: page 166 (top); Effie Waverlin: page 32 (bottom right), 33 (centre); Albany Wiseman: pages 34–35, 167 (top).
For permission to reproduce photographs: Jon Hibberd: page 50 (bottom), 52 (bottom), 54 (bottom left), 56 (bottom left), 64 (bottom left), 180, 238; Martin Norris: page 60 (bottom).

Special thanks must go to the following artists for their step-by-step demonstrations: Ray Balkwill: pages 244–249; Diana Constance: pages 88–93, 146–151; Martin Decent: pages 38, 82–87, 130–135; Joe Francis Dowden: pages 220–225, 232–237; Abigail Edgar: pages 49, 53, 58–59, 63, 67, 94–99, 112–115, 116–119, 156–159, 176–179, 188–191, 204–209, 216–219, 226–231, 238–243; Timothy Easton: pages 130–135, 192–197; Wendy Jelbert: pages 210–215; Beverley Johnston: pages 126–129; Vincent Milne: pages 51, 54–55, 56–57, 61, 64–65, 180–183, 184–187; Melvyn Petterson: pages 104–107, 136–139, 172–175, 198–203; John Raynes: pages 120–125; Paul Robinson: pages 152-155; Albany Wiseman: pages 44–45, 100–103, 108–111.

Contents

Introduction

Landscapes are probably the most popular of all subjects for artists – and with good reason. From high mountain peaks to lush valley floors, raging torrents to calm ponds, sylvan oases to arid deserts, the natural world is infinitely varied and endlessly fascinating. Man-made landscapes, too – whether they be remote, picturesque villages perched on a hillside or urban settings in which old and new are intriguingly juxtaposed – can have tremendous visual appeal.

Despite its popularity, however, landscape drawing and painting has its own particular challenges. With some subjects (still lifes, for example), pretty much everything – the composition, the background, the lighting – is under your control. You can spend time arranging your subject, moving things around until you are happy with the composition. If you choose to work with artificial lighting, you can ensure that the quality and intensity of that light remain constant throughout the painting session – and you can leave the set-up for days, or even weeks, in the knowledge that nothing will have changed when you return to it.

▲ Learning how to apply paint, charcoal or pencil and blend for atmospheric effect is essential for landscape artists.

▲ Capturing the tranquillity of a scene with reflective water is a great exercise in observation and composition.

▼ The form, colours and movement in swirling, crashing waves make a challenging project in watercolour.

Not so with landscapes! The vagaries of the weather mean that working in situ is often simply not feasible. Even when you are able to take your sketchbook and paints out on location, the quality and direction of the light are constantly changing, shadows come and go, and colours and tones can appear different from one minute to the next. Out of necessity, many artists are obliged to work at least part of the time from photographs. There is, however, no substitute for experiencing the landscape for yourself, even if all you are able to do at the time is make a few quick reference sketches. You will produce a far better result by painting a landscape that you have actually visited, where you have been able to explore different viewpoints and angles and pick out the essentials of the scene for yourself, than by working from a photo of a place you have never been to.

This book is designed to provide a thorough introduction to everything you need to become confident in this genre. After taking a look at the artists' tools and materials available, the book features a tutorial section, which sets out some of the technicalities of landscape drawing and painting. Here you will find guidance on how to tackle different lighting and weather conditions, as well on specific subjects

▶ Landscapes may be realistic, subdued, vivid or stylized – depending on the scene, time of day and the artist's style.

that often form an intrinsic part of a landscape, such as clouds, trees and foliage, or water. If you are a complete beginner, work through this section page by page, as it will help you build up the confidence to tackle more complex landscapes on your own. Alternatively, if you are more experienced and there are specific aspects of drawing and painting landscapes that you feel you need a little help with, dip into the book as a refresher course whenever you need to. Perhaps you want to experiment with different media, or bring more atmosphere or realism to your work – the projects and tutorials offer plenty of tips and inspiration.

The book is divided into two project sections: 'Town and Country' and 'Water and Sky'. Each part begins with a gallery of works by professional artists with commentary, and you may well find that this is useful as a source of ideas and inspiration. There follows a series of quick sketches and step-by-step projects covering a whole range of landscapes and media.

All the artists who have contributed to this book have many years' experience of drawing and painting. They work in a range of media, and their styles range from highly detailed, almost photo-realistic renditions to looser, expressive interpretations that explore the artist's personal and emotional response to the scene before his or her eyes. Even if a project is in a medium you do not normally use or in a style that does not particularly appeal to you, studying the way the artist has tackled the subject will give you invaluable insights that you can use in your own work. You may choose to copy the projects exactly, as a technical exercise to help you master new techniques or media; alternatively, you can use them as a starting point for your own explorations, picking out aspects that relate directly to your own chosen landscape. However you use them, they will add to your growing understanding of technical aspects of drawing and painting and enrich your awareness of the artistic choices open to you as a landscape artist.

◀ Aerial and linear perspective are essential for creating a sense of depth and distance.

▶ Close study of the effects of light and shadow can produce interesting results in any medium.

OIL PASTELS
DALER ROWNEY
OIL PASTELS
DALER ROWNEY
OIL PASTELS
DALER ROWNEY
OIL PASTELS
DALER ROWNEY
OIL PASTELS
PERMANENT MAGENTA
MAGENTA PERMANENT
PERMANENTMAGENTA
MAGENTA PERMANENTE
409
ROWNEY

Materials

If you are new to drawing and painting landscapes, you may well find the choice of materials on offer completely bewildering. This chapter sets out the pros and cons of each medium, and provides practical information on everything from selecting paper and brushes to priming and stretching canvases, so that you can make an informed choice about what is really essential.

Start with a selection of good-quality materials, adding new items as and when you need them. Think, too, about whether you are going to be working in the studio or outdoors, on location: you may well need a lighter, more portable kit for field work.

It is also worth trying out media that you might not previously have considered. If you love the luminosity of watercolour for portraying the fleeting effects of light, for example, why not see if you can create a similar effect with soft pastels? If you have mastered the art of applying layer upon layer of coloured pencil to create delicate, detailed nature studies, why not experiment with a looser, freer style for big, bold panoramas in oils or acrylics? Varying your approach will keep your work fresh by giving you new creative and technical challenges.

Monochrome media

For sketching and underdrawing, as well as for striking studies in contrast and line, there are many different monochrome media, all of which offer different qualities to your artwork. A good selection is the foundation of your personal art store, and it is worth exploring many media, including different brands, to find the ones you like working with.

Pencils

The grading letters and numbers on a pencil relate to its hardness. 9H is the hardest, down to HB and F (for fine) and then up to 9B, which is the softest. The higher the proportion of clay to graphite, the harder the pencil. A choice of five grades – say, a 2H, HB, 2B, 4B and 6B – is fine for most purposes.

Soft pencils give a very dense, black mark, while hard pencils give a grey one. The differences can be seen below – these marks were made by appying the same pressure to different grades of pencil. If you require a darker mark, do not try to apply more pressure, but switch to a softer pencil.

Water-soluble graphite pencils

There are also water-soluble graphite pencils, which are made with a binder that dissolves in water. Available in a range of grades, they can be used dry, dipped in water or worked into with a brush and water to create a range of watercolour-like effects. Water-soluble graphite pencils are an ideal tool for sketching on location, as they allow you to combine linear marks with tonal washes. Use the tip for fine details and the side of the pencil for area coverage.

Water-soluble graphite pencils

Graphite sticks

Solid sticks of graphite come in various sizes and grades. Some resemble conventional pencils, while others are shorter and thicker. You can also buy irregular-shaped chunks and fine graphite powder, and thinner strips of graphite in varying degrees of hardness that fit into a barrel with a clutch mechanism to feed them through.

Graphite sticks are capable of making a wider range of marks than conventional graphite pencils. For example, you can use the point or edge of a profile stick to make a thin mark, or stroke the whole side of the stick over the paper to make a broader mark.

Charcoal

The other monochromatic drawing material popular with artists is charcoal. It comes in different lengths and in thin, medium, thick and extra-thick sticks. You can also buy chunks that are ideal for expressive drawings. Stick charcoal is very brittle and powdery, and is great for broad areas of tone.

Compressed charcoal is made from charcoal dust mixed with a binder and fine clay and pressed into shape. Sticks and pencils are available. Unlike stick charcoal, charcoal pencils are ideal for detailed, linear work. As with other powdery media, drawings made in charcoal should be sprayed with fixative to hold the pigment in place and prevent smudging during and after working on the piece.

Thick and thin charcoal sticks

Pen and ink

With so many types of pens and colours of ink available, not to mention the possibility of combining linear work with broad washes of colour, this is an extremely versatile medium and one that is well worth exploring. Begin by making a light pencil underdrawing of your subject, then draw over with pen – but beware of simply inking over your pencil lines, as this can look rather flat and dead. When you have gained enough confidence, your aim should be to put in the minimum of lines in pencil, simply enough to ensure you have the proportions and angles right, and then do the majority of the work in pen.

Dip pens and nibs

A dip pen does not have a reservoir of ink; as the name suggests, it is simply dipped into the ink to make marks. Drawings made with a dip pen have a unique quality, as the nib can make a line of varying width depending on how much pressure you apply. You can also turn the pen over and use the back of the nib to make broader marks. As you have to keep reloading with ink, it is difficult to make a long, continuous line – but for many subjects the rather scratchy, broken lines are very attractive.

When you first use a new nib it can be reluctant to accept ink. To solve this, rub it with a little saliva.

Nibs and dipping pens

Rollerball, fibre-tip and sketching pens

Rollerball and fibre-tip pens are ideal for sketching out ideas, although finished drawings made using these pens can have a rather mechanical feel to them, as the line does not vary in width. This can sometimes work well as an effect. By working quickly with a rollerball you can make a very light line by delivering less ink to the nib. Fibre-tip and marker pens come in a range of tip widths, from super-fine to calligraphic-style tips, and also in a wide range of colours. Sketching pens and fountain pens enable you to use ink on location without having to carry bottles of ink.

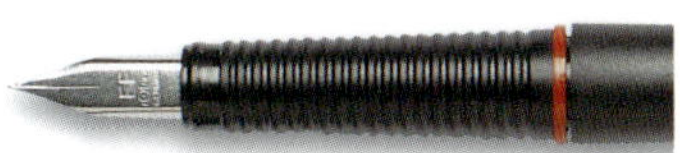

Sketching pen

Fibre-tip pen

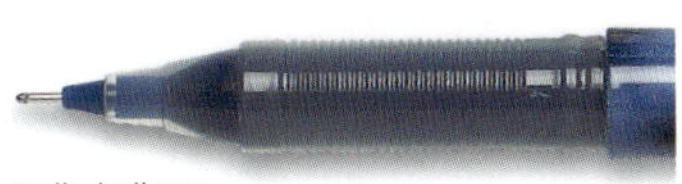

Rollerball pen

Bamboo, reed and quill pens

The nib of a bamboo pen delivers a 'dry', rather coarse line. Reed and quill pens are flexible and give a subtle line that varies in thickness. The nibs break easily, but can be recut with a knife.

Quill and bamboo pens

Inks

The two types of ink used by artists are waterproof and water-soluble. The former can be diluted with water, but are permanent once dry, so line work can be worked over with washes without any fear of it being removed. They often contain shellac, and thick applications dry with a sheen. The best-known is Indian ink, actually from China. It makes great line drawings. It is deep black but can be diluted to give a beautiful range of warm greys.

Water-soluble inks can be reworked once dry, and work can be lightened and corrections made. Do not overlook watercolours and soluble liquid acrylics – both can be used like ink but come in a wider range of colours.

Waterproof ink

Water-soluble ink

Liquid acrylic

Coloured drawing media

Containing a coloured pigment and clay held together with a binder, coloured pencils are impregnated with wax so that the colour holds to the support with no need for a fixative. They are especially useful for making coloured drawings on location, as they are a very stable medium and are not prone to smudging. Mixing takes place optically on the surface of the support rather than by physical blending, and all brands are inter-mixable, although certain brands can be more easily erased than others; so always try out one or two individual pencils from a range before you buy a large set. Choose hard pencils for linear work and soft ones for large, loosely applied areas of colour.

Box of pencils ▲
Artists who work in coloured pencil tend to accumulate a vast range in different shades – the variance between one tone and its neighbour often being very slight. This is chiefly because you cannot physically mix coloured pencil marks to create a new shade (unlike watercolour or acrylic paints). So, if you want lots of different greens in a landscape, you will need a different pencil for each one.

Water-soluble pencils

Most coloured-pencil manufacturers also produce a range of water-soluble pencils, which can be used to make conventional pencil drawings and blended with water to create watercolour-like effects. In recent years, solid pigment sticks that resemble pastels have been introduced that are also water-soluble and can be used in conjunction with conventional coloured pencils or on their own.

Wet and dry ▼
Water-soluble pencils can be used dry, the same way as conventional pencils.

Conté crayons and pencils

The best way to use Conté crayons is to snap off a section and use the side of the crayon to block in large areas, and a tip or edge for linear marks.

The pigment in Conté crayons is relatively powdery, so, like soft pastels and charcoal, it can be blended by rubbing with a finger, rag or torchon. Conté crayon drawings benefit from being given a coat of fixative to prevent smudging. However, Conté crayons are harder and more oily than soft pastels, so you can lay one colour over another, letting the under-colour show through.

Conté is also available in pencils, which contain wax and need no fixing (setting); the other benefit is that the tip can be sharpened to a point.

Conté crayons ▼
These small, square-profile sticks are available in boxed sets of traditional colours. Drawings made using these traditional colours are reminiscent of the wonderful chalk drawings of old masters such as Michelangelo or Leonardo da Vinci.

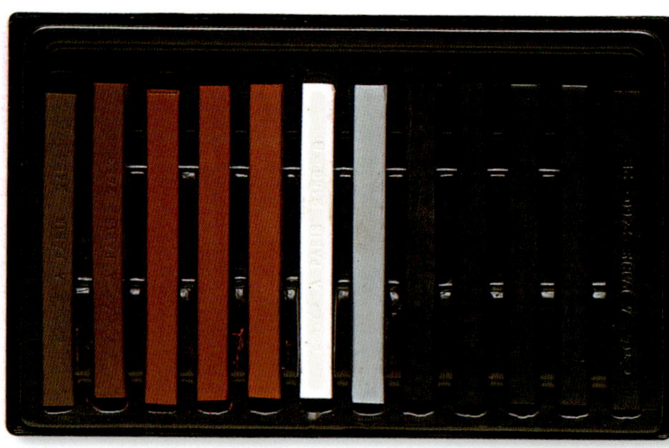

Conté pencils ▼
As they can be sharpened to a point, Conté pencils are ideal for drawings that require precision and detail.

Pastels

Working in pastels is often described as painting rather than drawing, as the techniques used are often similar to those used in painting. Pastels are made by mixing pigment with a weak binder, and the more binder used the harder the pastel will be. Pastels are fun to work with and ideal for making colour sketches as well as producing vivid, dynamic artwork.

Soft pastels

As soft pastels contain relatively little binder, they are prone to crumbling. For this reason they have a paper wrapper to help keep them in one piece. Even so, dust still comes off, and can easily contaminate other colours nearby. The best option is to arrange your pastels by colour type and store them in boxes.

Pastels are mixed on the support either by physically blending them or by allowing colours to mix optically. The less you blend, the fresher the image looks. For this reason, pastels are manufactured in a range of hundreds of tints and shades.

As pastels are powdery, use textured paper to hold the pigment in place. You can make use of the texture of the paper in your work. Spray soft pastel drawings with fixative to prevent smudging. You can fix (set) work in progress, too – but colours may darken, so do not overdo it.

Hard pastels

One advantage of hard pastels is that, in use, they do not shed as much pigment as soft pastels, therefore they will not clog the texture of the paper as quickly. For this reason, they are often used in the initial stages of a work that is completed using soft pastels. Hard pastels can be blended together by rubbing, but not as easily or as seamlessly as soft pastels.

Hard pastels

Box of soft pastels ▼
When you buy a set of pastels, they come packaged in a compartmentalized box so that they do not rub against each other and become dirtied.

Oil pastels

Made by combining fats and waxes with pigment, oil pastels are totally different to pigmented soft and hard pastels and should not be mixed with them. Oil pastels can be used on unprimed drawing paper and they never completely dry.

Oil-pastel sticks are quite fat and therefore not really suitable for detailed work or fine, subtle blending. For bold, confident strokes, however, they are absolutely perfect.

Oil-pastel marks have something of the thick, buttery quality of oil paints. The pastels are highly pigmented and available in a good range of colours. If they are used on oil-painting paper, they can be worked in using a solvent such as white spirit (paint thinner), applied with a brush or rag. You can also smooth out oil-pastel marks with wet fingers. Oil and water are not compatible, and a damp finger will not pick up colour.

Oil pastels can be blended optically on the support by scribbling one colour over another. You can also create textural effects by scratching into the pastel marks with a sharp implement – a technique known as sgraffito.

Less crumbly than soft pastels, and harder in texture, oil pastels are round sticks and come in various sizes.

A box of oil pastels

Pastel pencils

A delight to use, the colours of pastel pencils are strong, yet the pencil shape makes them ideal for drawing lines. If treated carefully, they do not break – although they are more fragile than graphite or coloured pencils. The pastel strip can be sharpened to a point, making pastel pencils ideal for describing detail in drawings that have been made using conventional hard or soft pastels.

Available in a comprehensive range of colours, pastel pencils are clean to use and are ideal for linear work. Ideally, store them in a jar with the tips upward to prevent breakage.

Pastel pencils

Watercolour paint

One of the most popular media, watercolour paint comes in pans, which are the familiar compressed blocks of colour that need to be brushed with water to release the colour; or tubes of moist paint. The same finely powdered pigments bound with gum arabic solution are used to make both types. The pigments provide the colour, while the gum arabic allows the paint to adhere to the paper, even when diluted.

It is a matter of personal preference whether you use pans or tubes. The advantage of pans is that they can be slotted into a paintbox, making them easily portable, and this is something to consider if you often paint on location. Tubes, on the other hand, are often better if you are working in your studio and need to make a large amount of colour for a wash. With tubes, you need to remember to replace the caps immediately, otherwise the paint will harden and become unusable. Pans of dry paint can be rehydrated.

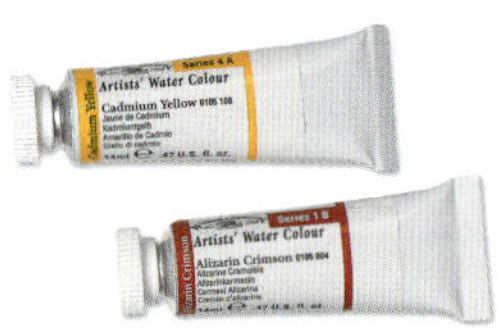

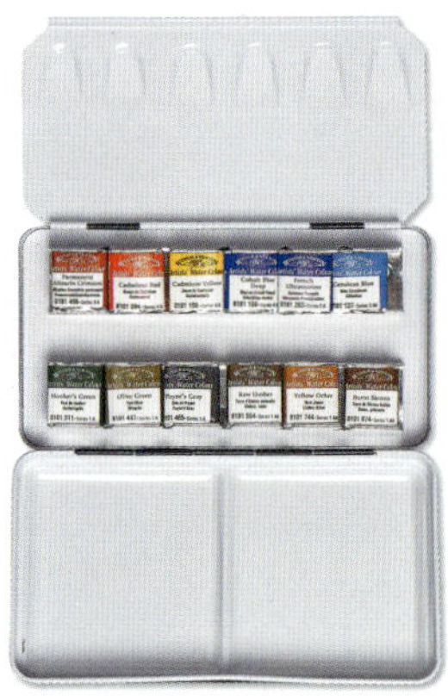

Tubes (above) and pans (right) of watercolour

Grades of paint

There are two grades of watercolour paint: artists' and students' quality. Artists' quality paints are the more expensive, because they contain a high proportion of good-quality pigments. Students' quality paints contain less pure pigment and more fillers.

If you come across the word 'hue' in a paint name, it indicates that the paint contains cheaper alternatives instead of the real pigment. Generally speaking, you get what you pay for: artists' quality paints tend to produce more subtle mixtures of colours. The other thing that you need to think about when buying paints is their permanence. The label or the manufacturer's catalogue should give you the permanency rating. In the United Kingdom, the permanency ratings are class AA (extremely permanent), class A (durable), class B (moderate) and class C (fugitive). The ASTM (American Society for Testing and Materials) codes for light-fastness are ASTM I (excellent), ASTM II (very good) and ASTM III (not sufficiently light-fast). Some pigments, such as alizarin crimson and viridian, stain more than others: they penetrate the fibres of the paper and cannot be removed.

Working with watercolour paint

Different pigments have different characteristics. Although we always think of watercolour as being transparent, you should be aware that some pigments are actually slightly opaque and will impart a degree of opacity to any colours with which they are mixed. These so-called opaque pigments include all the cadmium colours and cerulean blue. The only way to learn about the paints' characteristics is to use them, singly and in combination with other colours.

Judging colours

It is not always possible to judge the colour of paints by looking at the pans in your palette, as they often look dark. In fact, it is very easy to dip your brush into the wrong pan, so always check before you put brush to paper.

Even when you have mixed a wash in your palette, do not rely on the colour, as watercolour paint always looks lighter when it is dry. The only way to be sure what colour or tone you have mixed is to apply it to paper and let it dry. It is always best to build up tones gradually until you get the effect you want. The more you practise, the better you will get at anticipating results.

Appearances can be deceptive ▼ These two pans look very dark, almost black. In fact, one is Payne's grey and the other a bright ultramarine blue.

Test your colours ▼ Keep a piece of scrap paper next to you as you work so that you can test your colour mixes before you apply them.

Gouache paint

Made using the same pigments and binders found in watercolour, gouache is a water-soluble paint. The addition of *blanc fixe* – a precipitated chalk – gives the paint its opacity. Because gouache is opaque you can paint light colours over darker ones – unlike traditional watercolour, where the paint's inherent transparency means that light colours will not cover any darker shades that lie underneath.

Recently some manufacturers have begun to introduce paint made from acrylic emulsions and starch. The best quality gouache contains a high proportion of coloured pigment. Artists' gouache tends to be made using permanent pigments that are light-fast. The 'designers' range uses less permanent pigments, as designers' work is intended to last for a short time.

Working with gouache paint

All of the equipment and techniques used with watercolour can be used with gouache. Like watercolour, gouache can be painted on white paper or board; due to its opacity and covering power it can also be used on a coloured or toned ground and over gesso-primed board or canvas. Gouache is typically used on smoother surfaces than might be advised for traditional watercolour, as the texture of the support is less of a creative consideration.

If they are not used regularly, certain gouache colours are prone to drying up over time. Gouache is water-soluble so can be rehydrated when dry, but dried-up tubes can be difficult to use. On the support, you can remedy any cracking of the dried paint by re-wetting it. During your work on the painting, you need assured brushwork when applying new paint over previous layers to avoid muddying the colours. Certain dye-based colours are particularly strong and, if used beneath other layers of paint, can have a tendency to bleed. With practice, this is easy to cope with.

Tubes of gouache paint

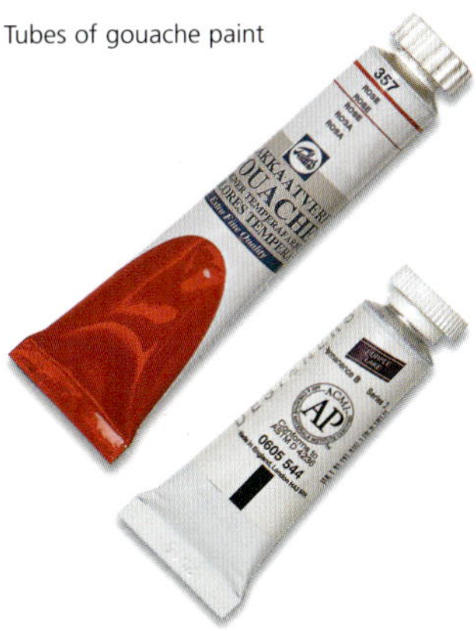

Change in colour when dry ▼
Gouache paint looks slightly darker when dry than it does when wet, so it is good practice to test your mixes on a piece of scrap paper – although, with practice, you will quickly learn to make allowances for this.

Wet gouache paint

Dry gouache paint

Bold brushwork ▲
Gouache remains soluble when it is dry, so if you are applying one colour over another, your brushwork needs to be confident: a clean stroke, as here, will not pick up paint from the first layer.

Wet into wet ▲
Like transparent watercolour paint, gouache paint can be worked wet into wet (as here) or wet on dry.

Muddied colours ▲
If you scrub paint over an underlying colour, you will pick up paint from the first layer and muddy the colour of the second layer, as here. To avoid this effect, see bold brushwork, left.

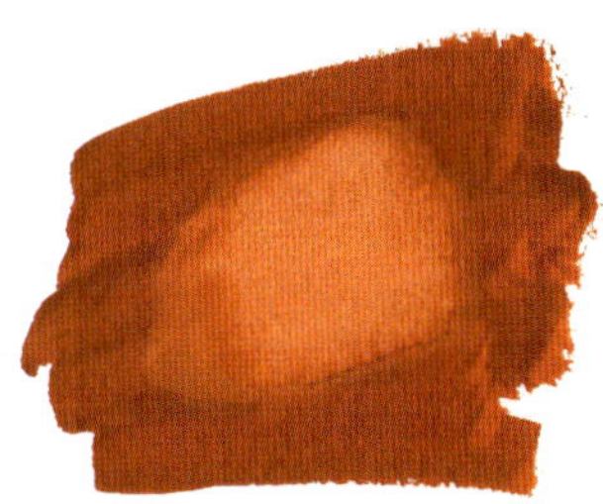

Removing dry paint ▲
Dry paint can be re-wetted and removed by blotting with an absorbent paper towel.

Oil paint

There are two types of traditional oil paint – professional, or artists', grade and the less expensive students' quality. The difference is that artists' paint uses finely ground, high-quality pigments, which are bound in the best oils and contain very little filler, while students' paints use less expensive pigments and contain greater quantities of filler to bulk out the paint. The filler is usually *blanc fixe* or aluminium hydrate, both with a very low tinting strength.

Students' quality paint is often very good and is, in fact, used by students, amateur painters and professionals.

Tubes or tubs? ▼
Oil paint is sold in tubes containing anything from 15 to 275ml (1 tbsp to 9fl oz). If you tend to use a large quantity of a particular colour – for toning grounds, for example – you can buy paint in cans containing up to 5 litres (8¾ pints).

Drawing with oils ▶
Oil bars consist of paint with added wax and drying agents. The wax stiffens the paint, enabling it to be rolled into what resembles a giant pastel.

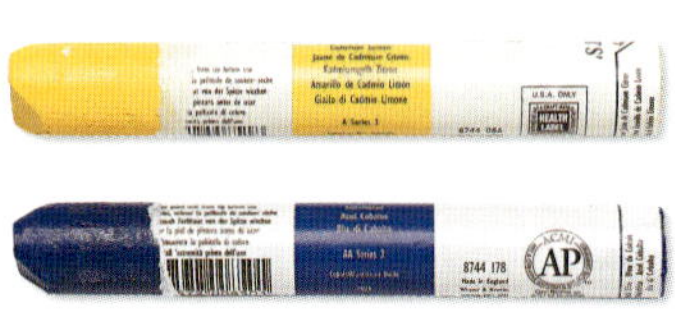

Water-mixable oil paint

Linseed and safflower oils that have been modified to be soluble in water are included in water-mixable oil paint. Once the paint has dried and the oils have oxidized, it is as permanent and stable as conventional oil paint. Some water-mixable paint can also be used with conventional oil paint, although its mixability is gradually compromised with the more traditional paint that is added.

Alkyd oil paints

Although they contain synthetic resin, alkyd oils are used in the same way as traditional oil paints and can be mixed with the usual mediums and thinners.

Alkyd-based paint dries much faster than oil-based paint, so it is useful for underpainting prior to using traditional oils and for work with glazes or layers. However, you should not use alkyd paint over traditional oil paint, as its fast drying time can cause problems.

Working with oil paint

However you use oil paint, it is most important to work on correctly prepared supports and always to work 'fat over lean'. 'Fat' paint, which contains oils, is flexible and slow to dry, while 'lean' paint with little or no oil, is inflexible and dries quickly. Oil paintings can be unstable and prone to cracking if lean paint is placed over fat. For this reason, any underpainting and initial blocking in of colour should always be done using paint that has been thinned with a solvent and to which no extra oil has been added. Oil can be added to the paint in increasing amounts in subsequent layers. You must allow plenty of drying time between layers.

Working 'fat over lean' ▲
The golden rule when using oil paint is to work 'fat' (or oily, flexible paint) over 'lean', inflexible paint that has little oil.

Glazing with oils ▲
Oils are perfect for glazes (transparent applications of paint over another colour). The process is slow, but quick-drying glazing mediums can speed things up.

Judging colour ▼
Colour mixing with oils is relatively straightforward: the colour that you apply wet to the canvas will look the same when it has dried, so (unlike acrylics, gouache or watercolour) you do not need to make allowances for changes as you paint. However, colour that looks bright when applied can begin to look dull as it dries. You can revive the colour in sunken patches by 'oiling out' – that is, by brushing an oil-and-spirit mixture or applying a little retouching varnish over the area.

Wet oil paint

Dry oil paint

Acrylic paint

Unlike oil paint, acrylic paint dries quickly and the paint film remains extremely flexible and will not crack. Acrylic paint can be mixed with a wide range of acrylic mediums and additives and is thinned with water. The paint can be used with a range of techniques, from thick impasto, as with oil paint, to the semi-transparent washes of watercolour. Indeed, most techniques used in both oil and watercolour painting can be used with acrylic paint. Acrylic paints come in three different consistencies. Tube paint tends to be of a buttery consistency and holds its shape when squeezed from the tube. Tub paint is thinner and more creamy in consistency, which makes it easier to brush out and cover large areas. There are also liquid acrylic colours with the consistency of ink, sold as acrylic inks.

You may experience no problems in mixing different brands or consistencies, but it is always good practice to follow the manufacturer's instructions.

◀ Liquid acrylics
The consistency of liquid acrylic is like writing ink.

Tubs ▲
Acrylic paint in tubs stores easily.

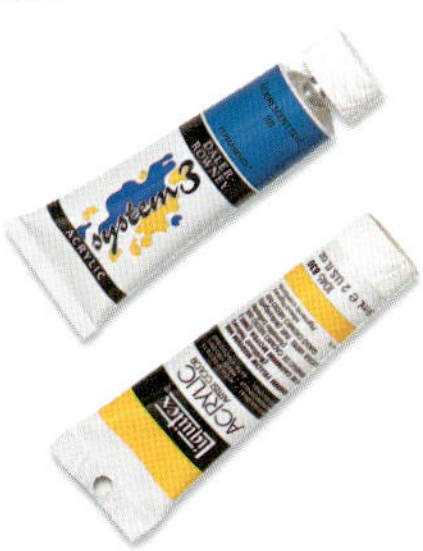

Tubes ▶
Acrylic paints in tubes are convenient to carry and use with a palette.

Working with acrylic paint

Being water soluble, acrylic paint is very easy to use, requiring only the addition of clean water. Water also cleans up wet paint after a work session. Once it has dried, however, acrylic paint creates a hard but flexible film that will not fade or crack and is impervious to more applications of acrylic or oil paint or their associated mediums or solvents.

Acrylic paint dries relatively quickly: a thin film will be touch dry in a few minutes and even thick applications dry in a matter of hours. Unlike oil paints, all acrylic colours, depending on the thickness of paint, dry at the same rate and darken slightly. A wide range of mediums and additives can be mixed into acrylic paint to alter and enhance its handling characteristics.

Another useful quality in acrylic mediums is their good adhesive qualities, making them ideal for collage work – sticking paper or other materials on to the support.

Extending drying time ▲
The drying time of acrylic paint can be extended by using a retarding medium, which gives you longer to work into the paint and blend colours.

Covering power ▲
Acrylic paint that is applied straight from the tube has good covering power, even when you apply a light colour over a dark one, so adding highlights to dark areas is easy.

Texture gels ▲
Various gels can be mixed into acrylic paint to give a range of textural effects. These can be worked in while the paint is still wet.

Glazing with acrylics ▲
Acrylic colours can be glazed by thinning the paint with water, although a better result is achieved by adding an acrylic medium.

Shape-holding ability ▲
Like oil paint, acrylic paint that is applied thickly, straight from the tube, holds its shape and the mark of the brush as it dries, which can allow you to use interesting textures.

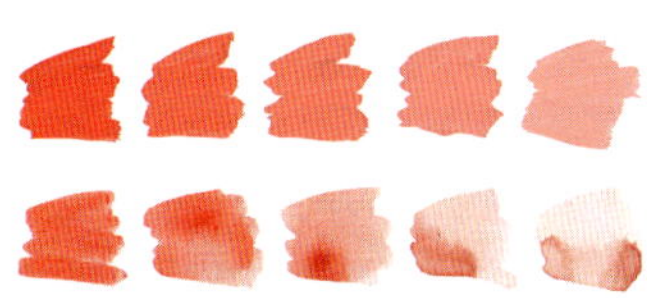

Lightening acrylic colours ▲
Acrylic colours can be made lighter by adding white paint, which maintains opacity (above top), or by adding water, which increases transparency (bottom).

Palettes

The surface on which an artist arranges colours prior to mixing and applying them to the support is known as a palette. (Somewhat confusingly, it is the same word that is used to describe a range of colours used by an artist, or the range of colours found in a painting.) The type of palette that you use depends on the medium in which you are working, but you will probably find that you need more space for mixing colours than you might imagine.

A small palette gets filled with colour mixes quickly and it is a false economy to clean the mixing area too often: you may waste usable paint or mixed colours that you could use again. Always buy the largest palette practical.

Wooden palettes

Flat wooden palettes in the traditional kidney or rectangular shapes with a thumb hole are intended for use with oil paints. They are made from hardwood, or from the more economical plywood.

Before you use a wooden palette with oil paint for the first time, rub linseed oil into the surface of both sides. Allow it to permeate the surface. This will prevent oil from the paint from being absorbed into the surface of the palette and will make it easier to clean. Re-apply linseed oil periodically and a good wooden palette will last for ever.

Wooden palettes are not recommended for acrylic paint, however, as hardened acrylic paint can be difficult to remove from the surface.

Holding and using the palette ▼
Place your thumb through the thumb hole and balance the palette on your arm. Arrange pure colour around the edge. Position the dipper(s) at a convenient point, leaving the centre of the palette free for mixing colours.

Wooden palette ▲
Artists working with oil paints generally prefer a wooden palette. Always buy one that is large enough to hold all the paint and mixes that you intend to use.

White palettes

Plastic palettes are uniformly white. They are made in both the traditional flat kidney and rectangular shapes. The surface is impervious, which makes them ideal for use with either oil or acrylic paint. They are easy to clean, but the surface can become stained after using very strong colours such as viridian or phthalocyanine blue.

There are also plastic palettes with wells and recesses, intended for use with watercolour and gouache. The choice of shape is entirely subjective, but it should be of a reasonable size.

White porcelain palettes offer limited space for mixing. Intended for use with watercolour and gouache, they are aesthetically pleasing but can easily be chipped and broken.

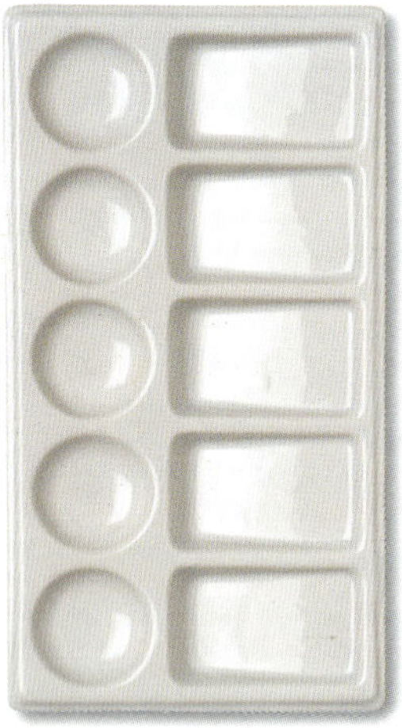

Slanted-well palette ▲
This type of porcelain palette is used for mixing gouache or watercolour. The individual colours are placed in the round wells and mixed in the rectangular sections.

Disposable palettes

A relatively recent innovation is the disposable paper palette, which can be used with both oils and acrylics. These come in a block and are made from an impervious parchment-like paper. A thumb hole punched through the block enables it to be held in the same way as a traditional palette; alternatively, it can be placed flat on a surface. Once the work is finished, the used sheet is torn off and thrown away.

Paper palette ▲
Disposable palettes are convenient and make cleaning up after a painting session an easy task.

Stay-wet palette

Intended for use with acrylic paints, the stay-wet palette will stop paints becoming dry and unworkable if left exposed to the air for any length of time. The palette consists of a shallow, recessed tray into which a water-impregnated membrane is placed. The paint is mixed on the moist membrane. If you like, you can simply spray acrylic paint with water to keep it moist while you work. If you want to leave a painting halfway through and come back to it later, you can place a plastic cover over the tray (many come with their own lids), sealing the moist paint in the palette. The entire palette can be stored in a cool place or even in the refrigerator, and will keep for up to three weeks. If the membrane does dry out, simply re-wet it using a spray bottle of water.

Stay-wet palette

Containers for water, solvents and oil

Although a regular supply of containers, such as empty jam jars, can be recycled from household waste and are just as good as a container bought for the purpose, several types of specially designed containers are available from art supply stores.

Among the most useful are dippers – small, open containers for oil and solvent that clip on to the edge of the traditional palette. Some have screw or clip-on lids to prevent the solvent from evaporating when it is not in use. You can buy both single and double dippers, like the one shown on the right. Dippers are useful when you want to work at speed, for example when painting on location.

Dipper ▼
Used in oil painting, dippers are clipped on to the side of the palette and contain small amounts of oil or medium and thinner.

Field box ▲
Most of the major manufacturers sell field boxes specifically for use on location, which include a small brush and perhaps a sponge as well as a selection of watercolour paints.

Acrylic and oil additives

Artists working with oils and acrylics will need to explore paint additives, which bring various textures and effects to their work. Although oil paint can be used straight from the tube, it is usual to alter the paint's consistency by adding a mixture of oil or thinner (solvent). Simply transfer the additive to the palette a little at a time and mix it with the paint. Manufacturers of acrylic paints have also introduced a range of mediums and additives that allow artists to use the paint to its full effect. Oils and mediums are used to alter the consistency of the paint, allowing it to be brushed out smoothly or to make it dry more quickly. Once exposed to air, the oils dry and leave behind a tough, leathery film that contains the pigment. Different oils have different properties – for example, linseed dries relatively quickly but yellows with age so is only used for darker colours.

A painting medium is a ready-mixed painting solution that may contain various oils, waxes and drying agents. The oils available are simply used as a self-mixed medium. Your choice of oil or medium will depend on several factors, including cost, the type of finish required, the thickness of the paint being used, as well as the range of colours employed.

There are several alkyd-based mediums on the market. They all speed the drying time of the paint, which can reduce waiting between applications. Some alkyd mediums are thixotropic; these are initially stiff and gel-like but, once worked, become clear and loose. Other alkyd mediums contain inert silica and add body to the paint; useful for impasto techniques where thick paint is required. Talking to an art stockist will help you decide which you need.

Types of finish

When acrylic paints dry they leave a matt or gloss surface. Gloss or matt mediums can be added, singly or mixed, to give the desired finish.

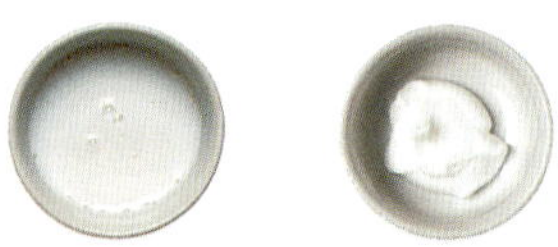

Gloss and matt mediums ▲
Both gloss (left) and matt (right) mediums are white liquids. Matt increases transparency and can be used to make matt glazes. Gloss will brighten and enhance the depth of colour.

Retarding mediums

Acrylic paints dry quickly. Although this is generally considered to be an advantage, there are occasions when you might want to take your time over a particular technique or a specific area of a painting – when you are blending colours together or working wet paint into wet, for example. Adding a little retarding medium slows down the drying time of the paint considerably, keeping it workable for longer. Retarding medium is available in both gel and liquid form – experiment to find out which suits you best.

Retarding gel

Gel mediums

With the same consistency as tube colour, gel mediums are available as matt or gloss finishes. They are added to the paint in the same way as fluid mediums. They increase the brilliance and transparency of the paint, while maintaining its thicker consistency. Gel medium is an excellent adhesive and extends drying time. It can be mixed with various substances such as sand or sawdust to create textural effects.

Modelling paste ▲
These pastes dry to give a hard finish, which can be sanded or carved into using a sharp knife.

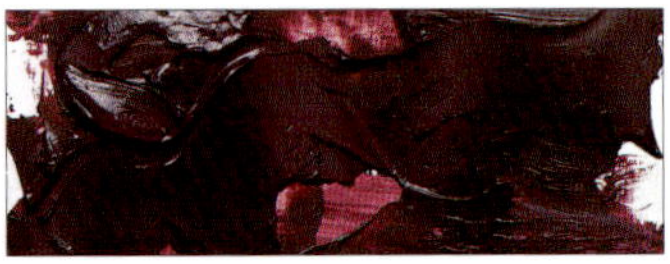

Heavy gel medium ▲
Mixed with acrylic paint, heavy gel medium forms a thick paint that is useful for impasto work.

Flow-improving mediums

Adding flow-improving mediums reduces the water tension, increasing the flow of the paint and its absorption into the surface of the support.

One of the most useful applications for flow-improving medium is to add a few drops to very thin paint, which can tend to puddle rather than brush out evenly across the surface of the support. This is ideal when you want to tone the ground with a thin layer of acrylic before you begin your painting.

When a flow-improving medium is used with slightly thicker paint, a level surface will result, with little or no evidence of brushstrokes.

The medium can also be mixed with paint that is going to be sprayed, as it greatly assists the flow of paint and also helps to prevent blockages within the spraying mechanism.

Without flow-improving medium

With flow-improving medium

Oils and thinners

If you dilute oil paints using only oil; the paint may wrinkle or take too long to dry. A thinner makes the paint eaiser to brush out, and then evaporates. The amount of thinner that you use depends on how loose or fluid you want the paint to be. If you use too much, however, the paint film may become weak and prone to cracking. Ideally, any thinner that you use should be clear and should evaporate easily from the surface of the painting without leaving any residue. There are a great many oils and thinners available. The common ones are listed below.

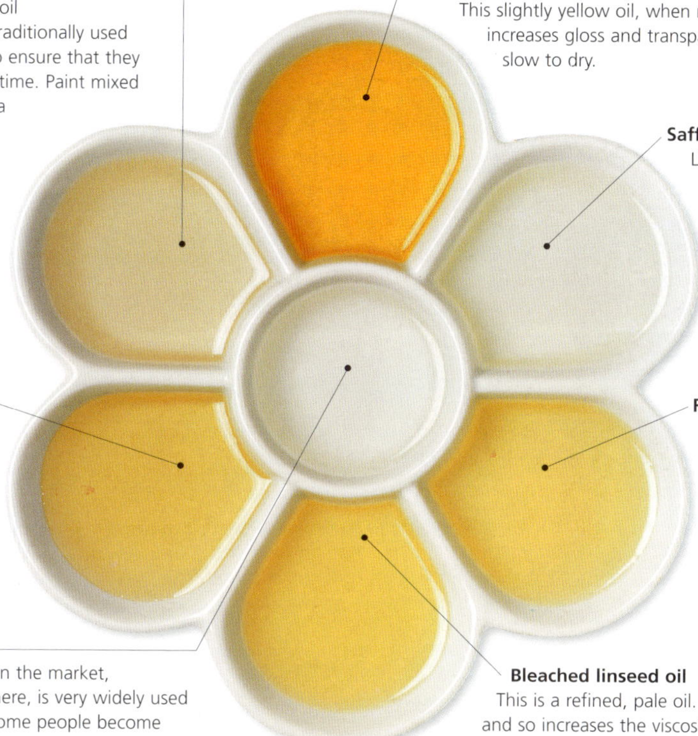

Poppy oil
Slow-drying poppy oil is very pale and is traditionally used with pale colours to ensure that they do not yellow over time. Paint mixed with poppy oil has a beautiful buttery consistency.

Cold-pressed linseed oil
This slightly yellow oil, when mixed with paint, increases gloss and transparency. It is reasonably slow to dry.

Safflower oil
Like poppy oil, safflower oil is traditionally used with light colours. It also slows down the drying time of the paint.

Stand linseed oil
A pale oil that is slightly thicker than other linseed oils. It is very slow to dry but leaves the paint with a tough, flexible finish.

Refined linseed oil
Slow to dry and pale yellow in colour, refined linseed oil increases gloss and flow.

Thinner
Of all the thinners on the market, turpentine, shown here, is very widely used but smells strong. Some people become allergic to it.

Bleached linseed oil
This is a refined, pale oil. It flows very easily, and so increases the viscosity of the paint. It dries slightly faster than other linseed oils.

Turpentine
The strongest and best of all the thinners used in oil painting, turpentine has an extremely strong smell. Old turpentine can discolour and become gummy if exposed to air and light. To help prevent this, store it in cans or dark glass jars.

White spirit
Paint thinner or white spirit is clear and has a milder smell than turpentine. It does not deteriorate and dries faster than turpentine. However, it can leave the paint surface matt.

Oil of spike lavender
Unlike other solvents, which speed up the drying time of oil paint, oil of spike lavender slows the drying time. It is very expensive. Like turpentine and white spirit, it is colourless.

Low-odour thinners
Various low-odour thinners have come on to the market in recent years. The drawback of low-odour thinners is that they are relatively expensive and dry slowly. However, for working in a confined space or for those who dislike turpentine's smell, they are ideal.

Citrus solvents
You may be able to find citrus thinners. They are thicker than turpentine or white spirit but smell wonderful. They are more expensive than traditional thinners and slow to evaporate.

Liquin
Just one of a number of oil and alkyd painting mediums that speed up drying time considerably – often to just a few hours – liquin also improves flow and increases the flexibility of the paint film. It is excellent for use in glazes, and resists age-induced yellowing well.

Paintbrushes

Oil-painting brushes are traditionally made from hog bristles, which hold their shape well and can also hold a substantial amount of paint. Natural hair brushes are usually used for watercolour and gouache, and can be used for acrylics and fine detail work in oils, if cleaned thoroughly afterward. Synthetic brushes are good quality and hard-wearing, and less expensive.

Brush shapes

Rigger brush

Liner brush

Rounded or 'mop' brush

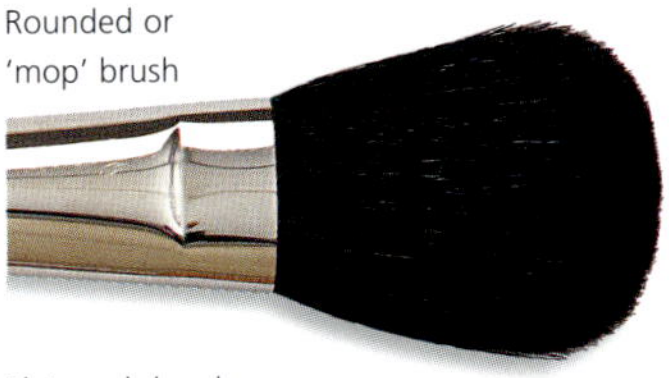

Flat wash brush

Flat brushes ▼
These brushes have square ends and hold a lot of paint. Large flat brushes are useful for blocking in and covering large areas quickly and smoothly, whatever type of paint you are using – ask your stockist to advise which type of bristle or hair is best for your preferred medium. Short flats, known as 'brights', hold less paint and are stiffer. They make precise, short strokes, ideal for impasto work and detail.

Short flat brush

Large flat brush

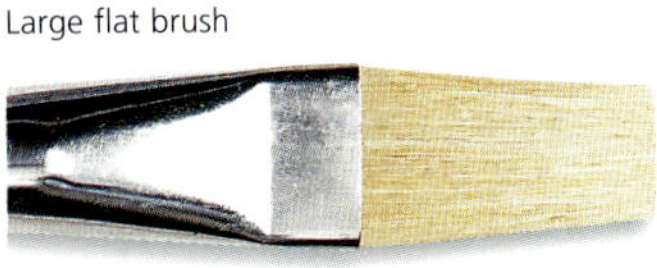

Brushes for fine detail ◄
A rigger brush is very long and thin. It was originally invented for painting the rigging on ships in marine painting – hence the name. A liner is a flat brush which has the end cut away at an angle. Both of these brushes may be made from natural or synthetic fibres.

Wash brushes ◄
The wash brush has a wide body, which holds a large quantity of paint. It is used for covering large areas with a uniform wash of paint. There are two types: rounded or 'mop' brushes are commonly used with watercolour and gouache, and flat wash brushes are more suited to oils and acrylics.

Round brushes ▼
These round-headed brushes are used for detail and for single strokes. Larger round brushes hold a lot of paint and are useful for the initial blocking in. The point can quickly disappear, as it becomes worn down by the rubbing on the rough support. The brushes shown here are made of natural hair.

Small round brush

Large round brush

Unusually shaped brushes ▼
Fan blenders are used for mixing colours on the support and drybrushing. A filbert combines some qualities of a flat and round brush.

Fan blender

Filbert

Cleaning brushes

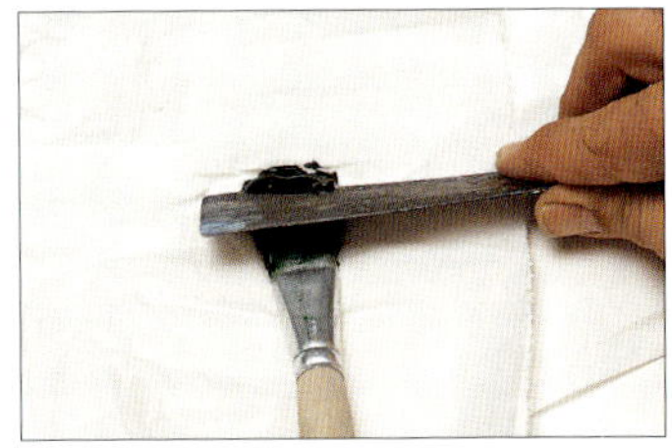

1 Cleaning your brushes thoroughly will make them last longer. Wipe off any excess wet paint on a rag or a piece of newspaper. Take a palette knife and place it as close to the metal ferrule as possible. Working away from the ferrule toward the bristles, scrape off as much paint as you can.

2 Pour a small amount of household white spirit (paint thinner) – or water, if you are using a water-based paint such as acrylic or gouache – into a jar; you will need enough to cover the bristles of the brush. Agitate the brush in the jar, pressing it against the sides to dislodge any dried-on paint.

3 Rub household detergent into the bristles with your fingers. Rinse in clean water until the water runs clear. Reshape the bristles and store the brush in a jar with the bristles pointing upward, so that they hold their shape.

Other paint applicators

Brushes are only part of the artist's toolbox. You can achieve great textual effects by using many other types of applicator, from knives to rags.

Artists' palette and painting knives

Palette knives are intended for mixing paint with additives on the palette, scraping up unwanted paint from the palette or support, and general cleaning. Good knives can also be found in DIY or decorating stores.

You can create a wide range of marks using painting knives. In general, the body of the blade is used to spread paint, the point for detail and the edge for making crisp linear marks.

Regardless of the type of knife you use, it is very important to clean it thoroughly after use. Paint that has dried on the blade will prevent fresh paint from flowing evenly off the blade. Do not use caustic paint strippers on plastic blades, as they will dissolve; instead, peel the paint away.

Steel knives ▲
A wide range of steel painting and palette knives is available. In order to work successfully with this method of paint application, you will need several.

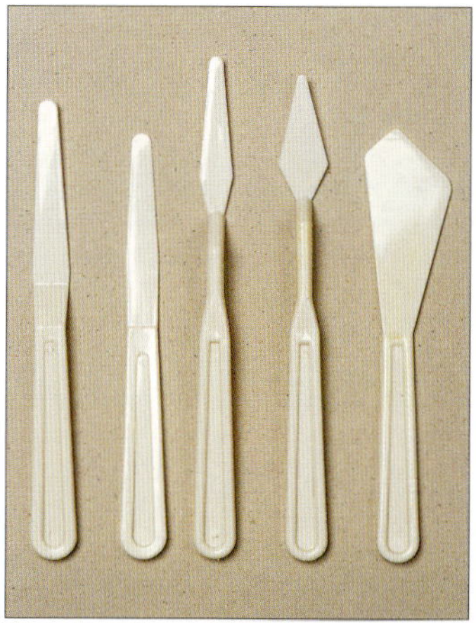

Plastic knives ▲
Less expensive and less durable than steel knives, plastic knives manipulate watercolour and gouache paints better than their steel counterparts.

Alternative applicators

Paint can be applied and manipulated using almost anything. The cutlery drawer and toolbox are perhaps a good starting point, but you will no doubt discover plenty of other items around the home that you can use. Card, rags, wire (steel) wool and many other objects around the house can all be pressed into service.

Rag (left) and wire wool

Natural sponge (left) and man-made sponge

Paint shapers, foam and sponge applicators

A relatively new addition to the artist's range of tools are paint shapers. They closely resemble brushes, but are used to move paint around in a way similar to that used when painting with a knife. Shapers can be used to apply paint and create textures, and to remove wet paint. Instead of bristles, fibre or hair, the shaper is made of a non-absorbent silicone rubber.

Nylon foam is used to make both foam brushes and foam rollers. Foam rollers can cover large areas quickly. Sponge applicators are useful for initial blocking in. Both are available in a range of sizes and, while they are not intended as substitutes for the brush, they are used to bring a different quality to the marks they make.

Paint shaper

Foam roller

Sponge applicator

Natural and man-made sponges ◄
With their pleasing texture, man-made and natural sponges are used to apply washes and textures, and are invaluable for spreading thin paint over large areas and for making textural marks. They are also useful for mopping up spilt paint, and for wiping paint from the support in order to make corrections. Man-made sponges can be cut to shape.

Supports

A 'support' is the name for the surface on which a drawing or painting is made. It needs to be physically stable and resistant to deterioration from the corrosive materials used, as well as the atmosphere. It should also be light enough to be transported easily. Importantly, choose a support with the right texture for the media, marks and techniques you intend to use.

There are many papers available and they vary enormously in quality and cost, depending on whether the paper is handmade, machine-made or mould-made. The thickness of a paper is described in one of two ways. The first is in pounds (lbs) and describes the weight of a ream (500 sheets). The second is in grams (gsm), and describes the weight of one square metre of a single sheet. Sheets vary in size.

Many papers can also be bought in roll form and cut to the size required. You can also buy pads, which are lightly glued at one end, from which you tear off individual sheets as required. One of the benefits of buying a pad of paper is that it usually has a stiff cardboard back, which you can lean on when working on location and means that you do not have to carry a heavy drawing board around with you. Sketchbooks have the same advantage.

Preparing your own drawing surfaces

It is both satisfying and surprisingly easy to prepare your own drawing surfaces. Acrylic gesso, a kind of primer that is used to prepare a surface such as canvas or board when painting in oils or acrylics, can also be painted on to paper to give a brilliant white, hard surface that receives graphite and coloured pencil beautifully.

To make a surface that is suitable for pastels, you can mix the gesso with pumice powder. You can also buy ready-made pastel primer.

To create a toned or coloured ground, simply tint the gesso by adding a small amount of acrylic paint to it in the appropriate colour.

Drawing papers

The most common drawing paper has a smooth surface that is suitable for graphite, coloured pencil and ink work. Papers for use with watercolour also make ideal drawing supports. These papers come in three distinctly different surfaces – HP (hot-pressed) papers, which are smooth; CP (cold-pressed) papers, also known as NOT, or 'Not hot-pressed' papers, which have some surface texture; and rough papers which have a rougher texture.

Art and illustration boards are made from cardboard with paper laminated to the surface. They offer a stable, hard surface on which to work and are especially useful for pen line and wash, but can also be used with graphite and coloured pencil. They do not buckle when wet, as lightweight papers are prone to do, and are available in a range of sizes and surface textures, from very smooth to rough.

Coloured paper ▲
The main advantage of making a drawing on coloured paper is that you can choose a colour that complements the subject and enhances the mood of your drawing. Coloured papers can be used with all drawing media.

Pastel papers ▲
Papers for use with pastels are coated with pumice powder or tiny cork particles that hold the pigment and allow for a build-up of colour. They are available in a range of natural colours that complement the pastel shades.

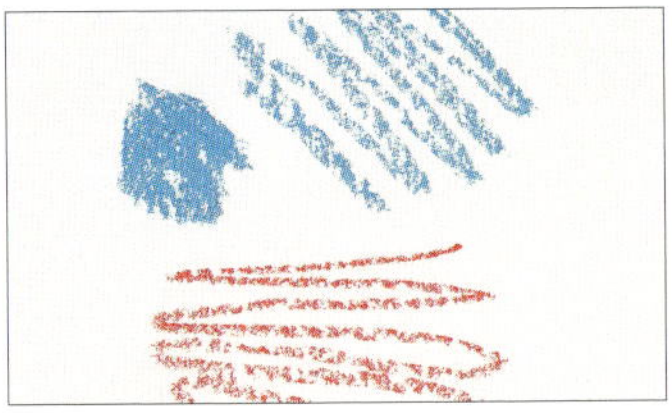

Drawing paper ◄
A medium-weight paper is suitable for most purposes, but if you are planning to use water-soluble pencils with water, a heavier paper is best. For fine, detailed work, choose a smooth paper. For charcoal and pastel work, a rougher paper with some 'tooth' to pick up the pigment is generally best.

Sketchbooks ◄
Available in a wide range of formats and containing all the above-mentioned papers, sketchbooks are great for sketching down rough ideas and drawing on location.

Painting papers

Papers for use with paints need to be carefully chosen. Some hold paint well, other papers are textured or smooth, and of course there are many different shades – all these factors will affect your work. Both oil and acrylic papers have a texture similar to canvas and sheets can be bought loose or bound together in blocks. Although they are not suitable for work that is meant to last, they are perfect for sketching and colour notes.

Types of paper ▼
From left to right: hot-pressed (HP), NOT and rough watercolour papers. Hot-pressed paper has a very smooth surface, while the other two are progressively more textured.

Smooth watercolour papers provide ideal surfaces for gouache and line work. The papers are found in various thicknesses and with three distinct surfaces – rough, hot-pressed (which is smooth) and NOT or cold-pressed, which has a slight texture. Rough paper has a prominent 'tooth' that will leave some deeper cavities unfilled when a wash is laid over.

Watercolour boards tend to have either a rough or a hot-pressed surface. Illustration board tends to be very smooth and is intended for use with gouache and linework.

Provided it is primed with acrylic primer, paper and illustration board can be used for painting in oils.

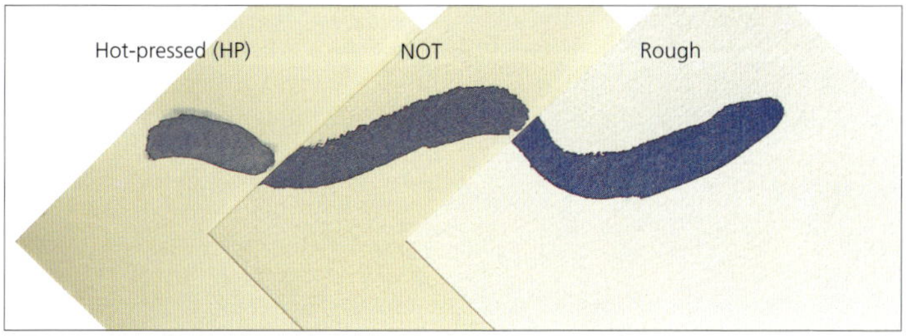

Canvas paper and board ▼
Artists' canvas boards are made by laminating canvas – or paper textured to look like canvas – on to cardboard. They are made in several sizes and textures and are ideal for use when painting on location. However, take care not to get them wet, as the cardboard backing will disintegrate. They can also be easily damaged if you drop them on their corners. They are ready sized and can be used for painting in both oils and acrylics.

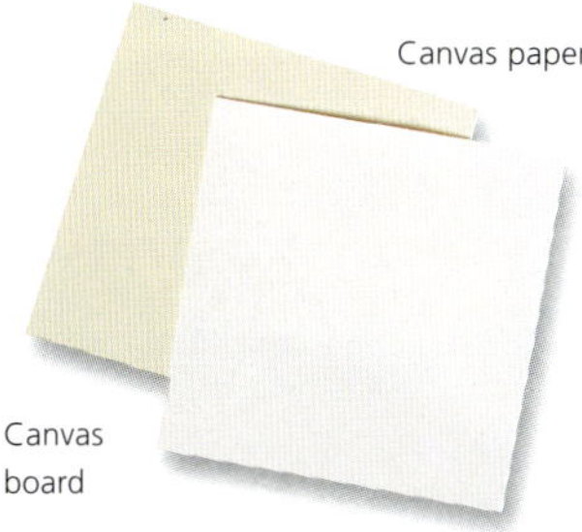

Tinted papers ▼
Although they are sometimes frowned upon by watercolour purists, tinted papers can be useful when you want to establish an overall colour key. Ready-made tinted papers are a good alternative to laying an initial flat wash.

Stretching paper for watercolours

Papers come in different weights, which refer to the weight of a ream (500 sheets) and can vary from 90lb (185 grams per square metre or gsm) to 300lb (640gsm) or more. The heavier the paper, the more absorbent. Papers that are less than 140lb (300gsm) in weight need to be stretched before use so that they do not cockle when wet.

1 Dip a sponge in clean water and wipe it over the paper, making sure you leave no part untouched. Make sure a generous amount of water has been applied over the whole surface and that the paper is perfectly flat.

2 Moisten four lengths of gum strip and place one along each long side of the paper. (Only gummed brown paper tape is suitable; masking tape will not adhere.) Repeat for the short edge of the paper. Leave to dry. (In order to be certain that the paper will not lift, you could staple it to the board.)

Canvases

Without doubt, canvas is the most widely used support for both oil and acrylic work. Several types of canvas are available, made from different fibres. The most common are made from either cotton or linen, both of which can be purchased ready stretched and primed to a range of standard sizes (although there are suppliers who will prepare supports to any size) or on the roll by the yard (metre) either primed or unprimed. Unprimed canvas is easier to stretch.

Cotton duck ▼
With a more regular (some people might say more mechanical) weave than linen, cotton duck is also less expensive than linen.

Linen canvas ▼
This tough material is made from the fibres of the flax plant, *Linum usitatissimum*. The seeds of the plant are also pressed to make linseed oil, used by artists. Linen canvas is available in a number different textures and weights, from very fine to coarse. The fibres are stronger than cotton fibres, which means that the fabric is less likely to sag and stretch over time.

Stretching canvas

Canvas must be stretched taut over a rectangular wooden frame before use. For this you will need stretcher bars and wooden wedges. Stretcher bars are usually made of pine and are sold in pairs of various standard lengths. They are pre-mitred and each end has a slot-in tenon joint. Longer bars are morticed to receive a cross bar (recommended for supports over 75 x 100cm/30 x 40in).

1 Tap the bars together to make a frame. Arrange the canvas on a flat surface and put the frame on top. Staple the canvas to the back of the frame, ensuring it stays taut.

2 Tap wooden wedges lightly into the inside of each corner. These can be hammered in further to allow you to increase the tension and tautness of the canvas if necessary.

Priming canvas

Canvas is usually sized and primed (or, increasingly, just primed) prior to being worked on. This serves two purposes. The process not only tensions the fabric over the stretcher bars but also (and more importantly in the case of supports used for oil) seals and protects the fabric from the corrosive agents present in the paint and solvents. Priming also provides a smooth, clean surface on which to produce work.

In traditional preparation, the canvas is given a coat of glue size. The most widely used size is made from animal skin and bones and is known as rabbit-skin glue. It is available as dried granules or small slabs. When mixed with hot water the dried glue melts; the resulting liquid is brushed over the canvas to seal it.

Increasingly, acrylic emulsions are used to size canvas. Unlike rabbit-skin glue, the emulsions do not have to be heated but are used diluted with water.

The traditional partner to glue size is an oil-based primer. Lead white, which is toxic, together with titanium white and flake white, are all used in oil-based primers. To penetrate the canvas the primer should be the consistency of single (light) cream; dilute it with white spirit (paint thinner) if necessary.

Traditional primer can take several days to dry, however; a modern alternative is an alkyd primer, which dries in a couple of hours.

Primers based on acrylic emulsion are easier to use. These are often known as acrylic gesso, although they are unlike traditional gesso. Acrylic primer should not be used over glue size, but it can be brushed directly on to the canvas. Acrylic primers can be used with both oil and acrylic paint, but oil primers should not be used with acrylic paints.

Primer can be applied with a brush or a palette knife. With a brush the weave of the canvas tends to show.

If you want to work on a toned ground, add a small amount of colour to the primer before you apply it. Add oil colour to oil primer and acrylic colour to acrylic primer.

Boards

Several types of wooden board make good supports for oil and acrylic work. There are three types of board in common use: plywood, hardboard (masonite) and medium-density fibreboard (MDF). You can obtain boards from DIY stores, and have them cut to size. Plywood is made up of a wooden core sandwiched between a number of thin layers of wood glued together. Hardboard is a composite panel made by hot pressing steam-exploded wood fibres with resin, and is less prone to warping than solid wood or plywood. MDF is made in the same way, with the addition of a synthetic resin. It has a less hard and glossy face side than standard dense hardboard. All these boards come in a range of sizes. If used at a size where they begin to bend, mount rigid wooden battens on the reverse to reinforce them.

Wood gives off acidic vapours that are detrimental to paint (for an example of how wood products deteriorate with age, think how quickly newspaper yellows). The solution is to prime the board with acrylic gesso, or glue canvas to the surface; a technique known as marouflaging.

Priming board

Wood was traditionally sized with rabbit-skin glue and then primed with a thixotropic primer in the same way as canvas; nowadays, most artists use ready-made acrylic primer or acrylic gesso primer, which obviates the need for sizing. Acrylic primer also dries much more quickly.

Before you prime your boards, make sure they are smooth and free of dust. You should also wipe over them with a rag dampened with methylated spirits to remove all traces of grease.

1 Using a wide, flat brush, apply primer over the board with vertical strokes. For a large surface, apply the primer with a paint roller. Allow to dry thoroughly, for at least an hour.

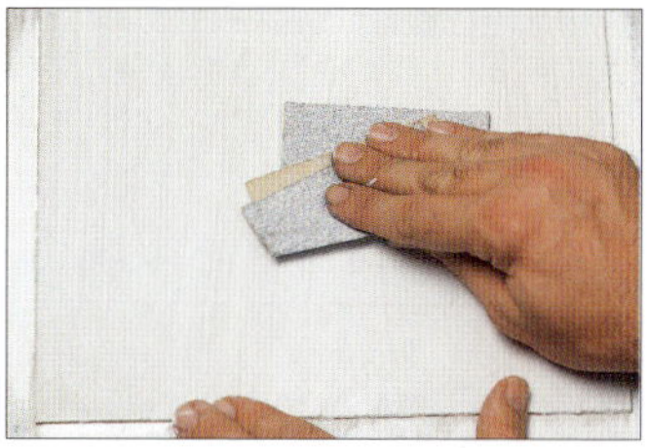

2 Rub the surface of the board with fine-grade sandpaper (abrasive paper) to smooth. Blow or dust off any powder to make the surface debris-free for the next coat of primer.

3 Apply another coat of primer, making smooth horizontal strokes. Allow to dry. Repeat as many times as you wish, sanding between coats.

Covering board with canvas

Canvas-covered board is a light painting surface that is useful when you are painting on location. It combines the strength and low cost of board with the texture of canvas. You can use linen, cotton duck or calico, which is cheap. When you have stuck the canvas let it dry for two hours in a warm room. Prime with acrylic primer before use.

1 Arrange the canvas on a flat surface. Place the board on the canvas. Allowing a 5cm (2in) overlap all around, cut out the canvas. Remove the canvas and using a wide, flat brush, liberally, but not thickly, brush matt acrylic medium all over the board.

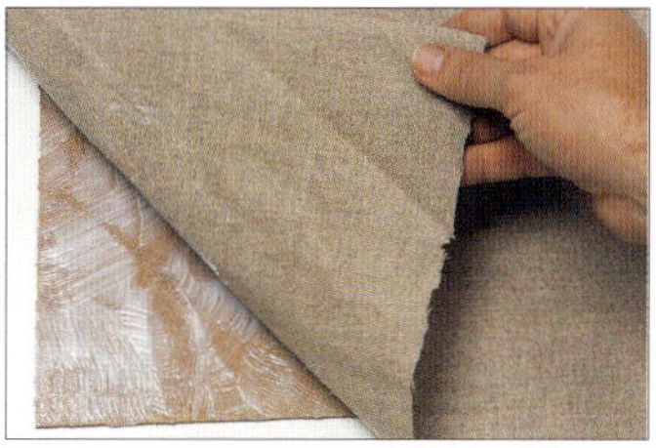

2 Place the canvas on the sticky side of the board and smooth it out with your fingertips, working from the centre outward. Brush acrylic medium over the canvas to make sure that it is firmly stuck down.

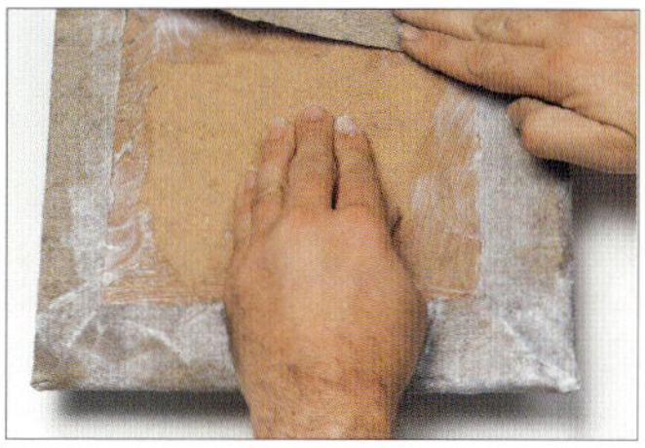

3 Place the board canvas side down on a bowl so that it does not stick to your work surface. Brush acrylic medium around the edges of the board. Fold over the excess canvas, mitring the corners, and brush more medium over the corners to stick them firmly.

Art essentials

There are a few other pieces of equipment that you will probably find useful in your painting, ranging from things to secure your work to the drawing board and easels to support your painting, to aids for specific painting techniques.

Boards and easels

The most important thing is that the surface on which you are working is completely flat and cannot wobble as you work. If you use blocks of watercolour paper, then the block itself will provide support; you can simply rest it on a table or on your knee. If you use sheets of watercolour paper, then they need to be firmly secured to a board. Buy firm boards that will not warp and buckle (45 x 60cm/18 x 24in is a useful size), and attach the paper to the board by means of gum strip or staples.

It is entirely a matter of personal preference as to whether or not you use an easel. There are several types on the market, but remember that watercolour paint is a very fluid liquid and can easily flow down the paper into areas that you do not want it to touch. Choose an easel that can be used flat and propped at only a slight angle. The upright easels used by oil painters are not really suitable for watercolour painting.

Portable box easel ▼
This easel includes a handy side drawer in which you can store all you need for a day's location work, as well as adjustable bars so that it can hold various sizes of drawing board firmly in place. Some easels can only be set at very steep angles, which is unsuitable for watercolour, so do check before you buy.

Table easel ►
This inexpensive table easel is adequate for most artists' needs. Like the box easel it can be adjusted to a number of different angles, allowing you to alter the angle to suit the technique you are using. It can also be stored neatly.

Other useful items

Various pieces of equipment come in handy, including a scalpel or craft (utility) knife: the fine tip allows you to prise up pieces of masking tape that have become stuck down too firmly without damaging the paper. You can also use a scalpel to scratch off fine lines of paint – a technique known as sgrafitto. Paper towel is invaluable for cleaning out paint palettes and lifting off or softening colour before it dries.

As you develop your painting style and techniques, you may want to add other equipment to the basic items shown here. You will probably assemble a selection of props, from bowls, vases and other objects for still lifes, to pieces of fabric and papers to use as backgrounds. Similarly, you may want to set aside pictures or photographs that appeal to you for use as reference material. The only real limit to what you can use is your imagination.

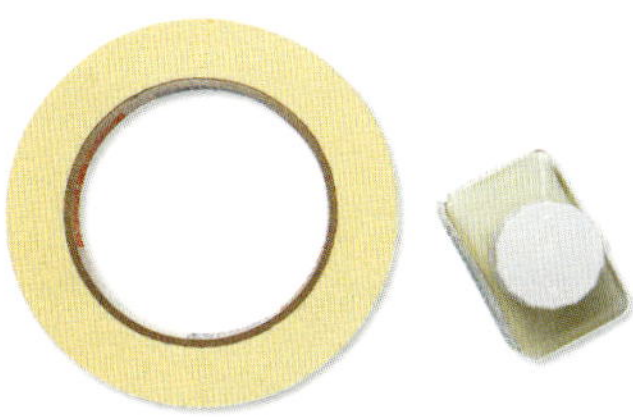

Masking tape and masking fluid ▲
One of the basic techniques in watercolour is masking. It is used to protect areas of the paper you want to keep unpainted. Depending on the size and shape of the area you want to protect, masking tape and masking fluid are most commonly used. Masking tape can also be used to secure heavy watercolour paper to a drawing board.

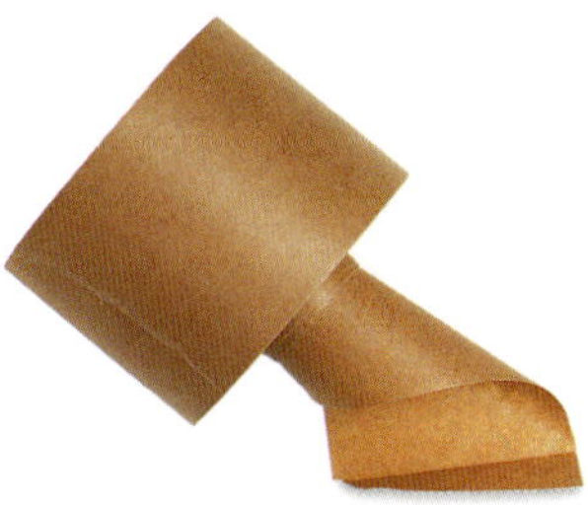

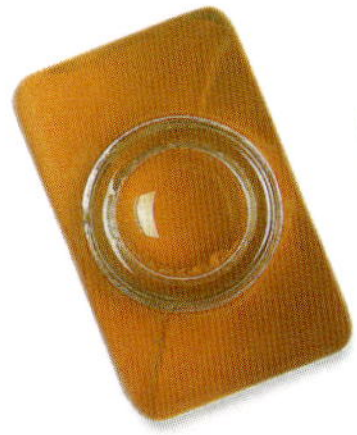

Gum arabic ▲
Adding gum arabic, a natural substance also called gum acacia, to watercolour paint increases the viscosity of the paint and slows down the drying time. This gives you longer to work. Add a few drops of the gum arabic to your paint and stir to blend. Gum arabic imparts a slight sheen on the paper, and increases the intensity of the paint colour.

Gum strip ◄
Gummed brown paper strip is essential for taping stretched lightweight watercolour paper to a board to ensure that it does not buckle. Leave the paper stretched on the drawing board until you have finished and the paint has dried, then simply cut it off, using a scalpel or craft (utility) knife and a metal ruler. Masking tape is not suitable for this purpose.

Eraser ◄
A kneaded eraser is useful for correcting the pencil lines of your underdrawing, and for removing the lines so that they do not show through the paint on the finished painting.

Sponge ▲
Natural or synthetic sponges are useful for mopping up excess water. Small pieces of sponge can be used to lift off colour from wet paint. Sponges are also used to apply paint.

Mahl stick ▲
This rod of wood (bamboo) with a soft leather ball at one end can be positioned over the work and leant on to steady the painting hand and protect your work from being smudged.

Varnishes

Used on finished oil and acrylic paintings, varnishes unify and protect the surface under a gloss or semi-matt sheen. Here are some of the most widely used.

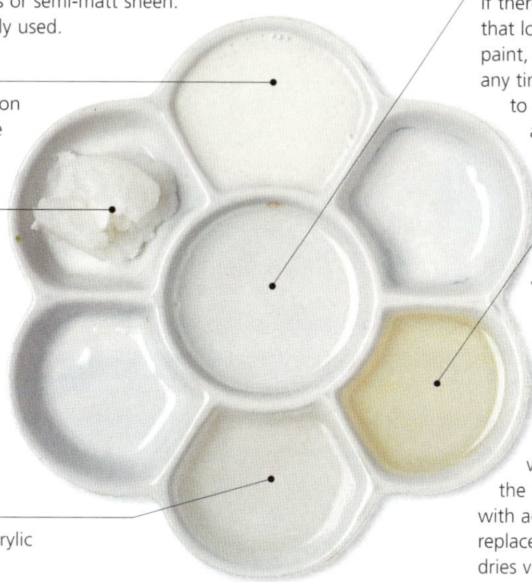

Acrylic matt varnish
Synthetic varnishes can be used on oil and acrylic paintings. The one shown here dries to a matt finish.

Wax varnish
Beeswax mixed with a solvent makes the wax varnish that is often used on oil paintings. The wax is brushed over the work and allowed to stand for a short time. The excess is then removed with a rag and the surface buffed. The more the surface is buffed, the higher the resulting sheen.

Acrylic gloss varnish
This synthetic varnish dries on acrylic paintings to a gloss finish.

Retouching varnish
If there are parts of your oil painting that look sunken, with dull looking paint, retouching varnish can be used at any time while the work is in progress to revive problem areas. Both damar and mastic thinned with solvent can be used as retouching varnish.

Damar varnish
For use on oil paintings, damar varnish is made from the resin of the damar tree, which is found throughout Indonesia and Malaysia. The resin is mixed with turpentine to create a slightly cloudy liquid. The cloudiness is caused by natural waxes in the resin, and clears as the varnish dries. Damar does yellow with age, but it is easy to remove it and replace it with a fresh coat. The varnish dries very quickly.

Tutorials

This chapter examines many of the most important elements of landscape drawing and painting. Skies, trees and foliage, lighting and weather conditions, close-up studies of bark and grasses, as well as more general topics such as perspective and composition, are all considered, as they are the keys to producing a good landscape picture.

In addition to sketches and other works by leading professional artists, you will find a series of short practice exercises in a range of popular media. By working through them, you will see how to apply the basic concepts in practice, and, once you have mastered the individual elements, you will have the necessary skills and confidence to use them in compositions of your own.

Whether you are a complete beginner or a more experienced artist looking for a refresher course on particular aspects of drawing and painting landscapes, this chapter is an invaluable resource that you can turn to time and time again.

Perspective

One of the many challenges in learning how to draw and paint is how to create the illusion of spatial depth on a flat suface. How can you make some objects appear close and others far away? This is done by using a technique known as perspective. At first sight, perspective may seem complex and confusing, but the basics are easy to understand and even a rudimentary grasp of the fundamentals will enable you to position elements in your work so that they appear to occupy their correct 'space' in the composition.

If you look straight down a road where only one façade of the buildings on each side is visible, the horizontal planes of the upper floors above eye level will appear to slope down through the length of the street. Horizontal lines below eye level will seem to slope upward. If the viewer of the picture is to be convinced that a road is receding into the distance, then you must reproduce these illusions. With practice, you may be able to do this by eye, but start by taking careful measurements.

Linear perspective

When extended from any receding surface all parallel lines ('perspective lines') meet at the 'vanishing point'. This point is on the 'horizon line', which runs across the field of vision. The horizon line is also known as the eye level, because it always runs horizontally across the field of view at eye level. All perspective lines that originate above the eye level run down to meet the vanishing point and all perspective lines that originate below the eye level run up. Vertical lines remain vertical.

The simplest form of perspective is one-, or single-point, perspective. This occurs when all the receding perspective lines meet at one single point. The vanishing point in one-point perspective always coincides with your centre of vision, directly in front of you.

Parallel lines receding away from the viewer ▼
In this simple illustration of one-point perspective the trees – which, in reality, are all of similar size – appear to get smaller the farther away they are. All perspective lines above eye level run down to the vanishing point (VP) and all perspective lines below eye level run up to the vanishing point.

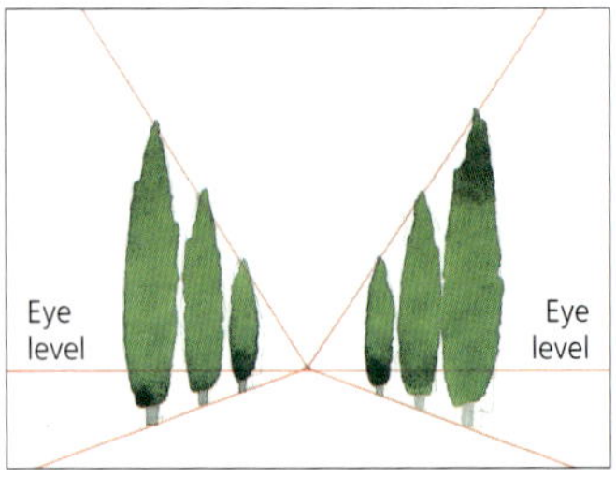

Parallel lines receding to one side ►
Here, all the elements on the front of the house are on the same plane and so they all meet at the same vanishing point (VP).

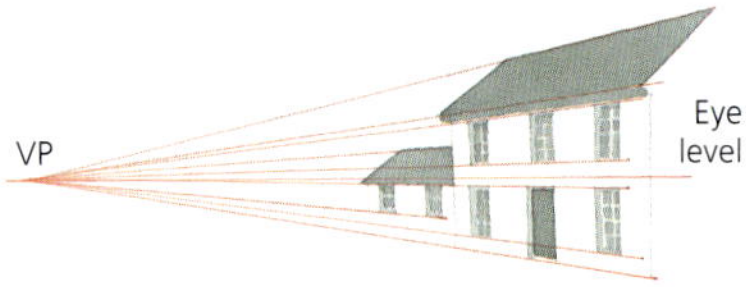

Street scene in single-point perspective ▼
In this scene, all the horizontal elements above eye level (for example, the roof lines and the tops and bottoms of the windows) appear to slope down toward the vanishing point, while those below eye level seem to slope up – although, in reality, the planes remain level along the road. If the houses were shown with equidistant planes (that is, without the lines of the roof and road appearing to slope toward the vanishing point), they would not look as if they were parallel to the viewer.

The roofs and many of the windows are above eye level and appear to slope down as the street recedes.

The pavement is below eye level and therefore appears to slope upward as the road recedes.

Two-point perspective

If two sides of an object can be seen at the same time, then two-point perspective comes into play. The principle remains the same, but because two surfaces are visible and both surfaces are at different angles, any parallel lines on those surfaces will eventually join together at their own vanishing point.

In two-point perspective, neither vanishing point falls at your centre of vision. Perspective lines on the right-hand side will converge at a vanishing point off to the right and perspective lines on the left-hand side will converge at a vanishing point off to the left. Even if you move to a position that is higher than your subject, the horizon line on which any vanishing points are situated will still run across your line of vision at eye level, so all perspective lines will run at an upward angle to meet it. Similarly, if you move to a position below your subject, so that you are looking up at it, all perspective lines will run down to meet the horizon line.

It is very easy to get so caught up in the technicalities of perspective that you lose sight of your drawing as a whole. Once you have mastered the basic principles of perspective, you should learn to trust your observational skills. Hold a pencil out in front of you to assess the angle of any horizontal lines as they recede toward their vanishing point. Now measure the distances between different elements of your subject carefully, ignoring any preconceptions that you may have about the relative sizes of things.

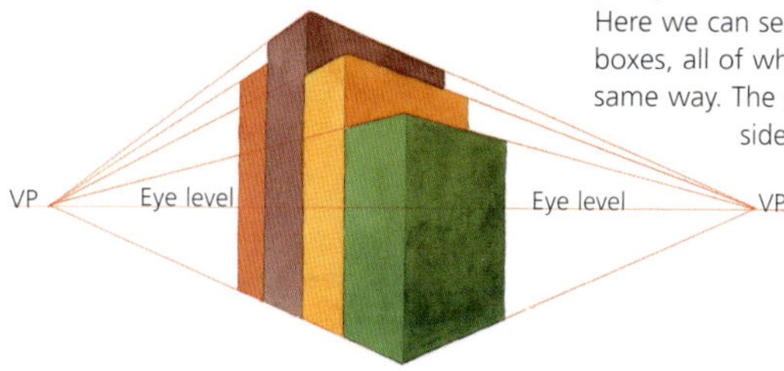

Two planes visible – two-point perspective ◄
Here we can see two sides of a row of boxes, all of which are oriented the same way. The perspective lines of each side of each box extend to the same vanishing point.

Multiple-point perspective

When several objects are arranged at different heights and angles, then multiple-point perspective comes into play. It looks a little more complicated, but the rules remain the same. Each object needs to be treated as a separate entity and its vanishing points and perspective lines should be plotted accordingly.

Several vanishing points in the same scene ►
Multiple-point perspective will be used if a building is viewed at a tangent, as the different sides of the building on view will have horizontal planes that extend to different vanishing points. In this example, both vanishing points are out of the picture; the moat façade, diminishing sharply, has a vanishing point close by, but the front elevation with the bridge is viewed at a less oblique angle and has a vanishing point that is farther out, far to the left of the picture area.

Objects at different angles – multiple-point perspective ▼
Here, three box-like shapes are resting on what might be a table top. Each box is facing in a slightly different direction, so each one needs to have separate vanishing points – as does the table, which is oriented differently to the boxes.

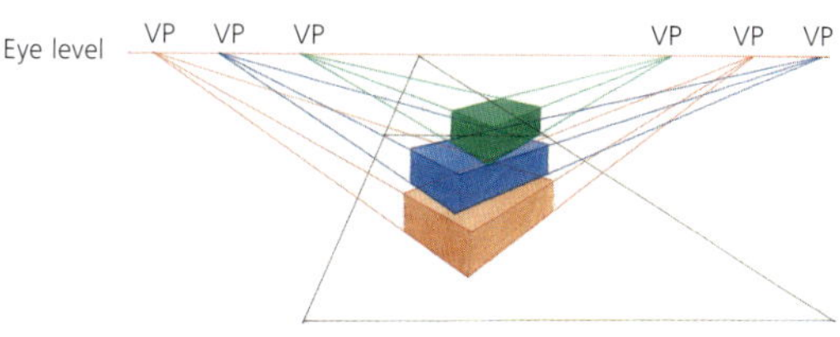

This side of the building is viewed from only a slight angle and so the horizontal lines recede only very gradually toward the vanishing points; the vanishing points themselves are far outside the picture area.

This side of the building recedes into the distance; the horizontal lines recede much more steeply, but the vanishing points are still outside the picture area. If you plot the vanishing points on a small-scale preliminary sketch you can then transpose the correct angles on to the full-size support.

Aerial perspective

Sometimes known as atmospheric perspective, aerial perspective refers to the way the atmosphere, combined with distance, influences and affects what you see. Being able to identify and utilize these effects will enable you to paint realistic and convincing three-dimensional landscapes.

Four things are directly influenced by distance: these are texture, colour, tone and size. The most obvious of these is size. Objects gradually appear smaller the farther away from you they are. You can see this most clearly by looking along a row of identically sized telegraph poles, fence posts or trees.

Second, detail and textures become less evident with distance. The texture and detail of objects that are nearby, in the foreground of a scene, are often large and in sharp focus; the texture and amount of detail visible in objects that are farther away is vague and less clearly defined. For instance, you could use textural techniques such as sponging or spattering to portray foreground pebbles and sand in a beach scene, or use vigorous brushstrokes to suggest foreground grasses, and reduce the amount of detail in the middle distance and background.

Third, colours seen in the foreground and near distance appear bright and vibrant because the warm colours – reds, oranges and yellows – are in evidence. Colours in the far distance appear much less bright. They are also cooler and contain more blue and violet. So use cool hues toward the horizon and warmer tones in the foreground.

Finally, tonal contrast is reduced with distance. If you were to paint all the trees in a scene the same tone, the spatial relationships would not be clear: it might look as if they were all standing in a row. Make the distant trees paler, on the other hand, and they will appear to recede. Sometimes, tonal contrast disappears completely: distant hills, for example, might appear as one pale mass of land.

The principles of aerial perspective apply not only to *terra firma* but also to the sky. Clouds appear larger when they are immediately overhead. The sky alters colour, too, being a warmer, deeper blue immediately overhead, gradually becoming paler and often with a cool yellow tinge as it falls towards the horizon and the far distance.

These effects of size, detail and colour are caused by our own visual limitations. They are also caused by the gases, dust and moisture present in our atmosphere, which create a veil through which light has to filter. In addition, all these effects are directly influenced not only by the time of day, but also by the season of the year, the location and the inherent local weather conditions.

As with any endeavour, planning is the key to success. You need to consider any perspective issues from the moment you begin a work and incorporate them from the outset. If you are unsure, make a sketch or working drawing before you begin work on the painting. This will allow you to resolve any possible problems in advance.

The effects of aerial perspective ▶ This simple landscape shows how atmosphere combined with distance influences the way we see things.

Landforms in the background are flat and uniform, whereas those in the foreground appear to have texture.

Colours in the foreground look warmer and brighter. Shapes are more defined than those in the background.

Detail is more apparent in the foreground, such as the long grasses shown by strokes of green.

A full range of tones can be seen in the foreground. Using very bright and very dark greens gives the effect of a sunny day, with contrasting sunlit and shaded leaves.

Clouds appear smaller the closer they are to the horizon.

Colours in the distance are cooler and less intense.

Clouds appear closer if they have more shape and depth of colour.

Tonal contrast is reduced in the background.

Composing landscapes

Although you may be painting what you can see, you still need to compose your picture. You have to make a decision about what viewpoint to take, which part of the scene to concentrate on, how much of the picture you will devote to the foreground and so on. Before you start, walk around to find the position that gives you the most interesting angle on the subject. It is a good idea to make a viewfinder, to help you decide how much of the scene to include. Just cut a rectangular aperture in a piece of card; you can then hold it up at different angles and at different distances from your eyes in order to isolate various sections of the landscape. This can help enormously when you are faced with a wide, panoramic view and you cannot decide which bit to focus on, or where the centre of interest lies.

Choosing a format

The next decision you need to make is which format to use. 'Format' simply means the shape of the painting. The three main formats are horizontal (also known as landscape), vertical (also called portrait) and square. Needless to say, landscapes can be painted on portrait-format supports and portraits on landscape ones. You can also alter the proportions to make what is known as a 'panoramic' format – that is, a wide-angle view, which extends beyond the field of vision that is normally encompassed by the human eye. Although panoramic formats are often horizontal, particularly when they are of landscapes, they can also be vertical – an approach that might be warranted with a subject such as a dramatic view of a tall cliff.

Your choice of format will be dictated largely by the shape of your subject. A tall subject such as a tree might demand a portrait format. If that tree has a long, horizontal shadow on a sunny day, and the play of light and shadow on the landscape is an important feature of your painting, then a landscape format that fits it all in might be more appropriate.

Landscape format ▲
The image of these cliffs in northern France, painted by Ian Sidaway, sits comfortably in the horizontal format. The curve of the waterline sweeps the eye around to the cliffs and into the painting. At the base of the cliffs, the viewer's attention is caught by the dark ripples and reflections in the water; these in turn bring the eye down to the breaking waves and round again.

Portrait format ▲
The vertical format of this work again suits the subject of this painting by Wendy Jelbert. The viewer's eye is pulled along the length of the craft, which is pointing diagonally into the centre of the painting, and up the steps towards the building. The golden yellow stonework pulls the eye down to the bottom of the picture and the journey begins again.

Dividing the picture area

Over the centuries, artists have devised ways of positioning focal points. The one that is considered to be the ideal division and aesthetically superior to others, is based on the 'golden section', also known as 'divine proportion', in which a line or area can be divided so that the 'smaller part is to the larger as the larger part is to the whole'. A simple grid is made by splitting the picture area into thirds, horizontally and vertically, to give nine sections, with lines crossing at four points. Positioning major elements near these lines or their intersections is supposed to result in a pleasing image.

In landscapes, there is a natural tendency to divide the picture into sky and land. This is not usually the best approach, particularly if it creates a central divide which can make pictures look dull. In a wide landscape you can often increase the sense of depth and space by letting the sky occupy more of the picture area, perhaps two-thirds, or even three-quarters of it. Conversely, with a mountain scene in which you want to express the upward thrust of the land, you could give minimum space to the sky.

Breaking the rules ◄
In this expansive view by Ian Sidaway, the landscape and sky are of equal importance. Placing the horizon on the halfway mark is risky, but the image works because the carefully arranged cloud formations balance the intricate landscape. Note, too, how the path and railings direct the viewer's eye through the scene.

Big sky ▲
In a wide, panoramic landscape, it is important to consider how to divide up the picture space and how much prominence to give to the sky. The area of England in which Geoff Marsters works is very flat, with the great expanse of sky one of its most noticeable features, so in *Fen Landscapes* he has given it three-quarters of the picture.

Divisions on the thirds ◄
The chairs and litter bin are the centre of interest in this painting by Ian Sidaway and are loosely positioned on the intersection grid lines to the right of the image, while the top third of the painting is filled with rows of leafless trees. Together, they balance the empty space in the bottom left of the image.

How much foreground?

A painting can easily be spoiled by a weak or over-dominant foreground. As a general rule, foregrounds should 'introduce' the rest of the picture and lead the eye into it. Too much detail or very strong shapes in the foreground can sometimes have the opposite effect, acting as a block. You can often solve the foreground problem in advance by choosing the best position from which to work – how much of the foreground you see is directly related to whether your viewpoint is high or low. If you look at a scene first standing and then sitting down, you will notice how it changes completely. In a flat landscape, particularly, some feature in the foreground that you may scarcely have noticed suddenly becomes dominant when you view it from low down, while objects in the middle distance are diminished in importance. There is no reason why you should not choose a low viewpoint – for a subject such as mountains, it could be ideal – but it is often better to stand at an easel to paint, or to find a vantage point such as a low wall.

Large foreground ▲
In *The View from Here* by Martin Decent, the foreground occupies roughly two-thirds of the picture space. This is not just empty space, however: the lines of the fence and furrows in the snow curve inward, leading our eye to the focal point of the image, which is placed on the third. In addition, the large foreground adds to the sense of open space, and contributes to the subject of a tough climb uphill.

Curving path ▶
In *Road to Ronda*, Pip Carpenter has organized the picture in such a way that the viewer's eye travels into and around the scene. The area of trees and barely defined grass on the left leads toward the curving path, which the eye naturally follows. The energetic brushwork also gives the painting a wonderful sense of movement and dynamism.

Leading the eye

Most landscapes have a centre of interest, or focal point, to which the eye is drawn. How obvious this is depends on the scene. Examples of an obvious focal point might include a group of buildings in a landscape, a tall tree, or some people sitting down having a picnic – people always grab our attention because we identify with our fellow humans. A less obvious focal point might be a ploughed field making a pattern in the middle distance, a particular hill, a gleam of light on a lake or river, or a light tree set against darker ones. In a successful composition, the viewer's eye should be directed toward the image's centre of interest and encouraged to linger on the picture.

Try to orchestrate the painting so that you set up a series of visual signposts toward the focal point. Diagonal lines or curves invite the eye to follow them, and a device frequently used in landscape is a curving path leading from the foreground in toward the middle distance – where the focal point is often located. A river snaking its way through a landscape, lines of ploughed fields or a line of trees receding into the distance could serve the same purpose.

Pathway into the picture ▲
A common device used to lead the viewer 'into the picture' is to use a path or river travelling from foreground to middle distance, and in *Vineyard in the Languedoc* Madge Bright has used the lines of the vineyard to lead toward the houses.

Clouds

The sky often makes up the largest area of a landscape painting, and can be vital in creating atmosphere, as well as in adding a sense of scale and perspective. At its simplest, a sky can be expressed by leaving the white paper, or laying a flat or graded wash of colour. More often it will include clouds, so it is worth exploring their characteristics and thinking about how to tackle them in different media.

Have a look at the clouds in your chosen scene. Are they light and wispy, large and heavy, high or low-lying? Do they blend softly into the sky or are the edges crisply backlit against the sun? There may be different cloud forms in the same vista: do you wish to describe them all, or would a simplification best suit your composition? Clouds are changing all the time, sometimes very rapidly, and you may need to work quickly or partly from memory if you are painting from nature. If you are working from photographs, you may find that you can be selective or inventive with your cloud shapes, so long as you have enough visual reference material to help you to convey them convincingly.

Remember that clouds follow the same rules of perspective as the rest of the landscape. They will appear not only smaller in size but also cooler in colour as they recede toward the horizon. Having said that, an interesting phenomenon is that clouds tend to look soft-edged when they are near to you, with crisp edges only taking shape when seen over greater distances, contrary to the usual way that objects lose their sharpness as they recede.

When choosing which medium to use, you may find that particular cloud forms suggest different materials. For example, the soft, fluffy forms of cumulus might be best handled in soft pastels, while higher streaks of cirrus clouds could work well with a wet into wet watercolour treatment. A dramatic sky or a vivid sunset might suit heavy impasto in oils or acrylics. Charcoal can be blended with the fingers or used on a textured ground to capture the graininess of stratus or rain-clouds, or lifted off with a kneaded eraser to convey complex shapes or light effects.

Colour is another factor in deciding your medium. Clouds are seldom a uniform grey, but often contain hints of violet, peach or ochre, depending on the time of day and conditions. Light from the landscape below can reflect colour up into the clouds, particularly in seascapes. Would these subtle variations be captured best in careful layers of watercolour wash, softly scumbled acrylics or swirling soft pastel? Try a few interpretations of the same clouds using different media. Becoming confdent with your materials will give you more options when you plan how to treat the sky within a landscape painting.

Giving clouds volume ▲
Clouds need to be given tonal value in order to create the illusion of three dimensions. When you identify the direction of light falling on the clouds and the shape of shadows (top), you might find it useful to think of clouds in terms of a cluster of spheres. Now the actual shape of the cloud can be described, and further shading added. The water vapour that makes up clouds gives soft outlines to shadows, so to create a convincing effect, avoid crisp or sharp edges (bottom).

Cirrus clouds ◄
Tending to be high, cirrus clouds are somewhat wispy and often stripy or linear in appearance. In this quick watercolour sketch, the paint has been applied mainly wet into wet, with a little sponging off toward the middle of the sky. Note the sense of perspective created by the larger cloud masses in the foreground giving way to flatter forms toward the horizon. The grey of the clouds is created with a mixture of alizarin crimson and phthalocyanine blue, with a touch of yellow ochre.

Stormy clouds ▲
The artist began this study by dampening the paper with water and dropping in a very pale grey, allowing it to spread of its own accord. She then blotted off paint in some areas with a paper towel to reveal the white paper, before adding the mid- and dark greys and the blue of the sky, wet into wet.

Cloudy sunset ▶
Here, thick acrylic paint was applied with a palette knife. The sketch aims to capture an atmosphere, rather than a realistic visual record. Note the limited range of greys and golds used here. It is a good idea to keep to a restrained colour palette when painting dramatic skies, to avoid a garish result.

Passing rain-clouds ▼
Charcoal has been applied swiftly to the dark areas of the foreground, and the paper allowed to show through in the middle distance and background. Blending has softened the texture and tonal contrast. The artist has used a kneaded eraser to suggest light breaking through and detail below.

Skyscapes

Having spent some time looking at clouds and how to portray them, you are better prepared for tackling the sky as a whole. Learn to think of the sky as an integral part of the composition, by including it in the planning stage rather than adding it when the rest of the painting is complete, which can leave it looking a little like an afterthought. Forward planning will also give you the practical advantage of being able to work out the best stage in the painting at which to tackle it. It can be difficult to work around complicated shapes with 'sky colour' and risks spoiling a picture you are otherwise happy with.

The sky can be vital in creating an atmosphere, as well as adding a sense of scale and perspective. As you have seen, clouds play an important part in establishing mood: billowing clouds in a bright summer sky, for example, evoke a different feeling to storm clouds. Clouds can be used as an aid to composition in various ways: the shapes and direction of them may lead the eye toward the focal point of the picture or a flat, uniform sky may act as a restful backdrop to a complicated scene below it.

Your viewpoint will dictate how much of the sky appears in your chosen scene. The same landscape will look vastly different when seen from a high viewpoint as opposed to a low one. In the first, you might see a large expanse of ground rolling away to a thin sliver of sky at the top of the picture. With a low viewpoint this area of land becomes compressed, foreground features loom large against the sky and the horizon line is near the bottom of the picture.

A conventional composition places the horizon line somewhere near a third or two-thirds of the way down the picture, but you may decide otherwise depending on your aims. You also need to think about how the sky relates to the rest of the image: is it the main subject or an adjunct to something else? This will help you decide where to put the horizon line.

Breezy sky ▼

This pastel drawing has a lovely sense of space and movement. The fluffy qualities of the cirrus clouds have been captured using blended soft pastels. Note small areas of blue breaking through the edges, giving a more natural outline. This view is a good illustration of the shadows of low clouds on a landscape, a device that helps to unify the land and sky within a painting, as well as being an interesting subject in itself. The tonal contrast is strongest near the centre of the picture, leading our eye toward the silhouetted trees and blueish hillsides beyond.

Glowing sunset ▲
A gradated pale blue wash provided the foundation for this sunset in watercolour. The pale orange strip of light on the horizon takes on an added brilliance against the dark landscape and the deep grey clouds above.

Big sky ▶
In this oil painting (*The Ploughed Edge* by Timothy Easton), the sky occupies just over two-thirds of the picture space and is crucial in creating a feeling of space and openness. The billowing clouds give a sense of movement and contrast well with the calm, still landscape below. Note how the artist has created a sense of distance through the converging perspective lines of the ploughed furrows and the use of paler, slightly cooler colours in the distance, along the horizon line.

▶

Practice exercise: **Simple sunset using a variegated wash**

One of the best things about learning to paint is that it does not take long before you are able to produce something that will look great hanging on your wall. For any budding landscape painter, a simple skyscape is a good, confidence-building first project. The technique used in this exercise is a variegated wash; this demonstration was done using watercolour, but the same method can be used with acrylics. This exercise works 'on the third' and is good practice for using aerial perspective, so it puts two important 'basics' into practice immediately. It is an excellent introduction to the study of light and movement in water, as well as light in the sky against the very dark buildings. The exercise also shows you how a silhouette can turn a simple variegated wash into an attractive landscape painting – relying on the eye to 'trick' the mind into seeing a landscape rather than actually putting in all the detail.

Some artists find it easier to dampen the paper first, using either sponge or a mop brush dipped in clean water. This allows the colours to blend and merge, without any risk of hard lines appearing between one colour and the next, because paint spreads more evenly on damp paper. When it is properly done, the transition from one colour to another in a variegated wash should be almost imperceptible.

You may need to allow the paper to dry slightly before you apply any paint. This is something that you will learn with practice. Equally, if you prefer, you can work on dry paper.

Make your initial pencil marks as light as possible so that they do not show through and spoil the end effect. If you are wetting the paper, do this after you have made your pencil marks. You will probably need to tape the paper firmly on to your table or easel with masking tape to prevent it from buckling. Apply the water sparingly with long smooth strokes of a clean, flat brush for very even coverage.

The scene

Striking colours, shimmering reflections and a bold silhouette – this picture has all the ingredients for a sunset with impact. Working quickly on dampened paper injects a lively quality into the work that complements the transience of the light and the movement of the water. The horizontal ripples in the water add a sense of depth and calm to the composition. Learning the effects of light is essential – a scene such as this provides excellent practice in observing where light catches and how you can use reflection.

Materials

- *2B pencil*
- *140lb (300gsm) rough watercolour paper, pre-stretched*
- *Watercolour paints: ultramarine blue, cadmium orange, cadmium red, ultramarine violet, alizarin crimson, sepia*
- *Brushes: large round, small round*

Damp versus dry paper

Variegated wash on damp paper
In the finished wash, the colours merge together almost imperceptibly, with no obvious division between the two.

Variegated wash on dry paper
Here, the division between the two colours is slightly more obvious. The pink and yellow are bolder.

1 Using a 2B pencil, lightly sketch the outline of the silhouetted trees on the skyline. Using a large round brush, dampen the paper with clean water. Mix a wash of ultramarine blue and, again using the large round brush, lay a gradated wash over the top half of the paper, adding more water with each brushstroke so that the blue colour pales to almost nothing just above the horizon.

2 Mix an orangey red from cadmium orange and cadmium red. While the paper is still damp lay this colour over the lower half of the paper, allowing it to merge wet into wet into the very pale blue around the horizon line. Leave to dry. Dampen the paper again very slightly. Brush a broad stroke of the same orangey red mix across the middle of the painting (this will form the basis of the silhouetted land area) and dot it into the sky. Leave to dry.

3 Mix a warm purple from ultramarine violet and a little alizarin crimson. Using a large round brush, brush this mixture on to the sky to represent the dark cloud shapes. Add a little more pigment to the mixture to make a darker tone and paint the outline of the silhouetted trees. Using the same mixture, paint a few broken brushstrokes on the water for the dark reflections of both the trees and the land area.

4 Mix a dark violet from ultramarine violet and sepia and darken the silhouetted area, adding a few fine vertical lines for the boat masts that stick up into the sky.

The finished painting
A two-colour variegated wash forms the basis of this colourful sunset, while a bold silhouette gives the viewer a strong shape on which to focus. Although the painting itself is very simple, the choice of rich colours and the careful placing of both the silhouetted land form and the reflections in the water combine to make an atmospheric little study.

The initial blue wash merges almost imperceptibly with the rich, warm colours of the sunset.

The white of the paper shows through in places – a simple but effective way of implying water sparkling in the last rays of the setting sun.

Trees

When drawing or painting trees, one of the most common mistakes that beginners make is to try to include every detail, without getting the underlying structure in place. Your first step should be to identify the basic shape of the tree. Start by concentrating on the contour or silhouette of the tree shape; it may be helpful to half-close your eyes to avoid the distractions of detail, texture and colour. You might even like to imagine the shapes as flat cut-outs to help see their true outline. Now think about this shape. Is it basically a round shape, such as an oak tree? Cylindrical, like a poplar or cypress? Conical, such as a pine? Once you have identified the basic outline shape, think about the tree's internal structure. Does the main trunk have one or two large branches coming off it or many? Does it split into two or more forks, and if so how far up the tree are they? Whether or not you can see much of the trunk, a knowledge of the tree's structure will make for a more convincing drawing. Remember that without external influences, such as strong winds, disease, or overcrowding, most trees seem to retain a kind of natural symmetry. The trunk of a gnarled fruit tree may lean at a wild angle, but the upper branches may cluster in the other direction.

Cedar tree ◄
This delicate watercolour by Trudy Friend carefully observes the way the branches spread and fall in layers around the thick trunk. Painted using a fine brush and wet-on-dry washes, the foliage colours consist of only three tones of the same silver-green colour.

Tips: Look at the tree's habit: do its branches spread upwards from the trunk or droop downwards? Lightly put in the underlying structure and make your brush or pencil strokes follow the direction of growth.

Tree shapes

Although tree shapes may look very complex to draw and paint, if you train yourself to view them as simple geometric shapes you will find them much easier to assess. They are actually no more difficult than any other subject. Breaking down complex forms into their most simple shapes is a good principle for any drawing or painting. It is also invaluable when you come to analyse the effects of light and shade.

In these sketches, the basic shape has been very lightly drawn around the outline of the tree. Remember, however, that these are generalizations and that the shape of a tree is often affected by the prevailing weather conditions; for example, on an exposed hillside trees may be lopsided because the wind tends always to blow from the same direction, while trees in poor soil may appear stunted.

Flattened top ▲
This distinctive umbrella pine tree looks as if it has been trimmed to a flattened shape on top.

Cone shape ▲
In many conifers, the branches grow horizontally from the trunk and are shorter toward the top of the tree, creating an overall cone shape.

What about groups of trees within the landscape? Again, try to think not of 'wood' or 'hillside' but instead in terms of abstract shapes – a cluster of flat-bottomed spheres, an elongated diamond shape. Seen from a distance, the base and trunk of trees are often obscured by shadow and perspective, so avoid the temptation, for example, to add neat rows of tree trunks along the edge of a wood. It is more likely that you can see one or two, at irregular intervals, while the rest have been swallowed by shade. From your viewpoint, the foreground fields or grasses may obscure the base of the trees, giving a flat-bottomed appearance to a stand of trees or wood. Having established the general shape of the tree or trees in question, the next stage is to give them three dimensions. As with cloud forms, the key to this is the depiction of light and shade. The shadows beneath a tree are crucial in anchoring it to the landscape so that it looks like it is growing, not floating. Light on the foliage, or bare branches in winter, help give it form. Light hits all objects consistently, but the surface texture and local colour will affect the appearance. Half-shut your eyes once more and think purely in terms of light and shade; you may notice, for example, that a softly rounded tree in the foreground is echoed by a distant stand of the same species.

Cylindrical shape ▲
Poplar and cypress tree branches grow upward and tend to be all the same length, giving a cylindrical shape.

Lozenge shape ▲
Some trees are characterized by a gently tapering, oval shape that narrows toward the top and bottom.

Broken shape ▲
Branches may grow asymmetrically, so that irregular gaps and shapes are created between them.

Rounded shape ▲
Oak trees, as well as beech and maple, have branches that radiate out from the main trunk, and a rounded top.

Gnarled, twisted forms ▲
Wind, harsh conditions or just the nature of the tree may dictate that it grows into twisted forms.

Two trunks ▲
Many shrubs have two or more trunks, with the branches closer to the ground than in trees.

Foliage masses

In depicting foliage, it is not a good idea to attempt to draw every leaf – aim for an overall impression, rather than putting in every detail.

Start by establishing basic facts about your scene. What season is being depicted? What direction is the light coming from, and is it bright or muted? What time of day is it? Low light may result in the undersides of the leaves being lit up, while midday sun will give a dark shadow on the ground. Is it windy, so that you need to show movement? Or rainy, so that the leaves are shiny and highly reflective?

Look for areas of light and shade within the foliage mass, to help create a three-dimensional effect. Study the direction of the light and whether it is hard or soft. Making a tonal study in charcoal or thinned paint can give you an excellent starting point.

Look also for gaps where you can see patches of sky or background colour showing through. These can be wiped out with a kneaded eraser in a drawing or blotted out of a watercolour; or dabs of opaque colour can be laid over existing paint. Few trees are so dense that no such gaps or spots of light are visible, so adding them lends realism.

Think about the way the leaves attach themselves to the branches. Some leaves form close clusters, whereas some spring upward from the branch, while others, such as willows, droop down. These differences can be represented with different marks and mediums. For example, a broad-leafed tree could be expressed by a dabbing movement of a round watercolour brush, while a tree with feathery foliage could be treated with a fan brush.

Finally, analyse the colour. Leaves can range from reddish-black to the palest of creamy yellows; from vibrant, lime green to a dusky blue-grey. Try mixing your own greens rather than relying on pre-mixed greens, which can be harsh. Experiment by mixing ultramarine and yellow ochre, then ultramarine and lemon yellow, for two useful greens. Looking for areas of your foliage colour within the surrounding landscape will also help to ground the tree within the composition and make for a harmonious whole.

Assessing tones ▲
It takes practice to assess tones, particularly when you are dealing with varying tones of the same colour. Try half-closing your eyes, so that you see the subject as a series of shapes. The strong evening sunlight on this loosely described park scene falls on the trees in the middle distance, while the foreground trees are plunged into deep shadow, becoming silhouettes.

Directional brushstrokes ▲
When painting foliage, it is essential to give an impression of the direction of growth. Do the leaves droop down, like willows? Are they grouped in tight, densely packed masses? In this study of a tree in summer, short vertical brushstrokes have been dabbed on to describe the leaves on the overhanging branches, while broad, horizontal strokes represent the shadows on the ground below. Fine vertical strokes are used for the grasses lining the path.

Separate foliage masses ▲
From a distance and, in the strong sunlight, the leaves almost seem to merge. By observing the different tones, colours and textures, the artist has made it clear that it is made up of separate trees and bushes.

Autumn foliage ▲
The rich reds and golds of autumn foliage have always attracted artists. Here, the leaves are an impressionistic mass of colour, with burnt sienna and cadmium yellow merging wet into wet on the paper to create sizzlingly vibrant tones. As the tree is viewed against the light, the detail is subdued, with the dense browns of the trunk and branches providing the structure for the painting. Note how well water-soluble pencils have been used to convey the gnarled texture of the bark.

Practice exercise: **Foliage mass in acrylics**

This is an exercise in assessing and mixing greens, from the yellowy greens of the pathway and grasses to the darker tones of the tree. Practise mixing different greens. You can create warm and cool shades to give the forms an illusion of solidity and depth. Try mixing in a warm yellow such as cadmium and then see how much brighter and more acidic the green is when you replace cadmium with lemon yellow.

Materials

- *Watercolour board*
- *Acrylic paints: cadmium yellow, phthalocyanine blue, yellow ochre, alizarin crimson, brilliant green, titanium white*
- *Brushes: Selection of round and flat brushes in different sizes*

The scene

Shining from the left, the sun clearly shows the spherical form of the tree and its dark interior.

1 Mix a bright green from cadmium yellow, phthalo blue and a tiny bit of yellow ochre and brush in the main shapes of the composition – i.e., the rounded shape of the tree in the background and the bushes and grasses on either side of the pathway.

2 Mix a deep violet from alizarin crimson and phthalo blue and paint in the trunk and main branches. Mix darker green from phthalo blue and a little cadmium yellow and, with a flat brush, block in the mid-tones of the foliage and the shadows under the tree.

3 Paint in the darker bushes in a mix of phthalo blue and a little yellow ochre. Create a thick light green from cadmium yellow, brilliant green and titanium white and, with short strokes and dots, put in the tree's mid-tones.

4 Vary the proportions of colours in the mixes to get a range of tones in the foliage. Put in dabs for the sky in a pale blue mix of phthalo blue and white. Mix a pink from alizarin crimson and white and dot in the flowers.

The finished painting

This sketch demonstrates the importance of creating an overall impression of the shape and direction of growth of a foliage mass, rather than attempting to put in every detail. The various tones of green have been carefully observed and the brushstrokes placed to create an impression of the way the leaves are attached to the boughs, hanging downward in loose, heavy fronds.

Those areas of foliage that receive the most light are painted in a very pale tone.

Dark green tones suggest shadow, and give the form a three-dimensional impression.

Bark

At first glance, bark might seem a rather specific topic for the average landscape painter's consideration, yet as a subject it will appear in most outdoor scenes and is worthy of attention.

Making a study of bark is an excellent way of 'getting inside' your subject, as it helps you to understand the way in which a particular tree grows. The more time you spend observing details of bark, the more the subtleties and nuances of its colour and texture will become part of your artistic vocabulary. Even if you need depict only a small area glimpsed through foliage, the time spent looking at it will ensure that you do not resort to using visual shorthand.

Bark can vary enormously depending on the age and type of the tree. It may be smooth and silky like that of a silver birch, or rough and knotted like an ancient oak; fine in texture like furled sheets of tracing paper or heavy and sculptural like a thick carving. The growth patterns may result in horizontal rings running across the circumference of the trunk or branch, or in deep vertical gouges running up and down it. Some trees, such as the ash, have criss-cross patterns of diamond-shaped furrows, like the opening and closing of a concertina. Some patterns are linear, others knobbly or seemingly random.

Look for the way in which bark expresses the growth of the tree. A twisted tree might have gnarled, convoluted bark forms; an upright one a more regular surface pattern. Bark patterns are likely to be wide and open on the trunk and older parts, closer and compact on younger branches. The texture of the bark changes where a branch meets the trunk, sometimes forming a cluster of rings like the wrinkles in an old stocking, and thick calluses will form over time around the circular space where a branch has been removed. The tiniest of twigs will have its own textured surface, a mirror of the larger tree in miniature. The perspective of rings around branches and trunks can help to convey the shape; for example, if a branch is leaning towards you the rings will appear foreshortened.

Think about how to capture these textures in different mediums. Flat washes of watercolour might be appropriate for the mottled layers of a young sycamore. Paint could be dragged or scraped for the ribbon-like bark of a eucalyptus, or laid on with a knife in thick slabs to suggest the patterns on a mature oak. The choice of support can come to your aid: dragging a pastel or dry brush over rough paper can create effective textures. Remember the direction of the light, so that you don't lose form while creating texture.

The colour of bark is rarely uniformly brown; in fact, it may be green or grey, with hints of purple or blue. Lichen or moss can look as if it's been sprayed on. Fungi and the effects of disease may also add their own character to the tree.

Gnarled bark ◄
This pen-and-ink sketch of weathered bark uses both hatching and a pale wash to add tone. The artist felt that relying solely on hatching would detract from the delicate textural forms of the bark. The ridges have been picked out with a variety of dashes and broken lines, which help suggest the organic quality of the natural material. Working in monochrome also seemed to suit the subject matter.

Practice exercise: **Bark close-up in acrylics**

In this exercise, the paint is applied using both a brush and a painting knife. You can create a surprisingly wide range of textures in this way, from delicate overall washes and fine details made with the brush to thin, smooth areas of paint, impasto ridges and jagged lines 'drawn' with the tip of the knife. As in the previous demonstration, it is vital to find points of reference so that you do not lose track of where you are. You will also need to decide whether you want to opt for a photo-realistic portrayal or, as here, exaggerate the colours.

Materials
- *Canvas primed with acrylic gesso*
- *Acrylic paints: burnt umber, naphthol red, yellow ochre, titanium white, ultramarine blue, raw umber, brilliant yellow green, lemon yellow*
- *Selection of round brushes in different sizes*
- *Painting knife*

The scene
Apart from the occasional splashes of green, at first glance this appears to be an almost monochromatic image of pinky-brown bark. Look closer, however, and you will see tiny paler-toned, almost white areas where the light hits raised patches, hints of a warm yellow ochre, deeper reds, and even dark, cool blues.

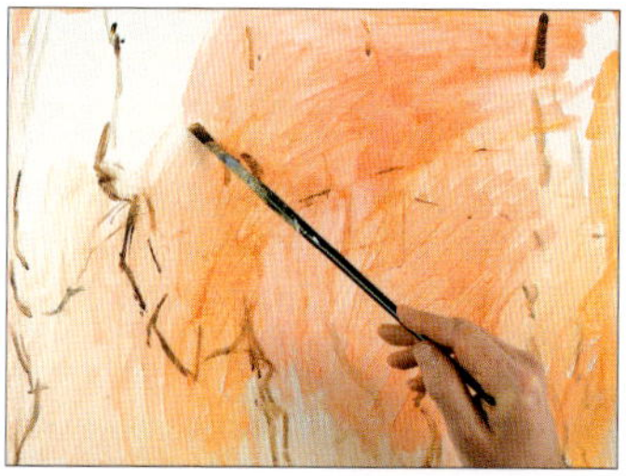

1 With a thin mix of burnt umber, put in the initial lines. Leave to dry. Mix an undercolour from naphthol red, yellow ochre and titanium white and scumble it over the canvas, varying the proportions of the colours to get some tonal variation. Leave to dry.

2 With a brush, paint over the crevices in the bark in ultramarine blue. Mix a thick but pale purple-pink from burnt umber, naphthol red and titanium white. Smear it over the surface with the back of a small painting knife, then use the tip of the knife to apply strong, thick lines of a rich raw umber.

3 Add more white to the purple-pink from the previous step and, using the back of the knife, smear it over larger areas of the bark to create the basic bark colour, varying the proportions of the colours in the mix as you work so that you do not get a flat expanse of just one tone.

4 For the moss in the crevices, mix a bright green from brilliant yellow green and lemon yellow and apply with a fine brush. Put in other darks as necessary – raw and burnt umbers, and blue-blacks mixed from ultramarine and alizarin crimson.

5 Continue in the same range of colours, alternating between the brush, knife back and knife tip, until you have built up the texture and range of tones that you want. Look for both warm and cool tones, as this will give the image a sense of depth.

The finished painting

This is both an experiment in mark making and a lively interpretation of a deceptively simple-looking subject. The underlying colour – various tones of purple-pink – holds the image together, while splashes of bold, acid greens and deep reds on top provide strong complementary colours that play against each other and create a dynamic, contemporary-looking image.

Bark is not flat: note how the artist has juxtaposed warm and cool tones to convey the different levels of the surface.

Linear marks made using the tip of the brush add texture, and contrast well with flatter applications of colour elsewhere.

Grasses

Whether you are painting a carefully tended park or an expanse of prairie, grass is a major feature of many landscapes. Portraying it convincingly requires a little planning, but can give a scene interest and texture.

Grasslands vary enormously. Vast expanses of rolling savannah, a meadow studded with wild flowers, manicured lawns, grassy sand-dunes, marshes or moorland each have their own character. There may be variations in the same view – scrubby grasses on a mountain slope giving way to cornfields lower down the valley, for example, or simply the contrast between long and mown grass in the more intimate confines of a garden.

In the foreground, a great deal of detail can be used to describe individual stems of grass; in the midground, less detail is visible, but highlights on certain clumps of grass may show the direction of its growth; in the background, one might see some indication of texture, but all detail is lost. By picking out a few foreground stalks and then hinting at others elsewhere, the eye will 'read' the whole area as grassy. This is how we naturally perceive objects.

Sunlight can produce interesting effects on grassland. Wiry grasses can be very reflective and add a silvery sheen to a hillside; long grass under trees makes patterns of light and shade when it catches the sun. Wind creates wave-like ripples and a sense of energy and movement.

Summer grasses ▼
Here, a strong shaft of sunlight falls across a summery garden scene. Softly blended oil pastels have been used on the closely cropped grass of the path, with horizontal strokes. In the long grass, the strokes become vertical with more of a hatching technique. Flower heads are suggested with dabs of horizontal colour. Individual stalks and seed heads have been scratched into the oil pastel, leaving the stained green colour of the paper beneath.

When drawing or painting foreground grass, use rapid upward strokes. The looseness and spontaneity of this approach can help capture the thick, criss-crossing growth without your marks becoming too rigid. Downward strokes can be added for bent stalks, and curls or seed heads added to some blades. Fine brushes or sharp pencils are useful, but you could also try dry-brushing with a brush splayed out between finger and thumb. Scratching through paint or oil pastel can also be effective. On a pencil drawing, an eraser can be used to pick out light grasses.

Echo the patterns for grasses in the background, remembering that clumps will seem small and closer together, and should follow the contours of the land. A smudge of paint may be enough to suggest grasses here. Perspective will give distant areas a pale appearance.

Practice exercise: **Grasses in charcoal**

This exercise gives you the opportunity to practise 'eraser drawing' – using a kneaded eraser to lift off charcoal pigment and imply light grasses growing against a darker background. For a broader line, use the edge of the eraser. To get a very fine tip on the eraser, simply pull it to a point.

Materials
- *Good-quality drawing paper*
- *Charcoal: thick and thin sticks*
- *Kneaded eraser*

The scene
Spiky clumps of grass growing on a sand dune form an interesting contrast in texture to the smooth undulations of the sand, which has been blown into small ridges by the wind. The strong lines within the subject suggested the simple, graphic approach of a monochrome drawing in charcoal.

1 Using the tip of a thick charcoal stick, draw in the base of the top clump of grasses. Wipe the side of the stick over the sand area and smooth out the charcoal marks with your fingers. Use the edge of a kneaded eraser to wipe off pigment to create light-coloured lines of sand, where the sun lights one side of the sand ridges.

2 Using thin charcoal, scribble in the dark areas within the grasses (the shaded area underneath) and draw in the blades of dark grass. For the lighter, yellowy grasses, pull the eraser to a fine point and wipe off charcoal. Also block in the underlying patches of earth.

3 Continue the process of putting in the grasses, alternating between drawing thin, curving marks and wiping off charcoal with the eraser. Draw in the foreground clump, again using a combination of positive marks with the thin charcoal stick and wiping off with the eraser.

The finished drawing

By carefully observing the different tones within the subject and using the eraser to pick out the brightest highlights, the artist has created a convincing portrayal of clumps of grass. This sketch demonstrates the versatility of charcoal. A fine layer smudged with the fingertips represents the sand, while crisp, sharp lines are used for the grasses themselves. The medium allows the artist to work at speed, which helps convey the windswept, natural energy of the scene.

The grasses are drawn using a combination of positive marks (that is, linear marks that depict the grasses themselves) and lifting off pigment with an eraser to create the negative spaces in between.

Note how shadows cast by the grass are not straight lines but are broken by the undulations in the sand.

The use of light and dark tones suggests ridges and makes the sand look realistic.

Rocks and stones

When drawing rocks or stones it is easy to be immediately seduced into trying to describe textural details, but it is important first to get a firm foundation. Try to think of rock shapes at their most basic, blocking in the largest shapes as roughly square or rounded forms. The light source is very important to give these complicated structures a sense of volume, so you may want to add tone at this stage. Remember to include shadows thrown by the rocks on to surrounding surfaces. Next the more complicated outlines and contours within the blocked-in shapes can be described – but keep thinking about light and shade. Finally, when you are happy with the shapes of the rocks, you can add colour and texture.

Many different mark-making techniques come into their own when describing the texture of rocks and stones. Pen-and-ink drawing, with different pressures applied to vary the strength of line, can be useful in suggesting lines of slate. Dry brushwork can create jagged or swirling patches of broken colour to denote craggy surfaces or the tracery of fossils within the rock. A palette knife can be used with thick paint to show stepping levels of stone. Torn paper can be used like a stencil, with paint spattered over, to give character to rock shapes while keeping unwanted paint off adjoining areas. There are numerous texture pastes and additives that can be used with oils or acrylics to give a sculptural effect.

Whatever your chosen techniques, think about applying them sparingly; one well-observed area of a cliff face may have more impact if the rest of the picture is treated more simply. The eye is grateful for a resting space within the picture when confronted by a complicated area of detail.

Light on rock and stone affects its colour enormously. Broad expanses of rock often reflect light, particularly when near the sea, so a shaded area can have warm or cool colours within it. Play around with different ways of creating colour mixes. Alizarin crimson and ultramarine blue with a touch of raw umber gives an interesting neutral that can veer toward warm or cool depending on the proportions in the mix; as can alizarin and viridian. Aerial perspective will soften shadows on any object, and cause colours to become cooler and paler as they recede. Think about how much prominence to give them to enhance your chosen subject. When portraying large rock faces or cliffs, a sense of scale can sometimes be achieved by including a figure, or a man-made structure.

Boulder ▼
Here, the artist experimented with watercolour and gouache to create texture. To the left, salt crystals were sprinkled over a purplish wash, then shaken off when completely dry to leave shapes that resemble pitted rock. Elsewhere, tonking (printing with scrunched-up paper dipped in paint) has been used. Sponging and dry-brushing add further texture.

Practice exercise: **Slate with lichen in soft pastels**

Soft pastel is great for capturing textures such as those on this lichen-covered slate as you can use the tooth of the paper. Once you study a subject like this in detail, you will be amazed at all the colours and differences in tone.

Materials

- *Dark blue pastel paper*
- *Charcoal*
- *Soft pastels: pale green, permanent yellow light, pale blue-grey, dark blue, yellow ochre, pale blue*
- *Pastel pencils: red violet, blue violet, black*

The scene
Here, the lichen and striations within the slate make a diagonal, which creates a dynamic composition.

1 Using thin charcoal on dark blue pastel paper, map out the main shapes and striations. Begin putting in some lichen, using pale green and permanent yellow light soft pastels.

2 Hatch the two violet pastel pencils over the purple-tinged area to the right of the yellow lichen. Using a pale blue-grey pastel, put in more of the lighter patches of lichen, varying your pressure and making range of marks from dots to small squiggles to get some textural variation.

3 Apply the base colour of the slate in pale blue-grey and dark blue, as appropriate, using the side of the pastels and making your marks follow the natural striations in the stone. Dot in yellow ochre for the darker yellow patches of lichen. Reinforce the very dark markings on the slate and within the patches of lichen with a black pastel pencil. These linear marks contrast well with the small dots used for the lichen.

4 Scribble in various pale blues and blue-greys for the lichen, using the tips of the pencils and a range of marks from dots to tight squiggles. Try not to be too literal in your depiction and attempt to put in every single element – an overall impression is what you should be aiming for.

The finished drawing

In this simple drawing, the texture of the paper has been used to good effect, in combination with an impressive range of pastel marks, from crisp dots and linear dashes to broad sweeps of colour made using the side of the pastel. The artist has carefully matched the pastel colours to those in the reference photograph, taking some time before commencing drawing to get this right. The choice of paper colour has a big effect on the end result, as patches of paper are showing through. The result is an interesting study in texture and a great exercise for observing colour in detail.

Soft, loosely blended areas of pastel are used to describe the underlying colour of the slate, with the texture of the support also contributing to the overall effect.

Carefully observed linear marks denote the striations and tiny undulations in the surface of the stone.

Still water

The smooth quietness of still water often gives tranquillity to a scene. We are all drawn to it visually, and it is a popular artists' subject. Still water takes its colour from surrounding objects, so any discussion of how to draw or paint it is primarily about reflections.

You need to be aware of three planes – the objects above the water, the reflections on the water's surface, and what can be seen beneath the surface. The interplay of these three worlds can be a fascinating subject in itself.

The direction of light on an object affects its reflection. For example, a sunlit tree produces a brightly coloured, sharp reflection on the surface of the water, whereas a tree silhouetted against the light produces a dark reflection, through which the third plane – the reeds or silt or whatever is beneath the water – can be seen clearly.

When water is completely still, the reflection is almost a mirror image of the objects above it. However it is very rare that there is no movement at all. Consequently, reflections are more often portrayed as a slightly less substantial version of the real world. This can be achieved by using less detail and tonal contrast to paint the reflected image; simply painting a paler version often looks amateurish. One or two horizontal lines of ripples or leaves floating on the surface of the water may be enough to convey its surface. Be careful to keep lines of ripples parallel to one another, and to the edge of the paper or canvas, or you may end up with a curved-looking surface to your pond.

It is crucial to keep reflections directly under the shape above the water. A tree trunk, for example, should mirror exactly the same angle in its reflection.

A reflection coming toward you over the horizontal plane of the water will appear longer than the real object. If the reflection is broken by ripples, they will elongate it, mainly vertically, toward the viewer.

Your viewpoint affects reflections. Only if your viewpoint is down at water level will you see the same above the water as on the surface.

Gently rippling water ◄
Wet-into-wet washes lay the foundation and general shape of these riverside trees. Wet-on-dry washes define the shapes further, while linear brush and coloured pencil work hint at a slight breeze rippling the almost still surface. The size of the ripples increasing as they come toward us is loosely but effectively described. Note that the reflections have less textural detail than the willows themselves, but retain the same strength of colour. Because of the artist's viewpoint we glimpse sky between the reflected willows, rather than the distant trees in the background.

Practice exercise: **Reflection in charcoal**

It's important to establish the surface of the water in a subject like this. Here, small ripples in the water help to create a sense of movement, which prevents the image from looking flat and bland.

The scene
Bare, skeletal trees and their reflections seemed to suit a treatment that is graphic and monochromatic – hence the choice of charcoal for this exercise. Note how some of the reflections of the branches are broken up by tiny ripples in the water.

Materials
- *Good-quality drawing paper*
- *HB pencil*
- *Charcoal*
- *Dark grey Conté stick*
- *Kneaded eraser*

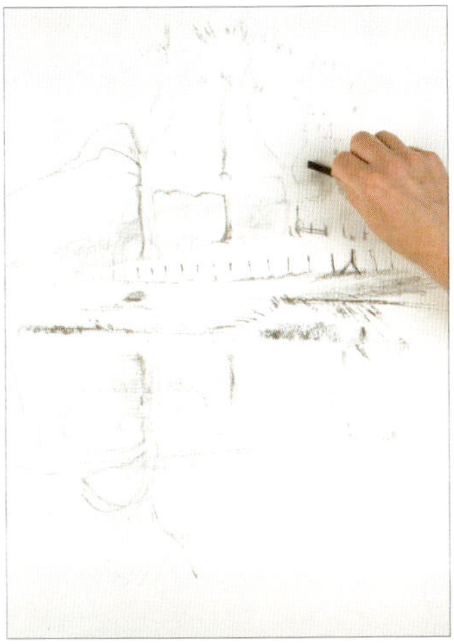

1 Carefully map out the scene, using an HB pencil. Using a dark grey Conté, draw in the branches and their reflections. Put in faint zigzag marks for the ripples. Use the Conté for the mid to dark tones in the grass and along the water's edge.

2 Use the side of the charcoal to put in the dark tones in the water. These negatives spaces help to define the shapes of the reflected branches. With a kneaded eraser, wipe out the highlight areas in the water, to show how the light catches the ripples.

3 Use the side of the charcoal to block in the hillside behind the trees and the dark reflections near the bank. Continue putting in the branches and their reflections in charcoal. Do not put in every single branch, otherwise the drawing may lose spontaneity.

4 Using the tip of the charcoal stick, make spiky lines for the thinnest branches. Check that you have put in all the reflections correctly – have you drawn in the same number of reflected fence posts as there are posts on the land, for example?

The finished drawing

In this monochrome study, the artist has taken great care to relate the reflections to the objects; careful measuring of the different elements in relation to one another has paid off. Note, too, how the water is darker than the sky: it takes its tone from the objects that are reflected in it – the bank and the trees. Note the variety of textural marks that can be achieved with charcoal.

Short, spiky marks describe the thinnest branches.

More flowing, linear marks are used for the bigger branches and trunks.

Bold 'scribbles' suggest the darkest tones under the grasses that grow along the water's edge.

In charcoal, particularly for small highlights, it is often easier to block in large areas and wipe out the highlights than to leave the white of the paper to stand for the brightest areas.

Moving water

Moving water is a challenge for the artist: how can one capture the energy of a force that is constantly changing? Photographs of water can look rather static – so if you use them for reference, try to take a series over the course of a few minutes.

When looking at waves on the beach, spend some time absorbing the scene and you might be able to detect a rhythm within the movement. Note how high the waves get, where they break on the shoreline, whether they unfurl in the same manner each time. Perhaps they crash attractively over a particular rock only once every few waves; make a few more marks in your sketchpad whenever that happens.

Aerial perspective is important in seascapes to create depth and distance. Think also about light on sand, pebbles and rocks, and how much detail is needed to enhance the composition.

The same principle applies when describing a cascading waterfall, rushing stream or gently flowing river. Look for the larger shapes that are created and use marks that best express their movement. The force of the waterfall might suggest an energetic approach with palette knife and oils. The stream might best be captured in loose pen and ink overlaid with washes.

Waterfall ►
In this watercolour sketch, white body colour was applied using a mixture of fluid wash and dry brush to capture the light catching on the falling water as it tumbles over rocks and boulders. The boulders were painted using a texture paste to give them added form.

Rocks and branches interrupting the flow of water can help suggest the force of the flow.

If you are working in watercolour, plan whether you need to leave white areas for surf or foam. Masking fluid can be spattered over the white paper to suggest spray, which may give a more effective result than using opaque gouache or Chinese white over your coloured washes. Resists of candlewax or oil pastel under watercolour can be an appealing way of conveying colours within the water or sunlight sparkling on the surface.

Remember that water gains its colour by reflecting its surroundings. A stream might look peaty-brown until it splashes over rocks, when it will reflect the sky. Cresting waves sometimes look green when seen against the light, blending back to a dark turquoise against the deeper water. Purples, yellows and greys may also find their way into water.

Practice exercise: **Crashing waves in acrylics**

In this demonstration acrylic paints are mixed with acrylic gloss medium, which increases the transparency of the paint and allows you to build up several thin glazes relatively quickly. When two colours are glazed over one another, the integrity of both remains intact – a perfect method for conveying the many different blues and greens that can be seen in the sea. Gloss medium also enhances the depth of colour. The white foam of the waves is created by applying the paint thickly, using a painting knife. When you are painting a scene such as this, describe one area in a spontaneous manner and keep the rest simple. This will often give more impact than a meticulous approach.

Materials

- *Watercolour board*
- *HB pencil*
- *Acrylic paints: phthalocyanine blue, brilliant green, cadmium yellow, alizarin crimson, titanium white*
- *Acrylic gloss medium*
- *Selection of round brushes in different sizes*
- *Small painting knife*

The scene
Waves break around the foreground rocks in foamy spurts of white, revealing the energy and force of the sea, while in the water itself can be seen myriad shades of blue and green. Note the way that these different tones within the water – dark blues and green on one side of the waves, lighter ones on the side that catches the light – give the sea dynamic form and show the movement and energy of the waves as they crash on the rocks.

1 Lightly sketch the shape of the rocks in HB pencil, putting in just enough detail to give yourself a guide to the different planes. Use a large round brush and short, slightly curved brushstrokes to imply the swirling waves. Apply dilute phthalocyanine blue over the sea, with a little brilliant green near the rocks, where the water is shallow. Leave to dry (acrylic paint dries quickly, especially when used thinly like this). Mix a pale brown from cadmium yellow and alizarin crimson and wash it over the rocks. Mix in some acrylic gloss medium and brush more phthalo blue over the darker parts of the sea to build up the intensity of colour.

2 Darken the sea with more phthalo blue and gloss medium, adding a greener mix of phthalo blue and brilliant green just above the rocks. Mix a dark violet from phthalo blue and alizarin crimson and, using a smaller brush, paint in the shaded sides of the foreground rocks.

3 Continue building up the form on the rocks, using various browns (mixed from cadmium yellow, alizarin crimson and a little phthalo blue) and purply greys as appropriate, mixing the paints with gloss medium as before. Brush phthalo blue over the sea at the base of the rocks to build up the density of colour.

4 Using a small palette knife and a thick mix of titanium white, apply the white 'foam' of the sea. Aim for a combination of broad, flat strokes made using the flat of the knife, and short flecks and linear marks made using the tip. Mix some white with the gloss medium to keep it translucent, so that the underlying sea colour still shows through – in the slightly calmer water to the right of the rocks, for example.

Using a small round brush and thicker versions of the brown- and purple-based mixes used before, continue building up the form on the rocks and add any linear detailing that you feel is necessary.

The finished painting

With bold, confident strokes that echo the shape and direction of the waves, the artist has created a colourful sketch that captures the energy of the waves and the colours of the sea very effectively. The thicker, impasto work on the foam of the sea and on the sculptural quality of the marks on the rocks contrast well with the flatter glazes of colour on the water.

The marks used for the foam range from thick strokes made with the side of the painting knife to lines made using the tip.

Varying the tones conveys the swell of the waves – dark blue farthest from the light, lighter blue on the side that catches the light.

With thin, transparent glazes, the integrity of each colour remains intact: both green and blue are clearly discernible.

Bright sunlight

When judging how to depict a sunny scene, it helps to imagine a series of graded tones, with pure white at one end through a deepening range of greys to black at the other. In flat, overcast light conditions you might just use the middle tones; in bright sun, the top and bottom tones are used too.

It might be tempting to think that a light, sunny picture will use mainly light tones or colours, but this can end up looking insipid; it is only when dark tones are introduced that the contrast is created to make the highlights really jump out. When you look at the proportion of light and dark areas within a composition, a painting might on balance be fairly dark, and yet still manage to convey a strong impression of light and heat. An evocative image in Mediterranean countries, where light conditions are strong, is the cool dark alleyway or doorway leading out onto the sunny square.

Very bright sunlight can affect our perception of colour within a scene, particularly on flat or reflective surfaces where it has a bleaching effect. An object can seem to lose its 'local' or actual colour; for example, a cafe awning that you know to be bright orange may appear to be almost white in strong sun. In watercolour this can be conveyed by using just a little pigment in a wash, so that the luminosity of the white paper shows through. In an acrylic or oil painting, you can simply mix plenty of white with the local colour, or alternatively use a scumbling technique, dragging a dry white or yellow-white mix over dry paint – useful when conveying textures.

Shadows play a crucial part in helping to depict sunshine. They shift position with the time of day, so you may need to take a decision on where they fall and block them in quickly. Remember that those closer to you will seem darker than those farther away. Shadows are not simply grey: they are usually affected by some reflected colour from nearby objects. Often they may appear to contain a hint of the complementary colour of the object: and even if this is not obvious, it can be a good idea to add a little for contrast.

Strong light ▼
The strong, clear light in this landscape gives dark shadows to the trees and highlights to the foreground stones and grasses. Aerial perspective gives the far hillside a softer green, and the receding shadows are a cool purple.

Practice exercise: **Alla prima landscape in oils**

In alla prima, the paint is applied in a single layer rather than waiting for successive layers to dry. The artist worked wet into wet and blended tones on the canvas, which often creates more energetic mixes than physically blending colours on the palette. The colours that you get depend on whether the underlying colour is warm or cool. It is this constant interplay of warm and cool, lights and darks, that is the key to an image such as this one, which celebrates the relationship of light against shadow on a furrowed hillside.

Materials

- *Canvas primed with acrylic gesso*
- *Oil paints: ultramarine blue, raw umber, yellow ochre, Venetian red, chrome green deep, lemon yellow, Winsor emerald, titanium white, cadmium yellow deep*
- *Brushes: selection of filberts in different sizes*
- *Turpentine/white spirit (paint thinner)*

The scene
Strong, low, late-afternoon sunlight illuminates the patch of ground in the centre of the image and casts long shadows across the field. The golden colours give the image a wonderful warm glow.

1 Tone the canvas in a pale blue-grey mixed from ultramarine blue and raw umber. Mix a brown from yellow ochre and Venetian red and, with a large brush, sketch in the fields. Map out the clump of trees in olive green mixed from chrome green deep and yellow ochre. Add a little of this mix to lemon yellow for the sunlit furrow tops.

2 Scumble a warm blue-green mixed from Winsor emerald, ultramarine and yellow ochre over the dark field in the background. Add more blue to the mix and put in the very darkest tones of the trees. Mix a light green from lemon yellow, Winsor emerald and yellow ochre and put in the light foliage tones and the brightest patches of grass.

3 Put in the long shadows with a mix of ultramarine, white and Winsor emerald. Build up the lights and darks, using lemon yellow with varying amounts of white for the lightest tones and an orangey mix of cadmium yellow deep and white for the next brightest. For the darks, use the same green and blue-green mixes as before, alternating for the warm or cool tones you need.

4 Alternate between lights and darks, and warm and cool tones, as you work across the painting, blending the colours wet into wet. Block in the long, cast shadows with the blue-green mix of ultramarine, white and Winsor emerald from Step 2.

5 Roughly scumble on the dark blue-green mix with vigorous, up-and-down brushstrokes for the straggly foreground bushes, for texture.

The finished painting

This contrast of light, bright yellows and oranges with dark, warm blue-greens makes an effective portrayal of sun on the landscape. The low, raking sunlight picks out texture in the furrows and casts long, deep shadows that form an integral part of the composition.

Although the sunlight is strong, note how dark the shadows are: the contrast is dramatic and atmospheric.

Bright, acidic yellow mixes convey the intensity of the sunlight.

Dappled light

An ordinary scene viewed in dappled light can be truly transformed by sparkling contrasts of light and colour. Sometimes a mysterious mood is evoked, as details are lost in shadows. The play of light and shade is a unifying element, bringing together the components of a scene. It can also give a work an abstract quality, as the subject may seem to become less important than the description of the light itself.

The very appeal of dappled light is that it forms a web of complicated patterns. This can be hard to replicate, even when seen upon a flat surface. Adding perspective and different textures to the equation requires further thought. Imagine, for example, a courtyard with a stairway and trees, and light filtering down. Perspective dictates that pools of light closer to you will have a rounded appearance, whereas those farther away will seem to flatten out into elongated shapes, as well as growing smaller. The shadows falling across the vertical sides of the steps will glance down diagonally, according to the direction of the sun, whereas those on the treads will be horizontally distorted. Further distortion would occur on a curved surface, such as a pillar or urn. Rather than getting bogged down in the detail, it can help to look through half-closed eyes, at blocks of light and shade. If you draw the shapes and the spaces around the negative shapes as you see them, you will achieve a surprisingly accurate result.

Textures will bring particular effects. On grass, for example, patches of sunlight may appear to be framed by a fringe of darker grasses in the foreground and lighter ones at the back.

Another point to note is that shadows will be stronger the closer they are to the object casting the shadow.

Once you are aware of these considerations, you are in a better position to use the effects of dappled light to your advantage. If you stick to the basic principles, you can play around with composition a little, perhaps leading the viewer's eye toward areas of interest or even adding contrast to a scene sketched or photographed on an overcast day.

High noon sunlight ▲
In this acrylic study, the artist studied the way the play of light and shade created a pattern of abstract shapes. The strong contrasts on the stones and paving at the base of the foreground tree are balanced by the sunlight on the buildings and awnings at the back of the square. Note the shape and direction of the light patches on the floor, as opposed to those on the vertical sides of the statue and tree trunk. The shadows also alter in density, from the deep shade on the right-hand side of the painting to the left-hand side, where the trees are more open and there is more reflected light.

Woodland light and shade ▼
In this lively study, oil pastels were used to create the impression of a low winter sun shining through trees on to the undergrowth of the woodland floor. The artist chose a dark brown oil pastel paper the same colour as the branches of the trees against the light, and scratched off pigment to reveal the colour of the support. Dashes of yellow were applied to depict leaves or grasses caught by the sunlight, and vertical strokes of reddish brown show the foreground foliage.

Practice exercise: **Dappled sunlight in soft pastels**

Soft pastel is a lovely medium for drawing the transient effects of light, as you can put down both broad areas and tiny, precise details and allow the colours to mix optically on the paper. It is a good idea to use a paper that is similar in colour to the mid tones in your subject. Here the artist selected a pale to mid beige.

Materials

- *Buff-coloured pastel paper*
- *Soft pastels: Dark brown, dark grey-green, white, bright yellow, mid green, very pale green, dark green*

The scene

Light filtering through the trees casts dappled shadows on the ground below, creating interesting patterns on what would otherwise be a bland area.

1 Using the side of the pastels, roughly block in the tree trunks in dark brown and the horizon and perspective lines in dark grey-green. Use white for the patches of sunlight on the ground and the sky visible through the trees. You do not need to be too precise at this stage – just map out the light areas. Using the dark grey-green again, put in the largest shadows and smooth the marks with your fingers.

2 Block in the leaves that are being hit by sunlight with a bright, acid yellow, then scribble in darker patches of foliage in a mid green. Using dark brown, strengthen the shaded side of the tree trunks and smooth out the marks with your fingers. Note how much more substantial the trees look now. Strengthen the shadows too, again smoothing out the marks with your fingers.

3 Using the tip of a dark brown pastel, loosely scribble in the dark shapes of the smaller shadows on the ground, then blend the marks. Add the blue-green area beyond the lowest branches, at eye level; this helps to give a sense of distance. Sharpen up the shapes of the patches of sky with a very, very pale green (so pale that it's almost white), then use the same colour for the corresponding patches of sunlight on the ground. Finally, use a dark green to sharpen up and give some definition to the shapes of the darkest patches of foliage.

The finished drawing

This atmospheric, expressionistic study relies on careful assessment of tones and on seeing the areas of light and dark as shapes, or blocks, of colour.

The use of light and dark greens in the foliage gives this area depth and texture.

Foliage shadows are loose, generalized shapes: do not get caught up in details!

Rain and mist

Unlike a sunny scene, where contrasts are strong and colours vibrant, in rain the scene is much more low-key. In overcast conditions the light is flat and muted, creating few sharp shadows. Colours are soft and subtle, with lots of grey tones, and may tend to merge together. The edges of shapes become blurred and ill defined. Rainy landscapes may also be quite dramatic.

Most painters portray rain by the general visual effect that it has on a scene. Perhaps the most obvious point to note is that many surfaces become reflective when wet. What light there is will be reflected back, creating unusual juxtapositions and a play of lights and darks. Puddles and other flat surfaces have an almost mirror-like quality, although the lack of light in the sky usually means that reflections are dark.

One of the most dramatic, if fleeting, visual effects is when a break in the clouds lights up part of the scene, resulting, for example, in sunlit foliage against heavy dark rain-clouds.

If your view includes figures, adding them huddling under umbrellas or hurrying from a downpour can give an element of charm.

Misty views have always attracted artists, lending as they do a romantic, mysterious atmosphere. Misty weather shares some of the visual characteristics of rain, without the reflective surfaces. Your approach will be influenced by the nature of the mist or fog: is it of a uniform thickness and likely to remain where it is, or is it broken and shifting around, in which case you might make notes in the same way you would with moving cloud formations. If it is static and uniform, it is simpler to portray.

Whether you are looking at an enclosed space such as a garden or out over a whole valley, the principles will be the same. Objects very close to you will appear normal, but as they become more distant, the water vapour in the air will flatten out the appearance of colours, texture and detail to the extent that they lose their three-dimensionality. Portraying this is a case of managing the decrease in tonal contrasts as shapes recede into the distance. If the mist is more broken, the challenge is to capture the effect of objects looming in and out of view, creating 'lost and found' edges, which can be immensely atmospheric and visually appealing.

Shanghai downpour ▲
The colours of the umbrella are the focus of this simple composition of an alleyway in Shanghai, China. They are framed by the buildings' muted colours, typical of rainy scenes. Note the shiny surface of the pathway and the dry brushwork that gives it texture. Leaving patches of white paper showing through helps to lighten the scene.

Practice exercise: **Misty scene in acrylics**

The challenge here is to control the decrease in tonal contrast as the shapes recede into the distance. Note how the colours become muted with distance; textural detail, too, is less evident.

Materials
- *Watercolour board*
- *Acrylic paints: yellow ochre, burnt umber, ultramarine blue, alizarin crimson, yellow-green, cadmium yellow, titanium white, turquoise*
- *Brushes: Selection of round and flat brushes in different sizes*

The scene ▶
Although this photo was taken as a portrait-format shot, the artist decided to make a landscape-format painting. Note how the sweeping curve of the path leads our eye to the bridge.

1 Establish the main shapes and structure. Apply a dilute wash of yellow ochre over the foreground path, dropping in a little burnt umber at the edges. Mix a pale purple from ultramarine and alizarin crimson and map out the shape of the bridge. Use the same colour for the left bank and any darker patches in the water. Leave space for the patches of sky.

2 Add more ultramarine to the purple mix, and darken the top of the bridge. Use the same colour for the brick edge of the towpath. Apply a very dilute wash of ultramarine over the foliage area on the right. Loosely 'draw' the trunks in burnt umber and a mix of burnt umber and yellow ochre. Using a range of greens (yellow-green on its own, mixes of ultramarine plus yellow-green and ultramarine plus cadmium yellow) begin to dot in some of the greens of the foliage, splaying out the bristles of the brush to create generalized shapes.

3 Use the same purple mix as before to put in the lines of the trunks on the left bank, in front of the bridge; these trunks are much less distinct in tone than those in the foreground. Put in the sharp line of the canal edge in the same colour. Dot in some greens, using paler, more muted versions of the foreground foliage colours.

Tip: It is generally better to mix greens than to rely on palette greens, as it gives you more control over the tones.

4 Mix a very pale, thin blue from turquoise and titanium white, then paint in the sky above the bridge and the light patches of water. Darken the underside of the bridge by glazing burnt umber over the previous colour. Dot in some greens for the fallen leaves in the foreground. Using a mix of burnt umber and purple, dot in the darker tones in the foreground towpath. If the tree trunks near the bridge are merging into the stonework, as here, strengthen them a little so that they come forward and the spatial relationships of the different elements become clearer.

5 Having more texture and detailing in the foreground helps to create an impression of distance, so continue building up the foreground, using the same mixes as before. Brush a very pale, dilute turquoise and white mix over the misted area to knock it back a little and make it appear less distinct. Vary the direction of your brushstrokes to convey the way the leaves are scattered over the ground and experiment with different techniques, such as spattering and stippling, to create texture.

The finished painting

This sketch captures the effects of mist well. All the detail is concentrated in the foreground, with the background being painted as indistinct shapes.

The diagonal lines of the brick towpath edging draw the viewer's eye deeper into the scene.

Mist obscures the detail of distant objects; this area is painted a cool, watery blue.

Snow and ice

For artists, the delight of snow is that it can transform a scene. Everyday objects lose their usual outlines and unexpected shapes appear; local colour is removed and new patterns of light and dark emerge. Sometimes the ground is lighter than the sky: normal rules seem to be suspended. With so few familiar features in evidence, you must analyse the scene accurately, so that the viewer is given sufficient clues to 'read' the landscape. Judgements about tone and colour are crucial in establishing a sense of form and distance.

At first glance, a snow scene may seem to be almost monochrome, but careful observation and faithful rendering of cool and warm colours will add depth and interest. Snow, sky, rocks and trees that look white or grey will all, on closer inspection, have subtleties of colouring. The snow itself may look white, but in fact it will contain warmer and cooler tones, depending on the light, as well as textural patterns where it has fallen on intricate forms such as hedgerows.

In watercolour painting, it might seem simpler to leave the white of the paper to suggest snow-covered areas, but applying even the most delicate of washes will bring the painting to life: for example, a pale warm wash on the side of a hill facing the light, and a cool wash on the side in shade.

Subtle shadows on the snowy surface of a field can hint at the forms lying beneath it – a ditch or furrowed track, a series of undulations, a frozen pond. Shadows on snow are full of interest due to the reflective surrounding surfaces. Like any shadows, they are not usually a flat, uniform tone or colour but carry touches of other colours within them. On a sunny day they often look bright blue or mauve against the brilliant white of the snow; as the sun moves lower in the sky, the snow takes on a warm, golden hue and shadows have a blue-green tint; by dusk the snow may look pink and the shadows a soft blue-grey. Shadows on ice are more reflective still. Look out for different characteristics that describe the snowfall in question. Perhaps the snow has been drifting; sometimes a tree trunk can look as if it has been sprayed from one side. Footprints can look crisp-edged or rounded depending on whether snow has begun to melt. Ice creates strange textures, making grass wiry and giving twigs a crystalline coating.

Ice takes its colour from the object beneath or behind it, for instance it may appear pale green on a mossy rock or clear and sparkling against the sky. A frozen lake loses most of its reflective qualities and becomes a solid mass. Try laying semi-opaque layers of white paint, thinned with water or medium, over a darker colour, to capture this effect; or use a scumbling technique with dryish paint over dark areas.

Snowy bank ▲
In this watercolour study white areas of paper have been saved where needed. The warm yellow of the backlit leaves makes a pleasing contrast to the blues of the snow in shadow. A warm wash has been applied to the top right-hand area of snow, to show the warmth of the sun.

Sunset on snow ◀
The artist made a quick, almost abstract watercolour sketch of the colours of the snow toward the end of a sunny day. A warm-coloured wash was applied first, to capture the pinky-orange colour of the winter sun on buildings and hillsides in the middle distance. A cooler wash added afterward allows some of that warmth to show through, suggesting reflected light on the snow and warm hazy clouds above. The foreground marks are only loose squiggles but the artist has made them convey a strong perspective. If the artist wished to work the piece up further in the studio, these marks are a good basis for foreground detail.

Practice exercise: **Winter scene in oil pastels**

Here, you can try out two ways of depicting snow. For the snow on the ground, block in the colour, looking for cooler, bluer tones that reveal hollows and dips in the land. Blend with a rag dipped in white spirit. On the branches, use the sgraffito technique to scrape off pigment and create thin lines of white.

Materials

- *Mountboard or acrylic board*
- *Oil pastels: pale peach, mid-grey, pale blue, raw sienna, white, dark grey, black, pale violet*
- *White spirit (paint thinner)*
- *Old rag or absorbent kitchen paper*
- *Scraperboard tool*

The scene

Skeletal trees, with their thin covering of snow, give the image a really interesting texture and an almost black and white tonal contrast.

1 Block in the sky with a pale peach oil pastel, then blend the marks with a rag dipped in white spirit. The colour gives a warm overall tone. Draw in the trees and the stream banks in a mid-grey then, using the side of the pastel, put in the darker patches of the water.

2 Using a very pale blue, put in the shaded snow on the left-hand bank and the snow on the branches, blending with a rag dipped in white spirit. Outline the foreground tree trunks in black, then go over the left-hand side in raw sienna. Strengthen the right-hand bank with mid-grey.

3 Block in the background, picking out the sky with peach and white and blending with your fingers. Use a mid-grey pastel for the branches over the stream and a darker grey for those in the foreground. Having more detail and warmth in the foreground is a way of creating depth.

4 Put in the reflections in the water, using white, pale blue, pale grey and pale violet. Using a scraper tool, scrape along the top edges of the branches to reveal the underlying white pastel and create the impression of a thin layer of snow on the branches.

The finished drawing

By using predominantly cool tones – white, pale blues and greys – this image has a wintry feel that is entirely in keeping with the subject. Using a scraperboard tool to reveal the 'snow' on the branches has enabled the artist to create thin, delicate lines far more easily than she could have done with a chunky oil pastel.

The scraperboard tool allows you to create flowing, twisting lines that would be difficult to achieve with the oil pastel.

Slight ripples in the water, created using horizontal dashes of oil pastel, add a hint of movement to an otherwise static scene.

Collecting visual material

Given the vagaries of the weather and how little free time we all have at our disposal, it is often not practical to draw and paint landscapes outdoors. Many landscape artists make preliminary sketches in situ, or take reference photographs of things that catch their eye, which they then work up into a finished piece back in their studio.

Sketches

The more you sketch, the more reference material you will have – and sketching also helps to polish up your observational skills. Making sketches for a painting, as opposed to simply sketching for the fun of it, is rather a special skill, as you must learn to provide yourself with sufficient visual information from which to work at a later date, bearing in mind that a considerable amount of time may elapse between your initial sketches and a more detailed work.

Depending on the kind of work you are planning, you may need sketches in colour, as well as in line. Trying to make a painting from a line sketch in pencil or pen and ink is virtually impossible; you will have no idea what colour the sky was or which areas were dark and which ones light. Get into the habit of including all the information possible on your sketches; it is better to have too much information than too little.

If you do not have time to sketch in colour, make written notes about the colours. Do not simply write 'blue' or 'green', but try to analyse the colours; as long as you can understand your notes, this can be more valuable than sketching in colour, particularly if you intend to use one medium for your sketches and another for the painting. A sketch in coloured pencil, for example, would be very difficult to translate into watercolour or oils.

Choosing a sketchbook ▲
The kind of sketchbook you require depends on your method of working and the kind of visual notes you wish to make. Some artists have two or three sketchbooks in different sizes and formats. John Townend uses a large book for coloured-pencil drawings like the one shown above, and a smaller one for quick pen and ink drawings.

Sketching for painting ◄
This sketch by Stephen Crowther was made as the first stage in planning an oil painting, and the artist has made copious written notes to remind him of the colours. Using a large spiral-bound sketchbook enables him to remove the sheet and pin it up near his easel to refer to when painting.

Materials for sketching

For sketching you can use any drawing media with which you feel comfortable. Pencil is a good all-rounder, as it allows you to establish tone as well as line. Pen and ink is useful for small sketches, but less so for tonal studies.

Coloured pencils are tailor-made for colour sketches, and so are pastels and oil pastels, although neither of the latter is suitable for small-scale work. Moreover, both soft pastels and oil pastels are quite messy media, so remember to take some rags or, better still, a packet of moistened hand wipes to clean your hands. For oil pastels, you will need paint thinner and rags to clean your hands, plus brushes if you intend to spread the colours. You will not need fixative for oil pastels, but you will for soft pastels, as it is easy to smudge work when you are carrying it.

If you prefer to paint your sketches, both watercolours and acrylics are quick drying and relatively easily portable, although you will also need a water container and a selection of brushes.

For supports, you can buy large sketching pads of drawing paper, pastel paper and watercolour paper, or clip individual sheets to a drawing board. Sketchbooks of all these kinds of paper are available in a wide range of sizes but, unless you like to work small, do not be tempted by a tiny address-book size, as you may find that it restricts and frustrates you.

You might also like to consider investing in a portable sketching easel and stool. And do not forget how easy it is to get sunburnt when you are engrossed in sketching outdoors, even on what might appear to be a dull day.

Collecting ideas ▲
David Cuthbert does not make sketches with a specific painting in mind, but he has several sketchbooks in which he notes down anything he sees, often taking photographs at the same time so that he has a 'library' of possible ideas.

Choosing the medium ◄
When you are out sketching it is wise to take a selection of different drawing media, as you may find that a particular subject is better suited to one than another. John Townend likes coloured pencil for landscapes, but prefers pen and ink for architectural subjects, where colour is less important than line.

Making colour notes ►
Gerry Baptist works mainly in acrylic, using vivid colours, and his watercolour sketches reflect his artistic preoccupations; a monochrome pencil sketch would therefore not provide the information that he needs for his paintings.

Taking reference photographs

Some purists might say that artists should never work from photographs, but this is a not realistic demand. Most painters have limited time at their disposal and the weather can make outdoor work impossible, so it is better to paint from photographs than not to paint at all. There are a few things to bear in mind when you take your photographs, however:

- Cameras cannot always capture very subtle nuances of colour. Dark colours, in particular, are often reduced to a formless mass with no detail. If possible make colour notes in the medium in which you plan to work, noting the colours you mixed to make shades.
- Remember that photographs tend to flatten out perspective and to reduce the feeling of three-dimensional space.
- Use your digital camera in situ as a compositional aid: you can review the image immediately and make minor adjustments to your viewpoint to see what effect they have.
- Take as many shots as you can, from different angles and viewpoints; close up and at a distance. With the advent of digital cameras, processing costs are no longer an issue.

221
Burnt Sienna
Series A ***
Transparent
620
Cadmium
Yellow (Hue)

Town and Country

Say the words 'landscape painting' and many people's first thought might be a romanticized image of a rural scene untouched by human hand – rolling hills, perhaps, or a majestic snow-capped mountain. But of course, human activity plays a crucial role in shaping the landscapes that we inhabit, from planted hedges to bustling scenes of urban life. This chapter demonstrates that the potential for interesting landscape subjects is all around us wherever we happen to live. It begins with a gallery of drawings and paintings, which gives you the opportunity to see how other artists have tackled a range of landscape challenges. This is followed by a series of quick sketches – a great way of grabbing a few minutes' practice when you are short of time. Finally, there are sixteen detailed step-by-step projects, covering topics as diverse as a summer poppy field and a city construction site. Recreate them as practice exercises or use them as a starting point for your own explorations. Even if they are in a different medium to the one you prefer, read through them carefully. They are all painted by professional artists with many years' experience, so you will find that they are packed with useful tips.

Gallery

In this gallery, you will find landscape drawings and paintings by professional artists in all the main media. Study them carefully to see what you can learn from their composition, use of colour, and technical approaches to painting this most fascinating of subjects. Many different forms, natural and man-made, are featured, and it may surprise you where inspiration can be found.

Line and wash ▸
In *White Village, South Spain*, Joan Elliot Bates has combined linear pen-and-ink work with light washes of watercolour. The paint has spread the ink in places, so there is no obvious boundary between line and colour. When you combine different media, it is important that they work together, or the drawing will lack unity.

Luminous colours ◂
In this pastel painting, *Window in Provence*, Patrick Cullen has built up the colours thickly, using short pieces of pastel to make broad marks. To create the gentle but luminous colours, he has restricted himself to light and mid tones, controlling them carefully and changing the direction of the strokes to give variety to the different surfaces that he is depicting.

Restricted colour palette ▾
In Patrick Cullen's atmospheric *Casa de Lido*, the pastel is again applied thickly and layered in places. Again the colour palette is restricted to mostly light and mid tones. Cullen usually works either on sandpaper or on heavy watercolour paper on which he first lays a ground of paint.

Man-made landscape ▶
In her oil painting *East End Pipes*, Karen Raney has found an exciting and unusual subject which has allowed her to explore strong contrasts of tone and the relationships between shapes and colours. This painting demonstrates that potential landscape subjects can be found everywhere, not just in conventionally 'pretty' rural settings. Note how the pipes on either side of the painting point inward, directing the viewer's eye into the painting. The patch of sky is relatively small, but it prevents the image from being too oppressive.

Watercolour plus soft pastel ▼
Hazel Harrison's unnamed painting combines watercolour (applied initially as an underpainting) with soft pastel. Some artists use a watercolour underpainting in much the same way as they would a coloured ground, covering most of it with pastel. Here, however, the two media work together, with the watercolour playing an important part in the overall effect. The brush marks of the watercolour show through in places – for example, in the foliage, where they are used to suggest the movement of the trees in the breeze – while the pastel is used to build up texture and create areas of broken colour.

Dramatic colour ▼
Oliver Bevan paints scenes using colour in a way that is not strictly naturalistic but which evokes a powerful atmosphere. In this oil painting, *Sharp Corner*, strong contrasts of tone and colour produce a highly dramatic effect, with a slight sense of menace reinforced by the two dark figures and the gravestone-like shapes in the foreground. Note how well the dark, silhouetted patches are balanced by the areas of light.

▶

Bold brushstrokes ▲

This unnamed oil painting of a Mediterranean landscape by Karen Raney illustrates what is meant by creating a sense of movement in a composition. The eye is led into and around the painting by the wing-like shape of the foreground roof and the directional brushwork. The bold brushstrokes also create a feeling of tremendous vibrancy and energy that is perfectly in keeping with the subject.

Landscape in close-up ◄

One of the most difficult decisions to make is how much to include and focus on. You can often make a more expressive statement by moving in close, as Doug Dawson has done in *The Edge of the Meadow*. The strong diagonal of the tree is balanced by the horizontal bands of colour formed by the foreground and by the light field in the middle distance.

Delicate brushstrokes ▶
The textures in this watercolour, *Birch Trunks* by Juliette Palmer, have been described with great care, with a succession of small, delicate brushstrokes used for the trunks and distant clumps of twigs.

Energetic pastel strokes▼
Pastel is often associated with delicate colours, but this powerful landscape, *Summer Hillside* by James Crittendon, shows that considerable depth of tone can be achieved by laying one pastel colour over another. The pastels have been applied vigorously, giving the painting a lovely feeling of energy; in the trees, particularly, the effect is very much like brushstrokes in an oil or acrylic painting.

▶

Precision strokes ◀
There is a luminous quality in Maureen Jordan's pastel painting, *Bluebells at Isabella*: one can almost feel the warmth of the sunlight. In a landscape setting, flowers usually need to be treated more broadly and simply than they would in an indoor group: the important features are the overall colour and the growth habit of the flowers. Here, even the flowers in the foreground are no more than dashes of pastel, the marks have been carefully placed and the flowers are immediately recognizable to anyone who has seen a bluebell wood.

Spontaneous use of line and wash ▶
Mike Bernard rarely uses one medium on its own; in *Cow Parsley and House*, he has combined watercolour with pen drawing. This has allowed him to introduce touches of detail into the foreground while keeping both the drawing and the watercolour washes free and unrestrained. The heads of the cow parsley are ink blots dropped from the pen, which have spread in places into the surrounding colours. The linear highlights were achieved by scratching into dry paint.

Complementary colours ▼
In *Pines on Beauvalla*, Gerry Baptist has controlled the juxtapositions of colour carefully, using complementary colours such as yellow and mauve to create maximum impact while giving a realistic account of the landscape.

Thick and thin paint ▲
Brushwork is an important element in David Curtis's oil painting, *Red Lane, near Dromfield*. The brushstrokes follow the direction of the tree trunks and branches, describing them with great economy. Depth and recession are suggested by the contrast between thick and thin paint: on the right-hand tree the paint is thick, while for the area of blue distance it has been brushed lightly over the surface. The effect is an energetic rendering of a very static scene.

Cool colours ►
The colour scheme in Ted Gould's *Snow Scene* is cool throughout; the yellow of the hat and scarf provides the only touch of contrast for the blues, blue-greens, greys and grey-browns. The painting is in acrylic, used thickly on canvas.

Quick sketches: Complex shapes

Trees can be a delight to draw – particularly old trees that have gnarled bark and twists and splits in their trunks – as they allow you to explore a wide range of textural techniques and approaches. Monochrome sketches are perhaps the most satisfying of all as, without the distraction of colour, the textures and shapes really come into their own.

However, trees are complicated forms and can be one of the biggest challenges to the inexperienced landscape painter. To get used to looking at them as simple shapes and assessing their growth patterns, practise making quick sketches. Set yourself a strict time limit – anything from 5 to 30 minutes – and, before you put pencil to paper, really look at your subject and analyse its structure. Look in particular at the way the branches grow out of the main trunk: do they spread out straight, veer upward in a v-shaped pattern on either side of the trunk, or droop down? Sketching deciduous trees in late autumn or winter, when they've shed their leaves, is a particularly useful exercise, as it allows you to become familiar with the underlying shape.

Once you have got the basic shape right, you can move on to adding tone so that your sketch takes on more of a three-dimensional feel. Experiment with different media, too – pencil, charcoal, pen and ink and even the humble felt-tip pen all create different moods and qualities of mark.

The scene

This tree was badly damaged in a winter gale. The artist came across it when she was out for a walk in the country and was attracted by the many shapes made by the broken and contorted branches and by the gnarled texture of the bark.

5-minute sketch: graphite pencil ▼

After putting down the outline with slightly jagged pencil strokes, the artist then scribbled in the darkest areas of tone, such as the undersides of the branches and the shaded interior of the split in the trunk. Even in a quick 5-minute sketch such as this, you can begin to capture something of the form of the tree.

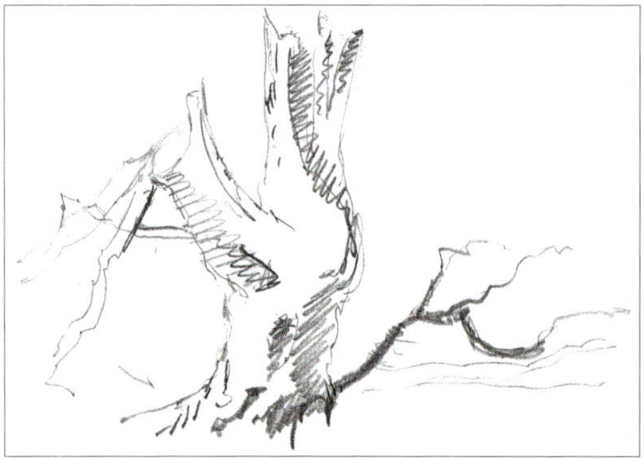

10-minute sketch: graphite pencil ▼

In a slightly longer sketch, you can begin to refine the detail, putting in tones that range from a mid-grey on the shaded parts to a much denser black in the hollowed recess near the base. In addition to providing information about the light and shade, the tone is applied in such a way as to hint at the pattern of the bark.

15-minute sketch: graphite pencil ►
The shading is more highly developed in this sketch and the tree looks more three-dimensional. Although the background is not drawn in detail, putting in the horizon and blocking in generalized shapes for the trees and bushes in the distance sets the tree in a recognizable context.

25-minute sketch: graphite pencil plus pen and ink ▼
Confident, scribbled pen lines over an initial pencil sketch give this drawing a real sense of energy and capture the character of the tree very well. Note the use of a wide range of marks, from simple hatching on the trunk to tiny flecks and dashes for the small leaves.

Quick sketches: Finding a focal point

When you are sketching on location, particularly when you have faced with a panoramic view, it is very easy to get carried away by the grandeur of the setting and lose sight of the fact that your image needs to work as a composition. Always look for something that you can use as a focal point, such as a large boulder or a tree, and place it at a strong point in the picture space so that the viewer's eye goes immediately to it. Placing the focal point 'on the third' almost always works well.

Look, also, for lines (real or imaginary) that lead the viewer through the scene – maybe a wall or a fence, a line of bushes or, as here, a stony track leading into the distance.

When you are out for a walk, take a sketchbook with you and spend a few minutes making quick sketches to improve your ability to compose a scene. After a while you will find that looking for a focal point and devising ways of directing the viewer's eye around the picture becomes second nature.

The scene
The track directs our attention to the mountains in the distance, while the rocks on the left provide a much-needed focal point.

5-minute sketch: charcoal ▼
Compositionally, the track is a way of drawing our attention to the backdrop, as are the wedge-shaped slopes on the left and right. Once she had worked out the composition, the artist scribbled down some very rough, linear marks for the pebbly track and rocks, and smudged charcoal to create broad areas of dark and mid-tone. The mountains were largely left untouched, so that they are paler than the foreground areas, which helps to create a feeling of recession.

15-minute sketch: chisel-tip pen ▶
You may never have thought of using a chisel-tip marker as a drawing tool but, although it is not the most sophisticated of implements, it can be very useful for making quick sketches on location as it is easily portable and clean to handle. By adjusting the angle at which you hold it and by applying differing amounts of pressure, you will also find that it can make a surprisingly varied range of marks. Here, the artist used spiky vertical marks to convey the texture of the grasses, while rough circles describe the pebbles on the track and wispy curves imply the fluffy clouds overhead. The chisel-shaped tip of the pen was used to block in larger elements such as the trees, bushes and boulders, creating a convincing sense of solidity in these areas. Note how the amount of visible detail decreases with distance: apart from a few sketchy lines to indicate the contours, the distant mountains are left blank.

30-minute sketch: soft pastels ▼
A cream pastel paper gives an underlying warmth to the image; the tooth of the paper also has an effect, as it helps to convey the texture of the pebble-strewn ground. Note how many different greens and yellows the artist has used. She has overlaid them to create lively colour mixes and blended them in parts so that areas of soft grass contrast effectively with the hard texture of the rocks.

Rolling hills in acrylics

Sometimes when you are painting a landscape, one element – a lone tree, a waterfall, a farm building, for example – attracts your attention; at other times, it's the sheer scale and drama of a broad panorama that draws you. In the latter case, it can be hard to evoke the same feeling of awe in the viewer that you felt on beholding the scene; more often than not, the reason for this is that you have failed to provide a focal point in your image.

In the landscape shown here, gently rolling hills sweep far away into the distance in an idyllic rural setting. But even in the most rural of settings, evidence of former industries can often be seen. Although the quarries in which they were cut have long since ceased to operate, these abandoned millstones provide the artist with a focal point for his painting. Without them, the scene would look like an empty stage set, with nothing to hold the viewer's interest.

This project uses acrylic paint in a similar way to traditional watercolour, with the colours being built up gradually in thin glazes, so that each layer is modified by the underlying colours. It also incorporates a wide range of textural techniques, from drybrush work to less conventional methods such as pressing bubble wrap into the paint and dabbing on paint with your fingertips. There is no 'right' or 'wrong' way to apply paint to the support: use whatever tools you have to hand to create the effect you want.

Materials

- *Card primed with acrylic primer*
- *B pencil*
- *Acrylic paints: cadmium yellow, cadmium red, phthalocyanine blue, burnt umber, magenta, titanium white, cobalt blue, cerulean blue*
- *Brushes: medium round, small round*
- *Rag*
- *Bubble wrap*

1 Using a B pencil, make a light underdrawing of the scene, taking care to get the ellipses and angles of the millstones right.

The scene

The millstones are the focal point of the painting. Note how they form a rough triangle, positioned just off centre at the base of the image, leading the viewer's eye up the line of the hill and back down again to the foreground. When you paint a scene like this, make sure you spend time selecting the best viewpoint.

2 Using a rag, spread cadmium yellow acrylic paint straight from the tube over the support, leaving a few gaps in the sky area for clouds. Drop a little cadmium red over the centre left of the image and blend it into the yellow paint with the rag so that the two colours merge on the support, creating an orange, wedge-like shape. Leave to dry.

3 Mix a dark green from cadmium yellow and phthalocyanine blue. Using a medium round brush, scumble the mixture over the wooded hillside in the middle distance to give a generalized impression of trees. While the first green is still damp, add a little more blue to the mixture and dot this in for the darkest areas of green.

4 Mix a dull but warm orange from cadmium yellow, cadmium red and a little burnt umber and brush it over the distant escarpment on the left of the image and over the fields in front of the wood. The warm colour helps to bring this area forward in the image.

5 Using a medium round brush, apply a thin glaze of magenta in a broad stroke over the slope of the hill on the left. Add a little phthalocyanine blue to the mixture and paint the crest of the escarpment behind it. While the paint is still wet, gently press bubble wrap into it to create some texture.

6 Add a little burnt umber to the warm orange mixture from Step 4 and brush it loosely over the bottom left corner of the painting, where the grasses and underlying soil are much darker in tone. While the paint is still wet, lift off some of the colour by 'drawing' the shapes of the light-coloured grass stems in the foreground with the tip of a paintbrush to reveal the colour of the support beneath.

7 Darken the hillside, using the same colours as in Step 5. Press bubble wrap into burnt umber paint and then press the bubble wrap across the bands of orange and magenta on the left to create loose, textured dots that echo the growth pattern of the vegetation. Paint the fence posts using a dark, reddish brown mixed from phthalocyanine blue and burnt umber. Mix a dark purple from cadmium red and phthalocyanine blue and brush it over the shaded sides of the millstones. For the darkest stones, use phthalocyanine blue.

8 Dot in the shapes of the isolated trees in the middle distance, using the same warm orange that you used to paint the fields. Following your initial pencil marks, mark out the field boundaries in burnt umber. Roughly block in the buildings in the middle distance in magenta. Brush a broad sweep of magenta over the hill to the right of the buildings and wipe a rag over it to blur the colour.

9 Brush titanium white over the sky area, allowing a hint of the underlying yellow to show through to maintain the overall warm colour temperature of the scene. Re-establish the highlight areas on the ground by smearing on titanium white paint with your fingertips, which gives a more spontaneous-looking and random effect than applying the paint with a brush.

Assessment time

It is becoming clear which parts of the scene are in shadow and which are brightly lit, and the underlying yellows and oranges give a warm glow to the whole scene. Now you need to concentrate on putting in the greens and browns of the landscape and on building up the textures so that the spatial relationships are established more strongly. Having more texture in the foreground than in the background is one way of creating a sense of scale and distance.

Note how the colours become paler in tone the farther away they are, which helps to create a feeling of distance and recession.

The yellow used as a base colour on these sunlit fields will modify any glazes that are applied on top.

More texture is needed in the grasses in the immediate foreground.

10 Reduce the starkness of the white areas by brushing over them with a thin glaze of the appropriate colour – cobalt blue over the wooded area, burnt umber over the shaded parts of the hillsides, and various yellow-orange mixtures over the sunlit fields. Note how the scene becomes more unified as a result.

11 Mix a bright green from cadmium yellow and cerulean blue and, using a medium round brush, paint over the mostly brightly lit fields in the middle distance. Note that some of the fields contain crops, so leave the underlying orangey-brown colour in these areas and take care not to go over the field boundaries.

12 Add a little more titanium white to the mixture to lighten it and paint the most distant fields. Mix a neutral brown from cadmium yellow, cadmium red and phthalocyanine blue and use it to tone down the reddish areas on the hill to the left, which look too harsh.

13 Mix a slightly darker green from cadmium yellow and phthalocyanine blue and paint the green grass in the immediate foreground. The use of a darker tone pulls this area forward and makes it seem closer to the viewer. The shaded sides of the millstones look too red in tone and jump forward too much. Mix a neutral brownish grey from cadmium yellow, cadmium red, cobalt blue and titanium white and paint over these areas, reinforcing the cast shadows with a slightly darker version of the same mixture.

14 Using a very small round brush, carefully paint a thin line of titanium white around the top edge of the millstone that is lying on its side, so that it appears to be rim-lit by the sun, keeping your hand as steady as possible.

15 Using a small round brush, dry brush thin strokes of burnt umber over the foreground to the left of the millstones to add texture and create the impression of grass stems blowing in the breeze.

The finished painting

Finally, put in the sky using a bright blue mixed from cerulean blue and titanium white. This tranquil landscape simply glows with sunlight and warmth. The scene covers a wide area but the millstones in the foreground, which are positioned slightly off centre, provide a strong triangular shape at the base of the image and a much-needed focal point. Although they occupy only a small part of the frame, the buildings in the middle distance provide a secondary point of interest, to which our eye is drawn by the gently sloping diagonal lines of the hills and fields.

Strong textures in the foreground help to pull this area forward and imply that it is closer to the viewer.

The sloping line of the hills leads our eye down toward the buildings, which form a secondary point of interest.

The greens and browns of the fields are modified by the underlying yellow, adding warmth to these rather subdued colours.

Rocky canyon in soft pastels

This is one of the best-known and most distinctive of all landscapes in the USA – Bryce Canyon in south-western Utah. The colourful rock formations, a series of eroded spires, are best viewed in early morning and late afternoon, when they glow in the sunlight.

When you are drawing formations such as these, look for tonal contrast within the rocks as this is what shows the different planes and makes them look three-dimensional. If a rock juts out at a sharp angle, there is a clear transition from one plane to another and the difference in tone between one side and another is very obvious. If the rock is smooth and rounded, the transition in tone is more gradual.

Drawing the many fissures and crevices also shows the form of the subject. If the shadows in these crevices are very deep, you might be tempted to draw them in black – but black can look very stark and unnatural. Instead, use a complementary dark colour for the shadows – so if the rocks are a reddish-brown, as here, try opting for a purple-based shadow colour.

Materials

- *Pastel paper*
- *Thin charcoal stick*
- *Soft pastels: pale blue, grey, violet, dark blue, browns, cadmium orange, pale pink, greens, yellow ochre*
- *Clean rag or paper towel*
- *Kneaded eraser*
- *Conté stick: brown*
- *Blending brush*

The scene

Trees in the foreground provide a sense of scale: without them, it would be hard to estimate how tall the rocks are.

Tip: If you are working from a photograph, you may find that it helps to grid up both the photograph and your drawing paper and then work systematically on one square at a time until all the elements are in place.

1 Using a thin charcoal stick, draw the rock formations and lightly indicate the main areas of shade. Using the side of a pale blue pastel, block in the small patch of sky that is visible above the rocks.

2 Using a cool grey pastel on its side, block in the darker, shaded areas of the rock formations. This gives the rocks some form and establishes the direction from which the light is coming.

3 Using a violet pastel on its side, put in the strata of the background rock-face. Note how the diagonal lines within this rock-face reveal the structure and add drama to the composition.

4 Again using the side of the pastel, strengthen the horizontal strata on the background rock, applying light shade of blue at the top of the rock and a darker blue at the base.

5 Begin applying colour to the rock formations, using brown and dark violet in the shadow areas, using the edge of the pastel to define the divisions between the sections. The crevices between the rocks are dark and deep: a deep violet provides the necessary dark tone and is a warmer and more lively colour than black.

6 Apply cadmium orange to the rock formations. On the shaded facets, where the orange is overlaid on the violet, a rich optical colour mix ensues. On the more brightly lit parts of the landscape, the orange represents the naturally warm, sun-kissed colour of the rock. The colour combination is sympathetic but striking.

Assessment time

The structure of the rock formations is beginning to emerge, but the contrast between the shaded and the more brightly lit facets is not yet strong enough: the tonal contrasts need to be much stronger and this is something that you can build up gradually, continually assessing the lights and darks as you work. The rock formations also need to be brought forward in the scene, so that they stand out clearly from the cliff in the background.

The main rock formations look rather flat and need more modelling.

It is hard to tell that this cliff is some distance behind the main rock formations. It looks as if it is joined to the foreground rocks, so the perspective needs work.

7 Lightly apply pale grey and pink over the foreground scrubland. Use grey for the shaded areas and pink for those illuminated by the late-afternoon sunlight.

8 Apply touches of pale green to the scrubland, then soften the whole area by blending the colours with a clean rag or piece of paper towel, using a gentle circular motion.

9 Using a kneaded eraser, wipe off the shapes of the trees in the foreground. If you accidentally wipe off too much, simply repeat Steps 7 and 8 for the right background colour.

10 Draw the trees, using a brown Conté stick for the trunks and their shadows, and bright green to roughly block in the masses of foliage.

11 Wipe a clean rag or a piece of paper towel over the top of the background rock-face and the sky to lift off excess pastel dust and soften the colour.

Tip: Turn the rag around in your hand so that you do not smudge violet over the sky.

12 Soften the violet on the lower part of the background rock-face by using a blending brush, brushing it both horizontally and vertically. If you have not got a blending brush, you could use your fingers or a torchon, but the bristles of the brush create very fine lines in the pastel dust, which are perfect for the striations in the rock. Although this rock-face is in the distance, it is important to create some subtle texture here.

13 Add more detail to the main rock-face, using the side of the deep violet pastel to overlay colour and the tip to draw on short horizontal and vertical lines to emphasize the different facets within the rock.

14 Now start working on the foreground scrubland. Using a pale green pastel on its side, roughly scribble in the base colour of the scrubby bushes that cover the ground immediately below the rock-face.

15 Build up the foreground foliage, using a range of pale and mid-toned greens and grey-greens. A general impression of the shapes is all that is required. Put in the roadway with a warm yellow ochre pastel.

16 Define the edges of the roadway in brown. Also add a range of browns to the scrubland, using jagged, vertical strokes of dark brown for the thickest stems and branches. Make sure your pastel strokes follow the direction of growth.

The finished drawing

This colourful drawing captures the heat and the mood of the scene very well. Warm oranges and purples predominate and are perfectly suited to the arid, semi-desert landscape. The artist used bold linear strokes to capture the striations and jagged texture of the rocks and the drawing is full of energy. Although some texture is evident on the background cliff, blending out the pastel marks in this area has helped to create a sense of recession. For the foreground scrubland, the artist opted for an impressionistic approach, describing the overall shapes and textures with dots and dashes of greens and grey-greens. This contributes to the liveliness of the scene and concentrates attention on the rocks, which are the main point of interest.

As the background cliff is less textured, it appears to be farther away.

The trees are dwarfed by the rocks that tower above, and give a sense of scale.

Tonal contrasts reveal the different facets of the rocks.

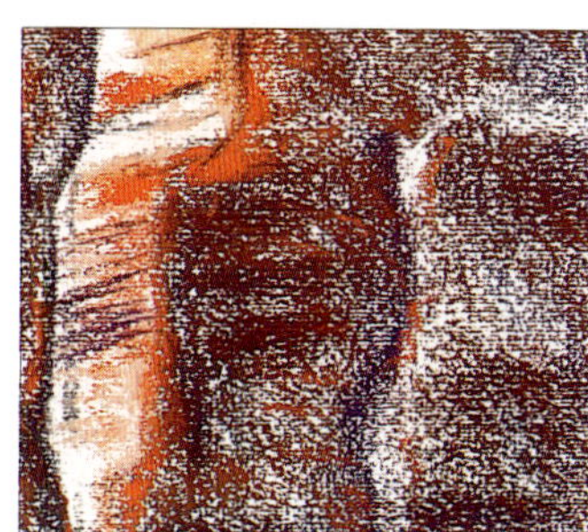

Craggy mountains in watercolour

In this exercise in aerial perspective, although the scene is very simple, you must convey a sense of the distances involved in order for it to look convincing. Tonal contrast is one way of achieving this: remember that colours are generally paler toward the horizon, so the mountains in the far distance look paler than those in the foreground. Textural contrast is another way to give a sense of distance: details such as jagged rocks and clumps of snow need to be more pronounced in the foreground than in the background.

The use of warm and cool colours to convey a sense of light and shade is important, too. Cool colours, such as blue, appear to recede and so painting crevices in the rocks in a cool shade makes them look deeper and farther away from the viewer. Warm colours, on the other hand, appear to advance and seem closer to the viewer. These should be used for the areas of rock that jut upward into the sunlight.

Although you want the painting to look realistic, do not worry about getting the shape of every single rock exactly right, If you try to put in every crack and crevice that you can see, you will get so bogged down in detail that you will lose sight of the images as a whole and your painting may become tight and laboured. It is more important to convey an overall impression.

Use short, jagged brushstrokes that follow the direction of the rock formations to convey the craggy texture and, above all, try to work freely and spontaneously.

Materials
- *2B pencil*
- *Rough watercolour board*
- *Watercolour paints: ultramarine blue, burnt sienna, cobalt blue, phthalocyanine blue, alizarin crimson, raw umber*
- *Brushes: large round, old brush for masking*
- *Sponge*
- *Tissue paper*
- *Masking fluid*
- *Scalpel or craft (utility) knife*

The scene

These craggy peaks make a dramatic image. The drama is enhanced by the billowing clouds, set against a brilliant blue sky, and the last vestiges of snow clinging to the rocks in the late spring.

Textural detail is most evident in the foreground; this also helps to create a sense of distance.

Note how the colours look paler in the distance, due to the effect of aerial perspective.

1 Using a 2B pencil, lightly sketch the scene, indicating the main gulleys and crevices and the bulk of the clouds in the sky. Keep your pencil lines loose and fluid: try to capture the essence of the scene and to feel the 'rhythm' of the jagged rock formations.

2 Mix a pale, neutral grey from ultramarine blue and burnt sienna. Using a large round brush, wash this mixture over the foreground mountain.

3 Mix a bright blue from cobalt blue and a little phthalocyanine blue. Using a large round brush, wash it over the top of the sky. While this is still wet, dampen a small sponge in clean water, squeeze out the excess moisture, and dab it on the sky area to lift off some of the colour. This reveals white cloud shapes with softer edges than you could achieve using any other technique.

Tips: The sponge is used in this project to lift off paint colour applied to the sky area, and to apply paint. The surface of the sponge leaves a soft, textured effect.

• Each time you apply the sponge, turn it around in your hand to find a clean area, and rinse it regularly in clean water so that you do not accidentally dab colour back on to the paper.

4 Mix a neutral purple from alizarin crimson, ultramarine blue and a little raw umber. Using a large round brush, dampen the dark undersides of the clouds and touch in the neutral purple mixture. While this is still damp, touch in a second application of the same mixture in places to build up the tone. If necessary, soften the edges and adjust the shapes of the dark areas by dabbing them with a piece of sponge or clean paper towel to lift off colour.

5 Study your reference photograph to see exactly where the little patches of snow lie on the foreground mountain. Using an old brush, apply masking fluid to these areas to protect them from subsequent applications of paint. Use thin lines of fluid for snow that clings to the ridges and block in larger areas with the side of the brush. Wash the brush in liquid detergent and warm water. Leave the masking fluid to dry completely before moving on to the next stage.

6 Mix a dark blue from cobalt blue and phthalocyanine blue and paint the distant hills between the two mountains. Dilute the mixture and brush it over the background mountain. Leave to dry. Mix a dark brown from burnt sienna with a little alizarin crimson and ultramarine blue, and wash this mixture over the background mountain. Add a little alizarin crimson and begin painting the foreground mountain.

7 Using a large round brush, continue to paint the foreground mountain. Use the same dark brown mixture that you used in Step 6 for the areas that catch the sun, and phthalocyanine blue for the areas that are in the shade. Paint with relatively short and slightly jagged vertical brushstrokes that echo the direction of the rock formations. This helps to convey the texture of the rocks.

Assessment time
Because of the careful use of warm and cool colours, the painting is already beginning to take on some form. Much of the rest of the painting will consist of building up the tones you have already applied to enhance the three-dimensional effect and the texture of the rocks. At this stage, it is important that you take the time to assess whether or not the areas of light and shade are correctly placed. Note, too, the contrast between the foreground and the background: the foreground is more textured and is darker in tone, and this helps to convey an impression of distance.

The rocks that jut out into the sunlight are painted in a warm brown so that they appear to advance.

The crevices are in deep shade and are painted in a cool blue so that they appear to recede.

The background mountain is painted in a flat colour, which helps to convey the impression that it is farther away.

8 Mix a deep, purplish blue from alizarin crimson, phthalocyanine blue and raw umber. Brush this mixture along the top of the background peak, leaving some gaps so that the underlying brown colour shows through. Using the dark brown mixture used in Step 6, build up tone on the rest of the background mountain, applying several brushstrokes wet into wet to the darker areas.

9 Continue building up the tones on both mountains, using the same paint mixtures as before. Leave to dry. Using your fingertips, gently rub off the masking fluid to reveal the patches of white snow. (It is sometimes hard to see if you have rubbed off all the fluid, so run your fingers over the whole painting to check that you have not missed any.) Dust or blow all dried fluid off the surface of the painting.

10 Using the tip of a scalpel or craft knife and pulling the blade sideways so as not to cut through the paper, scratch off thin lines of paint to reveal snow in gulleys on the background mountain.

11 Apply tiny dots of colour around the edges of some of the unmasked areas to tone down the brightness a little. Continue the tonal build-up, making sure your brushstrokes follow the contours of the rocks.

12 Dip a sponge in clean water, squeeze out any excess moisture and dampen the dark clouds. Dip the sponge in the neutral purple mixture used in Step 4 and dab it lightly on to the clouds to darken them and make them look a little more dramatic.

13 The final stage of the painting is to assess the tonal values once more to make sure that the contrast between the light and dark areas is strong enough. If necessary, brush on more of the purplish blue mixture used in Step 8 to deepen the shadows.

The finished painting

This is a beautiful and dramatic example of how contrasting warm colours with cool colours can create a sense of three dimensions. Although the colour palette is restricted, the artist has managed to create an impressively wide range of tones.

Jagged brushstrokes that follow the direction of the rock formations create realistic-looking textures on the foreground mountain and the white of the paper shines through in places, giving life and sparkle to the image.

The white of the paper is used to good effect, implying patches of snow clinging to the rocks.

The soft-edged clouds and brilliant blue sky provide a perfect counterbalance to the harshness of the rocks below.

The background mountain is painted in flat washes, with far less textural detail than the foreground.

Poppy field in watercolour

Lush expanses of wild flowers are always attractive, and when those flowers are a rich and vibrant red, like this stunning array of poppies, the subject simply cries out to be painted.

This project presents you with several challenges. First and foremost, it is an exercise in painting spontaneously and in creating an impression rather than trying to capture each individual flower. Work quickly and freely, and focus more on the overall tones than on specific details. Make sure you do not make the poppies look as if they have been planted in neat, straight rows. It is surprisingly difficult to position dots of colour randomly, but unpredictable techniques, such as spattering, can help.

Second, remember that this is not a botanical study: what you are trying to create is an overall impression of the scene, not an accurate record of how the flowers are constructed. You really do not want a lot of crisp detail in a scene like this, otherwise it will look stilted and lifeless. This is where watercolour really comes into its own. Wet-into-wet washes that merge on the paper create a natural-looking blur that is perfect for depicting a mass of flowers and trees swaying in the breeze.

Finally, take some time considering the tonal balance of the painting. Red and green are complementary colours so they usually work well together, but if the greens are too dark they could easily overpower the rest of the painting. On the other hand, if they are too light they will not provide a strong enough backdrop for the flowers.

Materials

- *2B pencil*
- *140lb (300gsm) rough watercolour paper, pre-stretched*
- *Watercolour paints: cobalt blue, alizarin crimson, gamboge, raw sienna, sap green, Delft or Prussian blue, viridian, burnt umber, cadmium orange, cadmium red, Payne's grey*
- *Brushes: large mop, medium mop, fine rigger, old brush for masking fluid, medium round, fine round*
- *Masking fluid*

The scene

This field is a blaze of red poppies as far as the eye can see, counterbalanced by a dark green background of trees. Although the horizon is very near the middle of the picture, which can sometimes makes an image look static, this effect is offset by the fact that the top half of the image is divided more or less equally into trees and sky. However, the sky is very bright, and this detracts from the poppies; so using artistic license with the colour here will improve the overall effect.

The sky lacks colour and needs to be made less dominant.

The dark trees provide a neutral background that makes the red of the poppies all the more vibrant.

1 Using a 2B pencil, lightly sketch the outline of the trees and some of the larger foreground poppies. Don't attempt to put in every single flower – a few of the more prominent ones are all you need as a guide at this stage. Using an old brush, apply masking fluid over the poppies in the foreground. In the middle ground and distance, dot and spatter masking fluid to create a more random, spontaneous effect. Draw some thin lines of masking fluid for the long grasses in the foreground. Clean your brush thoroughly and leave the painting to dry.

2 Using a medium round brush, dampen the sky area with clean water, leaving a few strategically placed gaps for clouds. Mix up a strong wash of cobalt blue and drop this on to the damp sky area, so that it spreads wet-into-wet up to the gaps left for the cloud shapes. The colour is more intense than it was in reality, but the sky needs to look dramatic and it is perfectly acceptable to use artistic licence and alter aspects of the scene in this way. Leave to dry.

3 Apply a strong wash of gamboge to the tree tops. Add raw sienna and brush over the base of the trees and the horizon. Touch raw sienna into the clouds. While this is still damp, touch a purplish-blue mixture of cobalt blue and alizarin crimson on to the underside of the clouds. Leave to dry.

4 Mix a dark green from sap green, raw sienna and a little Delft or Prussian blue. Using a medium round brush, brush this mixture over the trees to create dark foliage areas, allowing some of the underlying gamboge to show through in places.

5 Continue building up the foliage on the trees, leaving a few gaps. Mix a mid-toned green from gamboge and sap green and, using a large mop brush, brush this mixture over the lower part of the painting – the poppy field. Leave to dry.

6 Mix a darker green from viridian and cobalt blue and apply this mixture to the foreground, using a large mop brush. Use the same colour to touch in some dark lines for the long shadows under the main tree. Leave to dry.

7 Mix a dark green from sap green, raw sienna and burnt umber and, using a fine rigger brush, brush thin lines on to the foreground. Leave to dry. Spatter the same mixture over the foreground to represent the grass seed heads and add texture. Leave to dry.

Assessment time

Cool greens and yellows have been put in across the whole painting, establishing the general tones of the scene. As you continue to work, you will probably find that you need to darken some of the background colours to maintain a balance between them and the foreground. This kind of tonal assessment should be an ongoing part of all your paintings. Now it is almost time to start putting in the bright red poppies in the foreground, the finishing touches that will bring the scene to life. Try above all else to maintain a feeling of spontaneity in the painting as you work: the poppies must look as if they are randomly distributed over the scene.

The dark tonal masses of the background have been established.

Spattering in the foreground gives interesting random texture.

8 Mix a dark green from Delft or Prussian blue, viridian and burnt umber and, using a medium mop brush, darken the trees, leaving some areas untouched to create a sense of form. Add a little more burnt umber to the mixture and, using a fine rigger brush, paint the tree trunks and some fine lines for the main branches. Leave to dry. Using your fingertips, gently rub off the masking fluid.

9 Mix an orangey red from cadmium orange and cadmium red. Using a fine round brush, start painting the poppies in the background.

10 Continue painting the white spaces with the red mixture used in Step 9, leaving a few specks of white to give life and sparkle to the painting. Apply a second layer of colour to some poppies while the first layer is still wet; the paint will blur, giving the impression of poppies blowing in the wind, and the tone will deepen.

11 Using a fine, almost dry brush and the same dark green mixture used in Step 7, paint in the exposed foreground stalks and grasses. Finally, using a fine rigger brush, touch in the black centres of the poppies with a strong Payne's grey.

The finished painting

This is a loose and impressionistic painting that nonetheless captures the mood of the scene very well. It exploits the strong effect of using complementary colours (red and green), but the density of colour has been carefully controlled so that the whole painting looks balanced, with no one part dominating the rest.

The sky is darker than in the original photograph, which helps to maintain the tonal balance of the scene.

The shadow under the tree is painted with short brushstrokes that echo the direction in which the grasses and flowers grow.

Only the foreground poppies have painted centres. Those in the background are so far away that a blur of colour suffices.

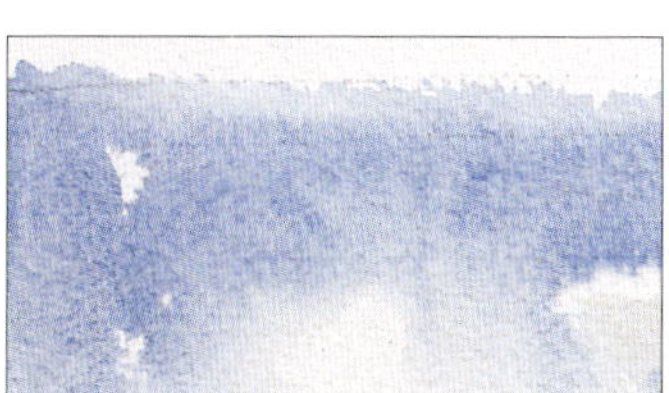

Snow scene in charcoal

Here is an interesting challenge: how do you draw a bright, white subject such as snow using charcoal, which is one of the densest and darkest drawing mediums available? The answer is not to attempt to draw the snow at all: allow the white of the paper to stand for the brightest parts of the snow and use the charcoal for the mid- and dark tones. Focus your attention on the clumps of earth that poke up above it and the thicket of trees on the right, rather than on the powdery, white covering on the ground.

Also, note that the snow is not a uniformly pure, unsullied white. The ground undulates, forming little peaks and shaded troughs. Tones of grey are required to make this distinction – smooth, pale tones without any sharp edges. To give the drawing impact, you also need to contrast the heavy, solid forms of the trees and background ridge with the much softer and less substantial shapes of the clouds and shadows. Use all the blending techniques at your disposal: smudge lines with your fingers or the side of your hand, or blend marks with a torchon, a sponge or tissue paper, as this allows you to build up areas of tone without creating a hard line.

If you get accidental smudges, do not worry. This is an unavoidable part of charcoal drawing and you can always wipe off powder with an eraser. A kneaded eraser gives a soft, smooth finish; for sharp edges, cut a plastic eraser or pull a kneaded eraser to a fine point. For an cheaper alternative, try small pieces of soft white bread.

Materials

- *Smooth drawing paper*
- *Willow charcoal sticks – thin and medium*
- *Kneaded eraser*
- *Compressed charcoal stick*
- *Large torchon*
- *Plastic eraser, cut to give a sharp edge*
- *Small sponge*

The scene

Here is a typical winter scene across a ploughed field. The thicket of trees on the right provides a focal point while the clumps of earth poking up through the snow form diagonal lines across the field that lead the viewer's eye through the composition.

1 Using a thin charcoal stick, map out the proportions of the scene. Look for specific points from which you can measure other elements. Here, the artist used the clump of trees as a starting point. When he measured it, he discovered that the distance from the base of the clump to the base of the ridge in the distance is roughly the same as the distance from the base of the trees to the base of the image.

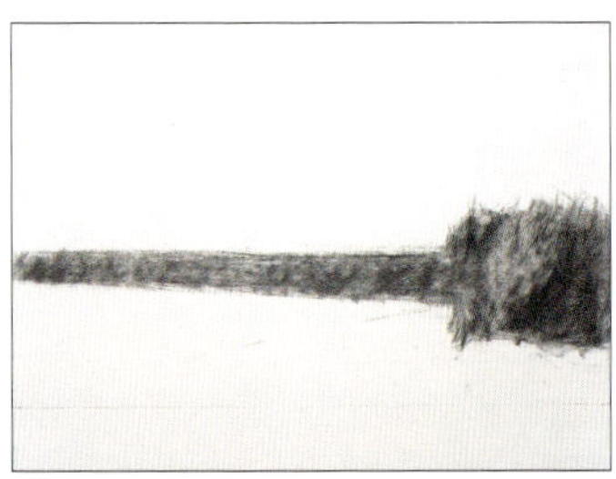

2 Using the side of the charcoal, roughly block in the wedge-shaped area of land in the middle distance and the thicket of trees on the right. Make jagged, spiky marks for the top of the thicket to convey the texture of the trees. Note also that some areas are darker in tone than others; although you will elaborate this later, it is a good idea to get some tonal variation into the drawing even at this early stage.

3 Using the tip of a medium charcoal stick, draw the darkest areas within the thicket of trees. Look for the negative shapes – the spaces between the branches rather than the branches themselves. Switch to a thin charcoal stick for the branches that stick out at the sides and top of the main mass. Using a kneaded eraser, lightly stroke off charcoal for the lighter-toned branches within the clump.

4 Start to introduce some form into the wedge-shaped area of land in the middle distance. The trees at the front of this area are very dark in tone, so build up the tone with heavy, vertical strokes. Use a thin charcoal stick to start dotting in the exposed clumps of earth peeping up above the snow in the field and make thin vertical strokes for the grasses on the right-hand side of the image.

5 Using a stick of compressed charcoal, put in some very dark blacks in the trees in the middle distance so that you gradually begin to build up texture and tone. Also use the compressed charcoal to draw more of the exposed clumps of earth that run across the field, making small, dotted marks of varying sizes and making the marks darker as you come toward the foreground.

6 Rub some charcoal on to a scrap piece of paper and press the end of a large torchon into the resulting powder. Gently stroke the torchon over the snow that leads down to the clump of trees to create soft shadows.

7 Using a plastic eraser, wipe off some of the charcoal to create the effect of snow on the edges of the fields in the middle distance. By carefully cutting the eraser down with a razor you can make it produce a crisp, sharp-edged line.

Assessment time

The main elements of the composition are in place, but the contrast between the sky (to which no charcoal has been applied so far) and the dark, dense tones of the trees is too extreme. This balance needs to be corrected. Even so, the thicket of trees on the right still needs to be darkened in places. Your task now that the essentials of the composition are all in place is to develop texture and tone across the image. In order to do this, you will need to continually assess the tonal balance of the drawing as a whole, to ensure that no one part becomes too dominant.

As yet there is no detail in the sky, which forms roughly half the image.

With the exception of a few foreground shadows, there is no texture or detail in the snow areas.

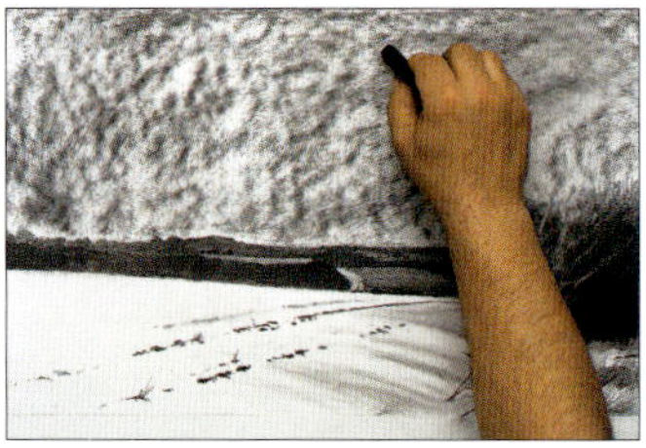

8 Wipe the side of a medium stick of charcoal over the sky area. Note how the coverage is uneven, creating lovely dappled marks.

9 Using a circular motion, vigorously rub a small sponge over the sky to smooth out the charcoal marks.

10 There is a band of blue in the sky above the land and below the mass of clouds. Block this in using the side of a medium charcoal stick and blend it to a mid-grey with a torchon, making it darker in tone than the rest of the sky. Using a kneaded eraser and a vigorous circular motion, lift off shapes for the looming storm clouds. Do not worry about the tones within the clouds at this stage; just try to get the approximate shapes. Note how putting some detail in the sky has changed the mood of the drawing from a tranquil winter scene to something much more dramatic, in which the threat of a storm is imminent.

11 Put in some very dark storm clouds and blend the charcoal with your fingertips or a sponge. Immediately, the scene looks much more dramatic; note how the dark areas of sky balance the thicket of trees on the right of the image. Scribble some charcoal on a piece of scrap paper to get some loose powder, as in Step 6. Dip a torchon in the powder and gently stroke it over the sky to create softly blended areas of mid tone between the clouds. This allows the white areas of the clouds to stand out more clearly.

12 The sky is now quite dark, so you may need to darken the land mass to make it more dominant. Compressed charcoal gives a very rich, intense black. Note how the snow also seems to sparkle and stand out more once the land mass has been darkened.

13 Using a thin charcoal stick, put in any remaining exposed clumps of earth on the field. Re-assess the whites in relation to the rest of the image. You may need to use a kneaded eraser to lift off some charcoal in the grasses on the right.

The finished drawing

This drawing demonstrates the versatility of charcoal. It can be blended to give a smooth, even coverage, as in the mid-toned areas of the sky, or used to create bold, highly textured marks, as in the clump of trees. The success of the image is due largely to the contrast between the very light and the very dark areas. In scenes like this, the key is often to darken the dark areas rather than to lighten the lights.

Charcoal is softly blended with a sponge to create the clouds.

The exposed clumps of earth are paler in the distance, creating a sense of recession.

'Drawing' some of the branches with an eraser creates fine, crisp-edged lines.

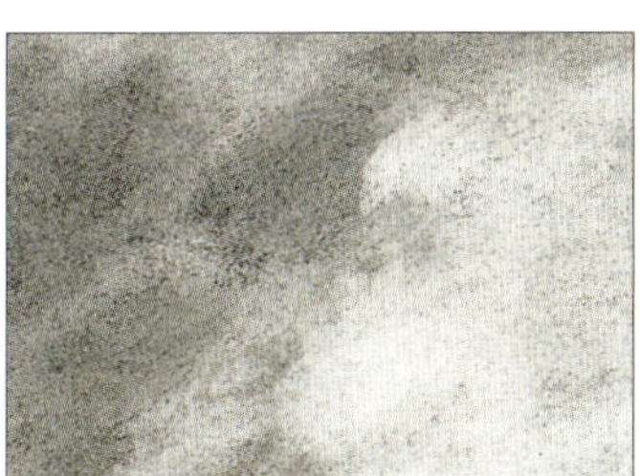

French vineyard in watercolour

This deceptively simple-looking scene is a useful exercise in both linear and aerial perspective. Take care over your underdrawing, as it underpins all the rest of the painting: if the rows of vines appear to be going the wrong way it will look very strange. It is worth taking plenty of time over this stage.

You also need to mix tones carefully. Note how the dark green vine leaves in the foreground give way to a much paler, yellower green in the distance – and then see how these pale greens gradually darken again above the horizon, shifting from a mid green to a very bluish green on the distant hills. Remember to test out each tone on a scrap piece of paper before you apply it.

Materials

- *2B pencil*
- *140lb (300gsm) rough watercolour paper, pre-stretched*
- *Watercolour paints: cerulean blue, Naples yellow, gamboge, light red, sap green, ultramarine violet, cobalt blue, viridian, Payne's grey, burnt umber*
- *Brushes: large mop, medium mop, fine round*

The scene

Sometimes one reference image simply does not give you enough information to create the painting you want. Do not be afraid to combine elements from several photos or sketches to create the desired effect. Here, the artist referred to the long panoramic-format photograph for the close-up detail of the vine leaves and the farm buildings, but based his composition on the larger photograph, in which the rows of vines are angled in a more interesting way.

1 Sketch the outline of the hills and vines, then dampen the sky with clean water, leaving some gaps. Mix a wash of cerulean blue and drop it on to the damp areas. Leave to dry.

2 Mix a pale wash of Naples yellow and touch it into the dry cloud shapes and along the horizon line. Leave to dry.

3 Darken the top of the sky with cerulean blue and leave to dry. Mix gamboge with light red and brush over the vines. Paint light red on the foreground and in between the vines.

4 Using a medium mop brush, loosely paint strokes of sap green into the foreground, heading along the perspective lines toward the vanishing point on the horizon, to indicate the rows of vines. Leave to dry.

5 Mix a deep blue from ultramarine violet, cobalt blue and viridian and wash it over the hills. Put a few dots along the top edge to break up the harsh outline and imply trees.

6 Mix a mid-toned green from viridian with a little cobalt blue. Using a medium mop brush, brush this mixture over the lower part of the hills. Mix a dark blue from cobalt blue, ultramarine violet and viridian. Using a large mop brush, darken the shadows on the distant hills. Use the same colour to stipple a few dots on the green hills to imply trees on the horizon.

Tip: It is often easier to assess colours if you turn your reference photo upside down. This allows you to concentrate on the tones without being distracted by the actual subject matter.

Assessment time

Once you are happy with the general lines and colours of the scene, you can start thinking about adding those all-important touches of detail and texture. Do not be tempted to do this too early: once you have painted the detail, it will be much harder to go back and make any tonal corrections to the background or the spaces between the rows of vines.

The perspective of the foreground has been established, leaving you free to add detail and texture.

The background is virtually complete, with darker shadows on the hills providing a sense of light and shade.

7 Mix a dark green from sap green, Payne's grey and a little burnt umber. Using a large mop brush, wet the foreground with clean water, leaving gaps for the vines. Using a medium mop brush, brush the dark green mixture on to the damp areas and let it flow on the paper to define the general green masses of the vines and their leaves. Paint the dark shapes of the foreground vine leaves.

8 Continue painting the vine leaves, as in Step 7. Do not try to be too precise or the painting may easily start to look overworked: generalized shapes will suffice. Mix a warm but neutral grey from ultramarine violet and burnt umber and, using a fine round brush, paint in the stems of the vines and the posts that support them, taking care to make the posts smaller as they recede into the distance.

9 Mix a dark shadow colour from ultramarine violet and a little burnt umber and brush this mixture across the ground in between the rows of vines. Again, take care over the perspective and make the shadows narrower as the vines recede into the distance.

10 Mix a warm, reddish brown from light red and a touch of Naples yellow and use this to paint the buildings in the background. This warm colour causes the buildings to advance, even though they occupy only a small part of the picture area. Using a fine brush and the same dark green mixture that you used in Step 7, touch in some of the detail on the vines.

11 Using an almost dry brush held on its side, brush strokes of light red in between the rows of vines. This strengthens the foreground colour but still allows the texture of the paper to show through, implying the pebbly, dusty texture of the earth in which the vines are planted.

12 Using a fine brush, brush a little light red on the top of the roofs. This helps the roofs to stand out and also provides a visual link with the colour of the earth in the foreground. Add a little burnt umber to the light red mixture to darken it, and paint the window recesses and the shaded side of the buildings to make them look three-dimensional.

The finished painting

Fresh and airy, this painting is full of rich greens and warm earth colours, providing a welcome dose of Mediterranean sunshine. Note how most of the detail and texture are in the foreground, while the background consists largely of loose washes with a few little dots and stipples to imply the tree-covered mountains beyond. This contrast is a useful device in landscape painting when you want to establish a sense of scale and distance.

Cool colours in the background recede.

Simple dots and stipples are enough to give the impression of distant trees.

Note how the rows of vines slant inward and converge toward the vanishing point.

Warm colours in the foreground advance.

Sun-bleached scene in acrylics

It could be said that contrast is the key to depicting bright sunlight in a work of art. In this scene of the landscape around a ruined temple in Sicily, the sunlight has the effect of bleaching out colour from all the pale-coloured stones and worn pathways – but unless you make the shadows really dark, the whole painting will look too pale and insipid. So it is the contrast that counts.

The key is to work gradually, building up the density of colour in stages. Even though this demonstration is in acrylics it's a good idea to leave the brightest highlights unpainted to begin with, just as you would in watercolour. Once you have put in the mid tones, it is much easier to judge how far you need to darken or lighten everything else. Keep assessing the darks and lights in relation to each other as you go: you may be surprised at how dark the deepest shadows turn out to be.

Another thing to remember when you are painting a deep panorama such as this one is the effect of aerial perspective. Colours look paler with distance, so this is one way of creating a sense of recession. Note, too, how the sky pales toward the horizon.

Texture is also less evident in things that are farther away, so concentrate on the textural detail in the foreground. There are a lot of trees and scrubby bushes in this scene that give you the chance to exploit dry brush and other textural techniques. However, beware of putting in too much detail. An impression of the shapes and textures will be sufficient, as it is really the intensity of the light and its effect on the landscape that are the subjects of this atmospheric painting.

Materials

- *Heavy watercolour paper*
- *HB pencil*
- *Acrylic paints: brilliant blue, alizarin crimson, cadmium yellow, yellow ochre, ultramarine blue, titanium white*
- *Brushes: Selection of rounds and filberts in different sizes*
- *Absorbent paper towel*

The scene
There is so much of interest in this scene that the artistic possibilities are huge. You might choose to walk along the path and paint the temple itself; you might decide that the twisted olive trees and dramatic shadows are to be the subject of your painting; or you might, as the artist has done here, elect for a broad panorama that concentrates on the play of light and shade. The dramatic shadows cast by the trees are counterbalanced by the patches of brilliant sunlight, lending a semi-abstract quality to the rocky forms. Whatever you choose, remember that a strong composition is essential; the viewer's eye has to be directed thorugh the image in some way, particularly when there is so much visual information to take in. Here, our attention is directed via the path to the ruined temple which, although it occupies only a small part of the picture space, is a strong focal point.

1 Using an HB pencil lightly sketch in the horizon, the square shape of the temple, and the main lines of the walls leading up to it. Wash a dilute mix of brilliant blue over the sky and then, using a paper towel, dab off some of the colour near the horizon to suggest a heat haze. Turn the work upside down to make it easier.

2 Mix a dilute, pale wash of alizarin crimson with a little cadmium yellow. Using a large round brush, wash it over the land in the background and over the parched earth on the left. Mix an earthy brown from yellow ochre with a touch of both ultramarine blue and alizarin and wash it over the land on the right for a warm undertone.

3 Mix a blue-green from ultramarine and yellow ochre and block in the dark foliage in the foreground, varying the proportions of the colours as necessary. Roughly put in the large foreground in a purple mix of alizarin and ultramarine. Touch in the blue of the distant hill in a mix of ultramarine and white.

4 Mix an olivey yellow from ultramarine, cadmium yellow and white and touch in the trees on the right – just the basic shapes. Mix a pinky white from alizarin crimson and white and block in the shapes of the temple. Add yellow ochre to the mix and scumble it on for the scrubland.

5 Continue putting in blocks of colour across the landscape, using the same pink- and ochre-based mixes as before. Remember that colours appear paler with distance, so add more white to your mixes for the background areas. Leave the brightest patches of earth in the foreground untouched for now.

6 Mix white, alizarin and cadmium yellow and put in the sun-bleached stones and earth in the foreground. Make this mix slightly thicker, for texture. Block in more shadows with a deep purple mixed from alizarin and ultramarine. With a fine brush, refine the temple in purples and pinks.

Assessment time

The artist has built up a good feeling of recession in the landscape, with darker tones in the foreground and lighter, paler ones in the middle distance and background. This could be improved by increasing the amount of textural detail in the foreground. However, the image is still lacking in form: the land in the middle distance, in particular, looks rather flat and it is hard to make sense of the different planes. To enhance the bright, sunny feel, the shadows need to be intensified for more contrast between them and the bright patches of ground.

This area is lacking in form.

There is insufficient contrast between the lights and the darks.

Although the foliage masses have been put in, these blocks of colour do not yet 'read' as trees.

7 Using a very fine brush, put in the trunks of the trees in a very dark purple. Define the shapes and tones of the foreground blocks of colour more clearly, so that the image becomes more three-dimensional. Look, in particular, at the purple-pink shadows the trees cast on the ground. Observe the shaded sides of the ruined walls in the foreground, which have a very dark tone compared to the sunlit patches.

8 Create more modelling on the left-hand side of the image, in the tussocky scrubland. By using different tones of purple-pink here, you can create a sense of light and shade and the undulations in the land. Dot in some darker trees and shrubs, too, remembering to keep the tone lighter than that used for the blue-green foreground foliage so that you create an impression of distance.

The finished painting

The heat and intensity of the bright summer sunlight is captured here. The piece is loosely painted, relying on blocks of colour and the interplay of light and shade. Very little detail is evident, but by carefully setting down the different tones the artist has created a convincing impression of depth and three-dimensional forms. The effects of aerial perspective have been well observed and the bold brushstrokes and dabs of colour give the painting energy.

Note how the land is paler and bluer in the distance than it is in the foreground.

The strong contrast between light and shade enhances the feeling of bright sunlight.

The different tones in the foliage masses make them appear three-dimensional.

Impasto landscape in oils

Impasto means thicker-than-usual paint. For some artists, one of the main attractions of oils and acrylics is that they can be built up thickly to create a range of exciting surface textures.

Impasto techniques are far from new. Both Rembrandt and the great 19th-century landscape painter J.M.W. Turner used thick, solid paint in some areas of their paintings, contrasting this with thinner applications elsewhere. Van Gogh was the first artist to use uniformly thick paint, applied in swirling or jagged brushstrokes; since then many artists have exploited the expressive and dynamic qualities of thick paint, sometimes squeezing it on to the canvas straight from the tube and then modelling it with a brush, or applying it with a painting knife or even using their fingers to create the right effects.

Impasto work of this nature requires a great deal of paint, so it is a good idea to bulk it out with one of the special media sold for impasto work in both oils and acrylics. This is particularly necessary if you are working in acrylics, as the paint is slightly runnier than oil paint. Adding an impasto medium enables you to produce two or three times the amount of paint, without changing the colour of the paint in any way.

With its scrubby vegetation and pebbly path, this Mediterranean cliffside scene provides many opportunities for working impasto. In a landscape such as this, however, it is generally helpful to include some quieter, flatter areas, such as the sea and sky, for the viewer's eye to rest on. This exercise is painted entirely with a painting knife.

Materials

- *Canvas-covered board primed with acrylic gesso*
- *HB pencil*
- *Oil paints: phthalocyanine blue, titanium white, ultramarine blue, alizarin crimson, cadmium lemon, sap green, burnt sienna, raw sienna*
- *Rag*
- *Small painting knife*

The scene

This is a classically composed scene, with the main cliff falling at the intersection of the thirds and the path leading our eye through the picture. The contrasting textures – the relative smoothness of the sea and sky versus the pebbly path and dense vegetation – make a picture that is full of interest.

1 Using an HB pencil, lightly sketch the scene so that you have a rough guide to where to place the different elements.

2 Mix a pale blue from phthalocyanine blue and titanium white. Using a rag, smear it across the sky. Add more phthalocyanine blue and, using a small painting knife, put in the sea in the distance, smoothing the paint out so that the coverage and density of colour are fairly even.

3 There are some deep shadows on the sea; paint these in using ultramarine blue. Still using the painting knife, apply strokes of thick titanium white for the clouds. The rough impasto work helps to give a sense of volume to the clouds.

4 Mix a dark purplish blue from alizarin crimson and ultramarine blue and smear it over the rocky, exposed area of cliff on the right, adding some sap green to the mixture as you work down toward the path. To capture the jagged feel of the rocks, pull the paint up with the tip of the knife to form small peaks. Mix a bright green from cadmium lemon, sap green and a little burnt sienna and begin putting in the lightest parts of the foreground vegetation on the left, dabbing in a more yellow version of the mixture in parts.

Tip: When painting the vegetation, angle the painting knife so that it follows the direction in which the plants naturally grow.

5 Mix a pale brown from raw sienna and white and paint the rough-textured ground to the right of the path.

6 Add more raw sienna to the mixture and include some darker browns in the vegetation.

7 Mix a pale purple from ultramarine blue, titanium white and a little alizarin crimson and use this to put in the shaded sides of the foreground rocks to the right of the path. Paint bright highlights where the sun hits the tops of the rocks in titanium white.

Assessment time

The impasto work has created bold, dynamic textures in the dark cliff and path, but the foreground of the image looks rather flat and featureless in comparison. Increasing the texture in the foreground plants and rocks will also help to create more of a sense of scale and distance in the painting.

The vegetation is little more than splashes of colour, with virtually no texture or detailing.

The path is distractingly bright.

8 Mix a very dark green from ultramarine blue and sap green and put in the very darkest areas of the plants that are growing on the cliff side, dabbing the paint on with the tip of the painting knife. Add some alizarin crimson to the mixture and put in some slightly curved strokes, using the side of the knife, for the taller stems and branches.

9 Continue to build up textures, using the same colours as before. Vary the way that you apply the paint, sometimes using the side of the knife and sometimes the tip. Paint the tall, thin grass on the right-hand side of the painting using a mixture of raw sienna and white, and dab on brownish stones on the path in mixes of cadmium yellow and raw sienna.

The finished painting

Impasto work adds great vitality to this image: you can almost reach out and feel the texture of the rocks and plants. The artist has also made full use of the range of marks that can be made with a knife, from smoothing out the sky and sea areas with the flat of the knife to dabbing on small blobs of paint with the tip, and even dragging the side of the knife over the canvas to create long, flowing marks for the thinnest stems and branches.

Note how the knife marks echo the direction in which the plants grow.

A flatter application of paint over the sea makes a calm area. The lack of texture here also helps to create a sense of distance.

Thick oil and acrylic paint can be pulled up with the tip of the knife to form small peaks, as here.

Woodland path in gouache

This project is about interpreting what you see and conveying the mood of the scene, rather than making a photo-realistic rendition. That does not mean that observation is not important. When you are painting a scene like this, look at the overall growth patterns. Are the tree trunks tall and straight or do they lean at an angle? Do the branches droop and spread on either side of the trunk, like weeping willows, or is the foliage weighted toward one side, like maples and Scots pines? Is the shape of the tree conical or rounded?

Look at where the shadows fall, too – and remember that the shape made by the shadows should match the shape of the objects that cast the shadows. Above all, make sure that the shadows are dense enough, as the contrast between the dark and the brightly lit areas is what gives the work a three-dimensional quality.

This scene gives you the opportunity to explore many different textures – the tangled undergrowth and criss-crossing branches, the rough texture of the path and the peeling bark on the trees. Again, do not try to place every detail precisely. Spatters of paint convey the rough texture of the ground, while the colour of the tree trunks and the patterning of the bark call for more carefully placed brushstrokes.

Here the artist also added a few small pieces of collage in the final stages. This is optional, and you may think that the image does not need it; however, provided you do not overdo things it is well worth experimenting with simple techniques like this, as they can bring an added dimension to your work.

Materials

- *Watercolour paper primed with acrylic gesso*
- *4B pencil*
- *Masking fluid*
- *Medium-nibbed steel dip pen*
- *Gouache paints: phthalocyanine green, brilliant yellow, raw umber, raw sienna, zinc white, scarlet lake, jet black, phthalocyanine blue*
- *Brushes: large wash, small round, old toothbrush*
- *Newspaper*
- *Gum arabic*

The scene

Although there is no real focus point of interest in this scene, the textures and the contrasting shapes (the sweeping curve of the path against the strong vertical lines of the tree trunks) make it very rewarding to paint. The shadows and bright sunlight over the foreground also add interest.

1 Using a 4B pencil, sketch the scene, putting in as much detail as you feel you need. Your underdrawing will help you to keep track of where things are once you start applying the paint.

Tip: You do not need to get all the branches in exactly the right place in your underdrawing, but you should try to be faithful to the general patterns of growth and the rhythms of the scene. Although this is a fairly loose, impressionistic painting, it must look convincing – but it is also important to try to capture a sense of spring-like growth and energy in the scene.

2 Using a medium-nibbed steel dip pen and masking fluid mask the lightest trunks and branches. Also mask any branches that are lighter than their immediate surroundings, even if they are brown in colour rather than a light, silvery grey. Using an old toothbrush, spatter some masking fluid over the undergrowth. Leave to dry: this will not take long, but it is essential that the masking fluid is completely dry before you apply the first washes of colour.

3 Before you begin the painting stages, take some time to make absolutely sure that you have masked all of the light-coloured areas of branches and foliage that need to be protected. Even though gouache is opaque and it is perfectly possible to paint light colours over dark ones, such corrective measures should only be used as a last resort – otherwise you run the risk of losing some of the freshness and spontaneity of the painting.

4 Mix a dilute, bright green from phthalocyanine green and brilliant yellow. Using a large wash brush, put in broad horizontal strokes for the band of undergrowth that runs across the centre of the scene. Mix a duller green from phthalocyanine green and raw umber and repeat the process in the foreground. For the tree trunks in the background, put in vertical strokes of raw sienna and raw umber, occasionally adding some green to them.

5 Mix a dilute yellowish brown from zinc white and raw umber and brush the mixture lightly over the earth in the foreground, allowing some of the support to show through to create some texture in this area. The earth on the far right, behind the band of undergrowth, is warmer in tone, so paint this in raw sienna. While the paint is still wet, touch a little scarlet lake into it so that it spreads of its own accord.

6 Mix a very dark greenish black from jet black, phthalocyanine blue and phthalocyanine green and paint the little stream in the background. Add raw umber to the mixture and paint the cast shadows on the ground.

7 Add more phthalocyanine green to the mixture and paint the shapes of the trunks in the background. Using the bright green mixture from Step 4, spatter colour over the foreground for the low-growing plants alongside the path.

8 Roughly cut masks from newspaper the same shape as the largest cast shadows on the ground and lay them in position. (There is no need to stick them down.) Mix brilliant yellow with white, load an old toothbrush with this mix, then spatter it over the foreground, pulling the bristles back with your fingertips.

9 Repeat the spattering process with a mixture of white and raw umber to create the rough, pebbly texture of the path in the foreground. When the paint is dry, remove the newspaper masks: the scene is now beginning to take on more depth and texture.

10 There are some warm, pinkish tones on the path, so mix scarlet lake and white and lightly spatter a little of the mixture over the foreground. Leave to dry completely, then rub off all the masking fluid.

Tip: When you have removed a little of the masking fluid, squash it into a ball and rub it over the surface of the painting like an eraser. Any remaining fluid will stick to it.

Assessment time

Now that you have removed the masking fluid, it is easier to see what must be done to complete the painting. Although the general shapes are all there, at this stage you can see that the painting lacks depth: you need to increase the density of the shadows to resolve this.

The exposed areas are too stark and bright and contain no detail.

Overall, the colours are too light; the image does not have the feel of dense, dark woodland.

11 Mix a pale brown from raw sienna and white. Using a small round brush, paint the shaded sides of the exposed tree trunks. Add raw umber to the mixture and paint the shadows cast on the tree trunks by other branches.

12 Mix brilliant yellow with a little phthalocyanine green and, using a small round brush, dot in the yellow flowers in the undergrowth, making the distant dots slightly smaller than those in the foreground.

13 Using various versions of the dull green mixture from Step 4, paint the exposed grasses on the bottom right of the painting, keeping your brushstrokes loose and flowing.

Tip: Vary the greens, as this will look more natural. Some grasses are more mature than others, and some are more shaded, hence the variations in tone.

14 The yellow flowers in the centre look a little too vibrant, so tone them down by dotting some of the dull green mixture from the previous step into this area. Put in some solid areas of green, too, obliterating the exposed whites and re-establishing any shadow areas that have been lost on the grasses. Using mid-toned browns, reinforce the lines of trunks in the background.

15 You might consider the painting finished at this point, but here the artist decided to enhance the three-dimensional quality of the upper part of the image by incorporating a little collage. If you do this, take care not to overdo it, or the result could end up looking messy and overworked.

16 Paint strokes of branch-coloured paint on a piece of scrap paper and leave to dry. Cut out curving, branch-shaped pieces and brush a little gum arabic on to the reverse side. Position the pieces on the painting and brush gum arabic over the top to fix them in place. Leave to dry. (The advantage of using gum arabic is that, unlike ordinary glue, it can be painted over if necessary.) The collage element adds depth and texture to the image.

The finished painting

This is a lively and atmospheric painting of a woodland path in dappled sunlight. The strong vertical lines of the tree trunks and the diagonal lines of their shadows give the picture a feeling of energy that is echoed by the textural details and bold applications of colour. The palette of colours chosen by the artist is muted but natural looking. Although the scene looks deceptively simple, there is much to hold the viewer's attention.

Spatters and dots of colour convey the texture of the path and the tiny flowers.

The use of collage on some of the branches is subtle but effective.

Carefully placed brushstrokes are used for the grasses and tree bark.

Miniature landscape in coloured pencils

On a cold autumn or winter's day, you could be forgiven if the idea of taking your sketch pad and drawing tools and working outdoors for several hours did not seem very appealing. So why not bring the landscape (or at least a small part of it) indoors? This project combines a reference photo of a tiny area of woodland floor with a real leaf to create a delicate but beautifully observed nature study.

This is a miniature in several senses of the word: the finished drawing measures only 10.5 x 7.5cm (4¼ x 3in.), and the subject itself is tiny.

Despite its size you do not need to depict every twig and particle, or worry if pieces appear in different places to where they are in reality.

With this kind of detailed coloured-pencil work, you need to put down a number of very light layers of pigment. If you apply too heavy a layer, the wax in the pigment clogs up the tooth of the paper, and subsequent layers will not go on as smoothly or as evenly. The key to success is to work slowly, building up the tones and textures gently. Try to maintain an even pressure, using the side of the pencil so that the coverage is smooth and there are no obvious pencil marks. Even an experienced artist could easily take a whole day to produce a work as detailed as this, so do not be tempted to rush things.

Materials

- *Smooth illustration board*
- *HB pencil*
- *Coloured pencils: Pale grey, light yellow, black, mid grey, reddish brown, light yellow ochre, raw umber*

The scene

On a walk through her local woods, the artist spotted this patch of ground covered in twigs and leaf litter, with delicate fronds of bracken in the top right corner adding an inviting splash of colour. She thought it would make an interestingly textured background for a small nature study and took a photo to use as reference in her studio, planning to incorporate a natural object such as a leaf, pine cone or feather to complete the composition. This is an interesting approach to composing an image, as it allows you to play around with the scale of your subject for artistic effect.

1 Make a frame from two L-shaped pieces of card and move them around over your reference photo until you see a composition you are happy with.

2 Place your chosen leaf, or other natural object, in position on the photo. Note how the artist has placed the leaf on the diagonal, to create a more interesting composition.

3 Draw the frame size you have created on smooth illustration board, then sketch in the shape of the leaf in HB pencil. Block in the base colours for the ground and the green leaves, using a pale, cool grey for the lightest colour on the ground (the twigs) and a light yellow for the leaves. The colour should be barely perceptible at stage, as you will be building up the layers of colour very gradually.

Tip: Do not apply the colours too strongly at this stage. If you do, dab at the surface with a kneaded eraser twisted to a point.

4 Now preserve the light, bright areas of the picture by drawing in the various pieces of woodland debris – the positive shapes of small twigs, pieces of leaves and small pebbles – in a cool grey. Begin drawing in the negative shapes, too – the dark areas of earth in between – in black. This helps the eye to flow from one shape to another.

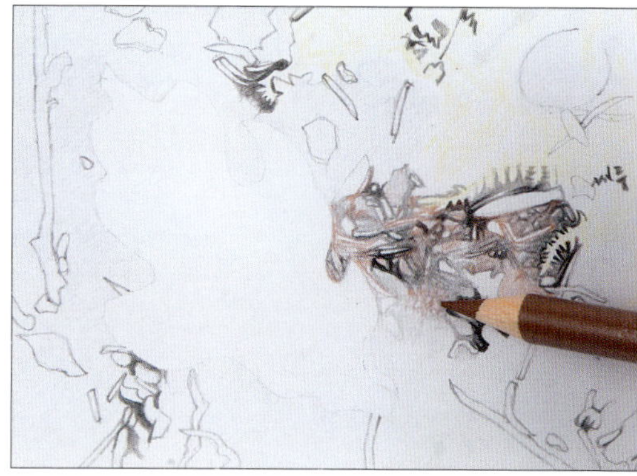

5 Start building up the layers of colour. Use a combination of linear strokes (for the debris, such as twigs) and squiggles for the mottled texture of the earth, alternating between mid and dark greys and a reddish brown.

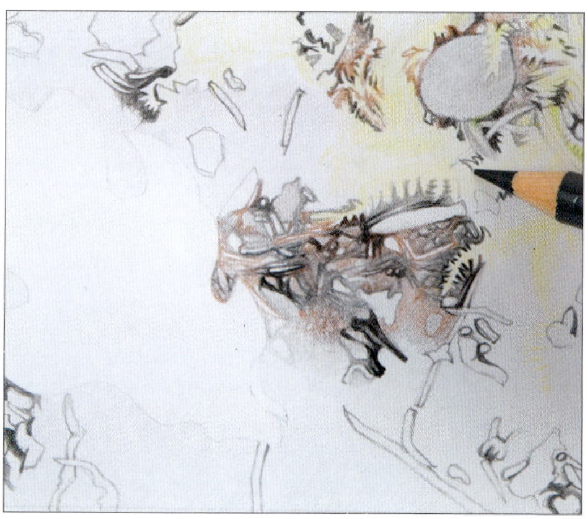

6 Continue building up the layers and colours in the background, alternating between greys and browns as before. Use a dark grey pencil to reinforce the edges of the tiny leaves. Effectively, you are repeating Step 3 – but this time, you will be using colour and refining the edges of the shapes.

7 Apply light yellow ochre to the leaf, leaving the highlight edges of the main vein uncoloured, as this is the very lightest part. Apply raw umber over the darker parts of the leaf, blending the colours very gently so that you do not get any harsh edges and allowing the underlying yellow ochre to show through to give a warm, golden glow. Draw in the dark edges of the other veins in raw umber.

Tip: It is important to keep your pencils very sharp for detailed work such as this. Keep a pot beside you for the shavings and sharpen often, using a razor or a pencil sharpener. Rotate the pencil as you work to keep the point for as long as possible.

Tip: With such a jumbled background, it is very easy to lose track of where you are in a drawing. Keep one finger of your non-drawing hand on your reference photo as you work, so that you can easily refer back to the right area.

8 Add shadows to the leaf in raw umber and darker reddish brown, so that it takes on a three-dimensional feel. Leave the highlight light.

9 Continue applying colour to the background. When you have put in the underlying moss, make tiny flicks of grey over the edge to create texture.

10 Redefine the leaf edge and darken the shadows within the leaf in the reddish brown.

Assessment time

The leaf (the main subject) has been left relatively light, with no more than a couple of layers of soft colour. When you have applied an initial layer of colour to the whole image, you will be able to assess how the leaf relates to the background. This allows you to build up the tones gradually, continually assessing each part of the drawing in relation to the rest and slowly refining the shapes which, at this stage, are not yet sufficiently well defined.

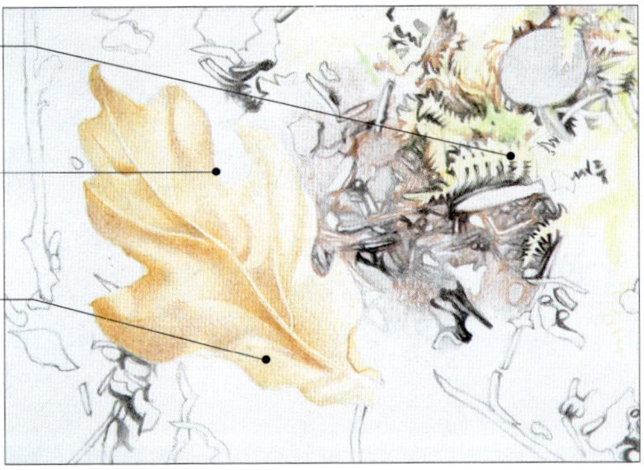

11 Some of the very brightest areas of the leaf may now look too pale in relation to the rest, so darken them if necessary, using the same colours as before. Using very sharp grey and reddish brown pencils, go over the edges of the leaf veins to really define them. Continue putting in the background, continually assessing the leaf in relation to it.

12 Using a black pencil, put in a small shadow under the leaf to help lift it away from the background and appear more three-dimensional.

The finished drawing

Although this is an impression of the scene rather than a very literal interpretation that includes every single twig and pebble, the amount of detail and the subtlety of tone that can be achieved using coloured pencils are very well demonstrated. Pencils are perfectly suited to this type of 'busy' subject. Within the leaf, the transitions from one shade to the next are virtually imperceptible. The background, drawn from a reference photo rather than from life, is muted in colour, allowing the leaf to stand out, while the tiny splashes of green moss add freshness and sparkle.

Crisp, linear detailing on the veins and subtle shading within the leaf make it look three-dimensional. It is realistically shaped without being overly detailed.

The shading under the leaf helps to 'lift' it from the background.

The bright yellows and greens of the moss add freshness to an image that is otherwise made up primarily of muted, earthy shades.

Landscape detail in gouache

Don't assume that landscapes have to be on a wide, panoramic scale. Little details that you come across – an old tree stump covered in fungi, a stretch of a mountain stream, or pebbles on a beach, as here – provide just as much scope for interesting compositions.

Here, a random arrangement of pebbles in a small fishing harbour, which the artist came across quite by chance, has been transformed into a colourful painting that is full of texture and interest.

Of course, subjects like this require careful planning on the part of the artist. You have to decide how much of the scene to include, and where to place the edges of the painting. You may even have to move things around a little to get the effect you want, just as you might when painting a still life indoors, although beware of doing too much as this can ruin the spontaneity.

In this project, the pebbles are painted more or less life-size. Painting a smaller subject than normal is a useful exercise, as you will have to look at things in a different way. Your normal tendency when painting a landscape might well be to scan the scene rapidly to gain an impression of the key elements; you will probably then decide how to make these elements stand out. When you concentrate on a small area everything counts; you need to look at how the parts relate to one another in terms of their size, shape and colour, and adjust your position until you have the best viewpoint. Moving a step to your left or right, backward or forward, can make a big difference.

Materials

- *Illustration board*
- *B pencil*
- *Gouache paints: cadmium yellow deep, cadmium orange, burnt umber, phthalocyanine blue, ultramarine blue, zinc white, ivory black, mid green, flame red, lemon yellow, cerulean blue*
- *Brushes: large wash, small round, fine round; old toothbrush*
- *Rag or absorbent paper towel*
- *Small painting knife*
- *Acrylic gold size*
- *Gold leaf*

The scene
Pebbles in a harbour, glistening with water left by the retreating tide, present an interesting challenge. When painting a subject like this, look for contrasts of size and colour.

1 Using a B pencil, mark a grid of squares on your paper. Many of the pebbles are similar in size and shape, so the grid will help you to keep track of which pebble you are painting. Again using the B pencil, make a light underdrawing.

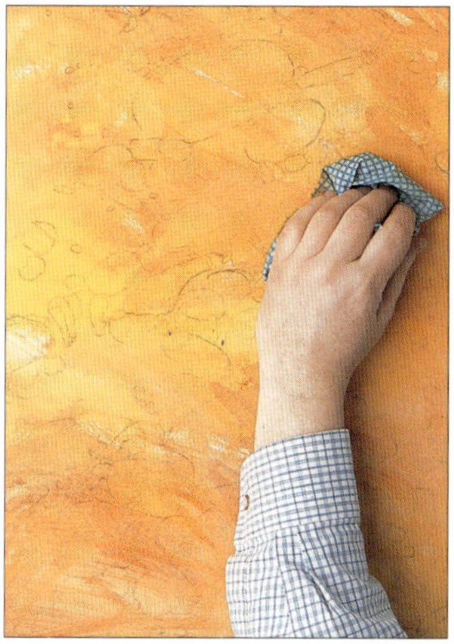

2 Mix separate washes of cadmium yellow deep and cadmium orange. Wash cadmium yellow deep over the whole paper. While it is still wet, brush in cadmium orange, leaving some areas as pure yellow. Press a clean rag or absorbent paper towel over the top right of the paper, to lift off some of the orange. Leave to dry.

3 Load an old brush or toothbrush with burnt umber and any other colours that you can detect in the sand, and drag a painting knife through the bristles to spatter paint over the paper, creating a background of large-grained sand. (If you do not have a painting knife, an ordinary kitchen knife will work just as well.) Leave to dry.

4 Mix various blues and greys from phthalocyanine blue, ultramarine blue, zinc white and ivory black. Using a small round brush, begin putting in the pebbles. Note that you are simply placing the pebbles at this stage; although they look like flat circles and ovals, you will begin to build up the form later.

5 Continue putting in the pebbles, varying the colours. Some have a purple undertone; others have a greenish tinge, created from a base colour of mid green plus zinc white or ivory black, as appropriate. Leave to dry.

6 Load the toothbrush with cadmium yellow deep. Drag a painting knife through the bristles, as in Step 3, to spatter both the pebbles and the sand with yellow paint. Repeat the process using flame red and lemon yellow.

Tip: To get the size of the spatters right, try practising on a piece of card, holding the toothbrush at different distances from the painting.

7 While the yellow spattering is still wet, drag a rag or a piece of absorbent kitchen towel over the spatters on some of the larger and darker pebbles to create streaked marks. On other pebbles, simply dab off any excess paint with a damp cloth to reveal the underlying colours, so that the spatters look like mica or other mineral crystals lodged within the stone, rather than lichen growing on top.

Assessment time

The initial blocking in of colours is complete, and the sand (which contains spatters of several different colours) looks convincingly textured, but at this stage the majority of the pebbles simply look like circles or ovals of dark colour positioned within the sand, rather than three-dimensional objects. The lighting is fairly flat and uniform, so there are no clearly defined shadows to help you, but if you look closely at the original you will see differences in both tone and colour temperature, with the sides of the pebbles that are turned away from the light being cooler (bluer) in colour. As you complete the painting, you should concentrate on reinforcing these tonal contrasts and on giving the pebbles more texture.

Smudging wet paint over dry has created streaks of paint that provide a good basis on which to build up more texture.

The shape of the pebbles is clear, but so far they all look flat and one-dimensional.

The texture of the sand has been built up well by blending colours wet into wet and by spattering.

8 Mix a bright but chalky blue from cerulean blue and a little zinc white. Using a small round brush, brush this mixture over the brightest parts of any blue-grey pebbles. Mix a pale yellow from cadmium yellow deep, lemon yellow and zinc white, and a pale pink from flame red and white, and dab these mixtures over the large, pale pebble near the top of the painting, using short horizontal brushstrokes. Mix a dilute, neutral shadow colour from phthalocyanine blue and a little burnt umber. Paint the small shadows to the right of the largest pebbles; they immediately look much more three-dimensional.

9 Continue to build up the texture and tonal contrasts within the pebbles, using all the colours on your palette – pale yellows and pinks, blue-greys, and almost pure white for the very lightest pebbles.

10 Vary your brushstrokes, stippling the paint in some places and using short strokes in others, but always allowing some of the underlying colours to show through.

11 Using a very fine brush, stipple all the colours on your palette on to the sand to create the appearance of large grains of sand or very tiny pebbles. Stand back from your work at regular intervals in order to see how the whole painting is progressing.

12 Many different colours have now been spattered and stippled on to the sand, creating a suitably granular-looking background for the pebbles. Take time to assess whether or not the texture of the sand is complete before you move on to the next stage.

13 If some of the stones look too dark in relation to the rest of the image, stipple or dab on some of your very pale yellow mixture. Use artistic licence where necessary in your choice of colours and keep looking at the balance of the painting as a whole.

14 Now for the final touch – the twine that twists and turns its way through the pebbles, creating a dynamic diagonal line that draws our eye through the composition. Using a fine round brush, 'draw' the line of the twine in acrylic gold size. Leave the size until it is tacky to the touch, following the manufacturer's instructions.

15 Lift a small piece of gold leaf by the backing paper and position it on the sized surface. Brush over the backing paper with a soft brush. Press a piece of kitchen towel over the gold leaf to ensure that it adheres firmly. Brush off any excess gold leaf with a clean, dry brush.

The finished painting

This is a deceptively simple-looking still life, but the gradual build-up of tones and textures makes it very convincing. A number of textural techniques have been used, and the artist has exploited the chalky consistency of gouache paint to give the pebbles solidity. The use of gold leaf for the twine is an imaginative touch that adds yet another texture to the image.

The trick with a painting like this is not to overwork it. Try to build up the image as a whole, rather than trying to finish one small area before you move on to the next. Taking time out at regular intervals, so that you can stand back and assess whether or not you have built up the textures to the degree that you want, is also important.

Just a hint of a shadow under the right-hand edge of the largest pebbles is enough to make them look three-dimensional.

The different facets of the stones have been carefully observed.

The twine, created by applying gold leaf, snakes its way through the image in a diagonal line.

Large-scale landscape in charcoal

Drawing on a large scale is very liberating, both physically and mentally. Physically, it allows you to use the full stretch of your arm and hand to make bold, sweeping marks that are full of energy. Mentally, you have to simplify things and stop yourself getting bogged down in unnecessary detail. Try to return to the essence of the scene – the aspects that made you want to draw it in the first place.

Charcoal is the perfect medium for a project such as this, as it is so versatile and easy to apply. You can drag the side of the charcoal across the support to cover large areas quickly, blend it using a variety of techniques, or use the tip to make expressive, linear marks.

If you cannot find sheets of purpose-made drawing paper large enough, a roll of lining (liner) paper from a DIY store makes an inexpensive alternative. Pin it to a drawing board (or attach it with masking tape), and then place the drawing board on a studio easel or hang it on a wall.

The composition of large-scale drawings needs careful thought and planning. Before you embark on the actual drawing, it is a good idea to make a schematic sketch of the composition, working out where the centre of interest falls and making sure that the viewer's eye is led to that point.

Materials

- *Drawing paper 1 x 1.25m (3 x 4ft)*
- *Charcoal: thick and thin sticks*
- *Kneaded eraser*

The scene

The rocky escarpment is surmounted on the left by a wooded area that echoes the bands of trees at the base of the escarpment and in the fields below. A narrow track leads the eye into the scene along the line of trees and up to the rocks. There are a range of shapes and textures in the grasses, trees and rocks that make the scene interesting.

1 First, decide how much of the scene you want to include in your drawing and map out the positions of the main elements. To make this process easier, divide the scene into quarters (either mentally or by making light marks at the edges of the paper) and mark out where things fall in each square. Use light marks at this stage, just to establish where everything goes. Lightly block in the slope of the cliff to give yourself a visual guide to where to position the trees that stand at its base.

2 Work out where the darkest areas of tone are going to be and roughly block them in with a thick charcoal stick. The wooded mass on the top of the cliff is very dark, so you can apply a lot of pressure to the charcoal for this area. However, it is not a solid, straight-edged wedge shape: look closely and you will see that the tops of the trees are gently rounded. Observe shapes closely at this stage, to bring together a convincing and realistic composition. Outline the trees at the back of the fields with light dots and dashes, then block them in with the side of the charcoal stick.

3 Turn your attention back to the cliffs and look for differences in tone: the contrasts between dark, shaded gullies and crevices and the more brightly lit areas that are in full sunshine give the cliffs some sense of form. Block in the larger areas of tone using the side of the charcoal stick and moving your whole arm, not just your hand, keeping the coverage fairly uneven so that some of the paper texture shows through. Note that the brightest areas are barely touched by the charcoal. Continue blocking in the band of trees at the back of the fields, putting in nothing more than generalized shapes at this stage.

4 Outline the trees at the base of the cliff, then sketchily develop some tone within them. Note the number of different shapes – the tall, elongated cypress trees and the more rounded shapes elsewhere. Start to put in some jagged, linear marks on the cliff to create some texture.

Tip: Continually check the size of the trees and the distances between them and other elements of the scene. It is very easy to make the trees too big and destroy the scale of the drawing.

5 Finish outlining the shapes of the band of trees that runs across the middle of the drawing. Now you can begin to develop the foreground a little. Put in the foreground grasses, using both the tip of the charcoal and the side.

Tip: Work across the drawing as a whole, rather than concentrating on one area. This makes it easier to get the tonal balance of the drawing right.

6 Continue working on the trees in the middle of the drawing, concentrating on the overall shapes. Add more tone to the trees at the base of the cliff so that they begin to stand out more. Using the tip of the charcoal, put in more jagged, linear marks on the side of the cliff. These dark fissures help to create a sense of form and texture.

Assessment time

Details in the image are taking shape, but it requires much more tonal contrast and texture. The trees are little more than generalized shapes at this stage and do not look truly three-dimensional; you need to develop more tone within them and also to put in the shadows that they cast. We are beginning to see the different facets of the cliff, but the darkest marks are not yet dark enough to give us any real sense of form.

Very little work has been done on the foreground. It is too bright in relation to the rest of the image.

The linear marks on the cliff need to be developed further to create a sense of form.

The foreground grasses are too indistinct. More texture is needed here.

7 Very gently stroke the side of a thin charcoal stick over the foreground to create some tone and texture. Note how using the charcoal in this way gives a slightly uneven coverage. Press slightly harder on the charcoal to put in the sides of the track that zigzags its way through the scene. Also indicate the shadows cast by the trees.

 **Tip**: Smooth out the long cast shadows with your fingertips, in order to make them less textured than the trees themselves.

8 Very gently make a series of horizontal marks over the fields immediately below the cliff, pulling the full length of the charcoal stick over the paper to create the effect of ploughed furrows. Using the tip of the charcoal and pressing down firmly, put in the dark trunks of the trees in the centre of the image.

9 The trees are now taking real shape. Look at how the light catches them. Darken the shaded sides, using the side of the charcoal to create broad areas of tone. Immediately the trees begin to look more three-dimensional as you add the shadows they cast. Developing this tone takes them away from generalized shapes.

10 Using a kneaded eraser, gently lift off some of the charcoal from the side of the trees that catches the light. If you lift off too much, simply go over the area in charcoal again. Using the tip of a thin charcoal stick, introduce more texture into the foreground grasses by making crisp, dark, vertical marks.

The finished drawing

Working on a large scale has allowed the artist to use the full stretch of his arm to make bold, sweeping marks that give the drawing a very energetic, lively feel. He has concentrated on the essentials of the scene, rather than trying to put in every single detail, but his clever use of tonal contrasts gives the image a convincing sense of form. The foreground track leads our eye through the scene to the trees and cliff beyond – a classic compositional device.

Note how the contrasts between light and dark areas reveal the different facets of the cliff-face.

Detail diminishes with distance; the amount of detail that we can discern in the grasses tells us that they are in the foreground.

Lifting off charcoal from the most brightly lit sides of the trees shows us which direction the light is coming from.

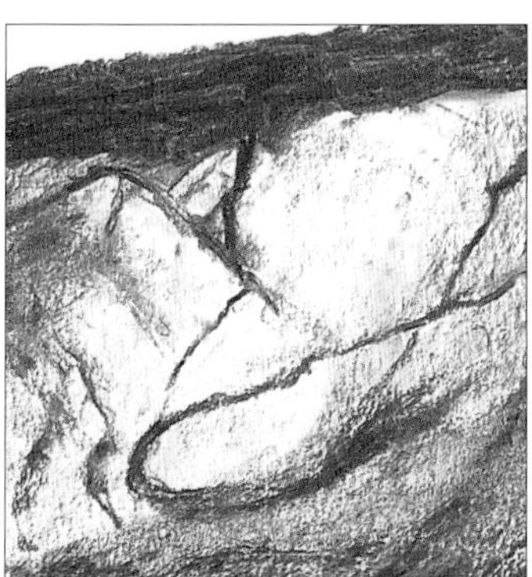

Church in snow in oils

Buildings are an integral part of many landscape paintings. Even when they are not the prime focus of attention, they add an element of human interest by implying the presence of man, and they also help to give a sense of scale.

In this project, the church in the background brings another dimension to a tranquil rural setting. Its solid form, positioned roughly on the third, contrasts well with the surroundings.

Begin by establishing the basic shape of the building and painting it as a flat area of tone. You can then develop this, creating contrasts of light and shade that reveal the different sides of the building, and finally putting in just enough detailing to tell us about the architectural style and period. The human brain is amazingly adept at interpreting a few general indications of shape and texture, and too much information can actually destroy the balance of the painting as a whole – particularly when the building is in the background, as here. The farther away something is, the less detail is required.

For this project, the artist began by toning the canvas with dilute olive green oil paint. The cool colour suits the wintry scene and gives a good, neutral mid tone from which to start painting.

Just like water, snow reflects colour. Where the sun strikes, the snow may be tinged with warm yellows or even pinks, depending on the time of day, while shadows will contain shades of blue and violet. Do not paint everything as a brilliant white: shadowy areas contrasting with small patches of bright, sunlit snow will have far more impact. The shadows in the snow also reveal the contours of the land beneath.

Materials

- *Stretched and primed canvas*
- *Oil paints: olive green, permanent mauve, titanium white, cobalt blue, raw sienna, viridian, burnt sienna, Indian yellow, cadmium red, lemon yellow*
- *Turpentine*
- *Brushes: selection of small and medium filberts*

The scene

Although the church is far away and relatively indistinct, it is still the main focus of the scene. Along with the trees, it provides a strong vertical element on which the viewer's eye can alight, while the curve of the water leads us around the scene.

1 Make an underdrawing of the church, main trees and water area, using a small brush and thin olive green paint. When you paint buildings it is particularly important to get the proportions and angles right, so measure carefully and take your time over this stage. Also indicate the shadows on the snow in the foreground and roughly scumble in the largest reflections in the water.

2 Block in the trees on the far bank, using a mid-toned purple mixed from permanent mauve, titanium white, cobalt blue and raw sienna, and a blue-green mixed from olive green, viridian and a tiny amount of burnt sienna. Using a small brush, begin putting in the cool shadows on the snow on the far bank, using a blue-grey mixed from cobalt blue, titanium white and permanent mauve.

3 Continue putting in the shadows on the snow on the far side of the water. Block in the reflections of the trees in the water, using olive green for the darkest trees and lighter olive green and purple mixes elsewhere, and leaving gaps for the brightest areas of water.

4 Mix a pinkish brown from burnt sienna, titanium white and cobalt blue and paint the walls of the church. Paint the snow-covered roof, which is in shadow, in a cool blue-grey. Overlay some pale blue on the purple trees in the background; this helps to link the trees with the snow.

Assessment time

Lively scumbles are a quick way of establishing basic shapes and tones in the early stages of a painting, and are particularly useful when you are painting outdoors. The underpainting is now virtually complete. For the rest of the painting, concentrate on texture and detailing, checking periodically to ensure that you maintain the tonal balance.

The church, which has been roughly blocked in, adds solidity to the scene.

Lively scumbles establish the basic shapes and tones.

5 Indicate the grasses on the near bank by scumbling on a little of the dark green mixture from the previous step and raw sienna. The warmth of the raw sienna helps to bring them forward in the painting. Brush on more blue for the shadows in the foreground snow, using horizontal strokes that follow the direction of the shadows. For the unshaded areas of snow, use a warm off-white colour mixed from titanium white and a tiny amount of Indian yellow.

6 Using a fine brush and the purplish-grey mixture from Step 2, put in the bare branches that poke up from the ivy-covered trees in the background. Do not try to put in every single detail or the painting will start to look overworked and fussy; you can create a general impression of the shape and texture of these thin branches by means of a series of short parallel lines. Reserve the main detailing and texture for the foreground of the scene.

7 Put in the thin saplings along the bank, as well as their reflections. Darken and strengthen the colours of the reflections: once you have established the general area, you can smooth out the brushstrokes, blending the colours together on the canvas.

8 There is an overly bright and distracting area of water near the centre of the image, which needs to be toned down in order to blend in with the rest of the painting. Leaving the brightest areas untouched, lightly brush a very pale purple over this area.

9 Mix a warm but pale yellow from Indian yellow and titanium white. Lightly touch it into the sky, where the winter sun shines through from behind the clouds.

10 Continue with the linear, dry brush detailing on the bare branches of the trees, as in Step 6, again resisting the temptation to put in too much detail.

11 Using a fine sable brush and a pale blue-grey mixture, put in the branches of the young saplings on the bank. Adjust the proportions of the colours in your mixture: the shaded branches are bluer in tone, while those branches to which the snow is clinging are whiter.

Tip: If the marks look too sharp, soften them by blending them with your fingers.

12 Strengthen the colours of the low bushes on the far side of the water, using short vertical strokes of reddish browns and dark olive greens. The warm colours help to bring this area forward in the painting.

13 Using thin paint, draw the shapes of the box topiary and geese on the near bank. Roughly block in the shapes of the topiary with a pale blue-green mixture, adding more white on the side that catches the light. Using the same colours as before, brush in the shadows cast by the topiary and the geese.

14 Warm up the foreground snow by scumbling the off-white colour from Step 5 over those areas that are not in shadow. Paint the geese in a blue-tinged white, adding more blue to the mixture for the markings on the feathers. Paint their feet, legs and beaks in cadmium red mixed with white and a little lemon yellow.

15 Using a paler version of the pinkish brown from Step 4, paint the sunlit sides of the church so that the building looks three-dimensional. Paint the lines on the tower in a blue-grey, adding more white where the snow clings to the ridges. Paint the castellations on the turret by overpainting some of the sky colour. Use the brush handle to blend colours around the edge of the church and create a crisp outline.

16 Paint the windows of the church in a dark brown, leaving the underlying colour showing through for the stonework.

The finished painting

This is a muted scene that nonetheless captures the feeling of thin, early-morning winter sunlight very well through its use of pale blues and pinks. The church is rendered indistinctly and almost appears to be seen through a haze, but there is enough detail to tell us about the architectural style. The geese in the foreground are painted in more detail and add life to what might otherwise be a rather static scene. Note how many different tones there are within the snow.

The brushstrokes in the reflections have been softly blended.

Warm but pale yellow in the sky lightens the scene.

The geese and their shadows enliven the foreground.

Moroccan kasbah in watercolour

The location for this striking project is the World Heritage site of Ait-Ben-Haddhou, in southern Morocco. It is a traditional-style village made up of several earthen fortresses, each one some 10m (30ft) high.

With its straight-edged buildings and clean lines, the scene looks deceptively simple, but it demonstrates well how important it is to train yourself to assess tones. The earthen buildings are all very similar in colour (predominantly ochre and terracotta), so without strong contrasts of tone you will never succeed in making them look three-dimensional.

If you are painting on location, you may find that the light, and therefore the direction and length of shadows, changes as you work. It is a good idea to make light pencil marks on your paper, just outside the margins of your painting, indicating the angle of the sun. This makes it easier to keep the lighting consistent when you are painting over a period of several hours.

Materials

- *2B pencil*
- *140lb (300gsm) NOT watercolour paper, pre-stretched*
- *Watercolour paints: cerulean blue, yellow ochre, light red, vermilion, mauve, white, alizarin crimson, Hooker's green, Winsor yellow, Payne's grey, ultramarine blue, burnt umber*
- *Brushes: large wash, medium round, medium flat, fine filbert*

Tip: Use a pencil to measure the relative heights of the buildings. Hold the pencil out in front of you and align the tip with part of your subject (say, the top of the tallest building), then run your thumb down the pencil until it aligns with the base of the building. You can transfer this measurement to your watercolour paper, again holding the pencil at arm's length. It is important to keep your arm straight and the pencil vertical, so that the pencil remains a constant distance from the subject.

The original scene

The artist took this photograph around midday, when the sun was almost directly overhead. Consequently, the colours looked somewhat bleached out and there were no strong shadows to bring the scene to life. She decided to use a little artistic licence and enhance what she saw by intensifying the colours in order to make her painting more dramatic.

The sky looks pale and does not have the warmth that one associates with hot African countries.

Here, the mud-brick buildings look pale and bleached out; in the right light, however, they glow a warm orangey-red.

1 Using a 2B pencil, lightly sketch the scene, taking careful note of the relative heights of the buildings and their angles in relation to one another.

2 Using a large wash brush, dampen the sky area with clean water, brushing carefully around the outlines of the buildings to get a neat, clean edge. Mix a wash of cerulean blue. After about a minute, when the water has sunk in but the paper is still damp, quickly brush on the colour. (You may want to switch to a smaller brush to paint up to the edge of the buildings. Use the side of the brush and brush the paint upward, to avoid accidentally getting any of the blue colour on the buildings.)

3 Mix a pale but warm terracotta colour from yellow ochre, light red and a tiny amount of vermilion. Using a medium round brush, wash this mixture over the buildings, working around the fronds of the foreground palm trees and adding a little more yellow ochre as you work across from right to left.

Tip: Vary the tone of the buildings. If they are too uniform in tone they will look newly built and mass produced.

4 Add a little mauve to the mixture to make a deeper tone. Paint the wall at the base of the picture, painting around the trunks of the palm trees. Hold the brush at an angle as you do this and make jagged marks, as this helps to convey the texture of the trunks and shows that they are not straight-edged.

5 Continue working across the painting until you have put in all of the lightest tones of the buildings.

6 Mix a mid tone from yellow ochre and a tiny amount of mauve and, using a medium flat brush, stipple this mixture on to the buildings in the centre of the painting to give them some texture as well as tone. Add more mauve to the mixture for the darker left-hand side.

7 Brush white watercolour over the top edge of the building in the centre. This reduces the intensity of the yellow and makes it look as if it has been bleached by the sun.

8 Mix a dark terracotta from light red, yellow ochre and a touch of alizarin crimson and start painting the darkest tones – the sides of the buildings that are in deepest shade.

Assessment time

The light, mid and dark tones are now in place across the picture and, although the tones have not yet reached their final density, we are beginning to get a clear sense of which facets of the buildings are in bright sunlight and which are in shade. From this stage onward, you need to continually assess the tonal values as you work, because even slight changes in one area will affect the balance of the painting as a whole. Take regular breaks, propping your painting up against a wall and looking at it from a distance to see how it is developing.

Stronger contrasts of tone are needed in order for the buildings to look truly three-dimensional.

Details such as the recessed windows and doors will help to bring the painting to life.

9 Mix a very dark terracotta colour from light red, yellow ochre and a touch of alizarin crimson, and begin putting in some of the fine details, such as the door in the exterior wall and some of the small windows. You are now beginning to establish a feeling of light and shade in the painting.

10 The right-hand buildings, which are in the deepest area of shade, look too light. Darken them as necessary by overlaying more washes of the colours used previously. Also darken the mid-toned wall in the centre of the picture and put some dark windows on the light side.

11 The lightest walls now look too light in relation to the rest of the painting, so darken them with another wash of the pale terracotta mixture used in Step 3. Build up the tone gradually. You can apply more washes if necessary, but if you make things too dark there is no going back.

12 Mix a yellowy green from Hooker's green and a little yellow ochre and, using a fine filbert brush, start putting in the green palm fronds in the foreground. Make short upward flicks with the brush, following the direction in which the palm fronds grow.

13 Continue painting the palm fronds, adding a little Winsor yellow at the point where the fronds spring out from the trunk. Paint the shaded sides of the palm trunks in Payne's grey, using short, broken strokes to indicate the knobbly surface texture of the trunks.

14 Lighten the grey by adding a little yellow ochre. Using the side of the brush, dab this mixture on to the left-hand side of the painting to indicate the scrubby texture of the bushes that grow in this area. Mix a very pale green from Payne's grey, yellow ochre and Hooker's green and dot in the sides of the palm trunks that catch the light. Mix a grey-green from Payne's grey and Hooker's green and dot this mixture into the foreground shrubs. Mix a pale purple from alizarin crimson and ultramarine blue and paint the dry earth and the shadows around the base of the palm trees.

15 Mix a pale wash of alizarin crimson and darken the wall in the foreground. Feel free to use some artistic licence in your choice of colours. Although the wall is, in reality, more terracotta than pink, you are trying to put colour into a subject that does not have much in order to create some drama and variety in your image. Adjust the tones over the painting as a whole if you feel that it is necessary.

16 Mix a dark brown from light red and Payne's grey and put in the dark details, such as the windows. Dry brush a pale mixture of Hooker's green over the foreground to give it some tone. Mix a dark brown from burnt umber and Payne's grey and dab it on to the palm trunks to give them more tone and texture. Paint the shadows of the palm trees on the wall in a pale tone of Payne's grey.

17 Mix a dilute wash of white watercolour paint and brush it over the tops of the highest buildings. Because the paint is transparent the underlying colour shows through, creating the effect of strong sunlight shining on the buildings and bleaching out the colour. Do not worry if the white looks too strong when you first apply it to the paper as it will quickly sink in and look natural.

The finished painting

The artist has managed to create a surprisingly wide range of tones in this painting, and this is one of the keys to its success, as the variety helps to convey not only the weathered textures of the mud bricks but also that all-important sense of light and shade. Rich, warm colours – far warmer than in the original reference photograph – help to evoke the feeling of being in a hot country. The foreground trees and bushes contrast well with the buildings in both colour and shape.

Transparent white watercolour paint allows some of the underlying colour to show through, and this creates the impression of sun-bleached brick.

In reality, this wall is the same colour as those behind. Painting it a warm pink brings it forward in the picture and helps to create an impression of distance.

Note the use of complementary colours – the orangey ochres and terracottas of the buildings against the rich cerulean blue of the sky.

Venetian building in pen and ink

This project is an exercise in perspective. The bottom of the balcony is more or less at the artist's eye level – so this is the horizon line. If you look at the initial pencil sketch in Step 1, you will see that the artist has drawn the bottom of the balcony to form a straight, horizontal line across the centre of the image. Any parallel line above this point (such as the line of the roof) will appear to slope down toward the vanishing point, while anything below it (such as the base of the building) appears to slope upwards. Take time over your initial pencil sketch to make sure you get the angles and proportions right. Texture is important, too, and the rough texture of the ancient brickwork is very pleasing to the eye. Do not try to draw every single brick, as this would make the image too 'busy' and detract from the overall effect. Leaving some areas empty gives a much-needed contrast of texture and implies the smooth render that would once have covered the whole façade.

Pen and ink is an ideal medium for architectural drawings, as it allows you to make very precise marks. Here, both permanent and water-soluble inks are used, creating a combination of crisp, linear details and ink washes, which soften the overall effect. For this project, the artist chose to use sepia ink, rather than black, as it is a much softer colour and helps to give the drawing a rather nostalgic, old-fashioned feel.

Materials

- *Heavy drawing paper*
- *HB pencil*
- *Permanent and water-soluble sepia inks*
- *Steel-nibbed pens*
- *Fine paintbrush*
- *Gouache paint: white*

The scene

Old buildings such as this one, with the canal lapping at its foundations, are common in Venice, and can evoke a strong sense of the past. The decorative lines of the balconies are not overly ornate, but they hold our interest, and the beautiful arched doors and windows form a repeating pattern that runs through the whole image.

1 Using an HB pencil, make a light, detailed sketch of the scene, making sure you measure all the different elements.

Tip: The buildings are receding. Put in the perspective sight-lines as a guide; you can erase them later.

2 Following your pencil lines and using permanent sepia ink, carefully ink in the windows and balconies. It is very important not to use water-soluble ink here, as you want to retain all the crisp detail of these lines in the finished drawing.

3 Continue with the ink work, using water-soluble sepia ink for the foliage and brickwork. Also hatch the windows behind the open shutters on the top right of the drawing in water-soluble ink, drawing the lines close together as this area is very dark.

4 Continue working on the brickwork, alternating between permanent and water-soluble sepia inks. Put in the lines of the Venetian blinds in permanent ink. Here the artist has put the blinds in at different heights to add interest.

5 Using water-soluble ink, put in some light hatching around the window recesses, in the windows below the blinds, and under the balconies to introduce some shading. (The ink will be washed over at a later stage, so that the hatching marks blend together to create an area of solid tone.)

Assessment time
The main lines are now in place. However, although there is some indication of the shading around the windows and balconies, the image overall looks rather flat and two-dimensional. From this point onward, concentrate on creating more depth and texture.

Although there is some texture and detail, the image as a whole is rather lifeless. Washes of colour will help to counteract this.

6 As the light is coming from the right of the scene, the balconies cast oblique shadows on the façade of the building. Put them in lightly, using an HB pencil. (The pencil lines act as a positional guide – they should be covered up by washes of ink later.)

7 Using permanent ink and zig-zagging vertical lines, draw the ripples in the water. Hatch the darkest areas of the water, using water-soluble ink. The ripples will remain visible when a wash is applied, while the hatching will blend to an area of solid tone.

8 Erase all the remaining pencil lines, apart from the cast shadows that you put in in Step 6. Load a paintbrush with water and brush over the shaded parts of the building. The lines drawn in water-soluble ink will dissolve, allowing you to create areas of solid tone.

9 Continue brushing water over the water-soluble ink, including the canal. Brush colour over the doors, darkening them with more ink if necessary. Dilute some sepia ink (or use sepia watercolour paint) and brush it over the cast shadows on the building, keeping within the pencil marks.

10 Using a fine paintbrush and white gouache, paint in the reflections of the doors in the water. Gouache paint used straight from the tube can be quite thick so only dip the tip of your brush into it.

The finished drawing

This is an evocative and elegant pen-and-ink study of a classic Venetian building. Permanent ink was used for the linear details in the most important areas, while brushing water over the water-soluble ink has helped to create areas of tone that soften the harshness of the pen work, transforming an architectural study into something much more picturesque. Although only one colour of ink was used, a good range of tones was created by washing water over different densities of hatched marks.

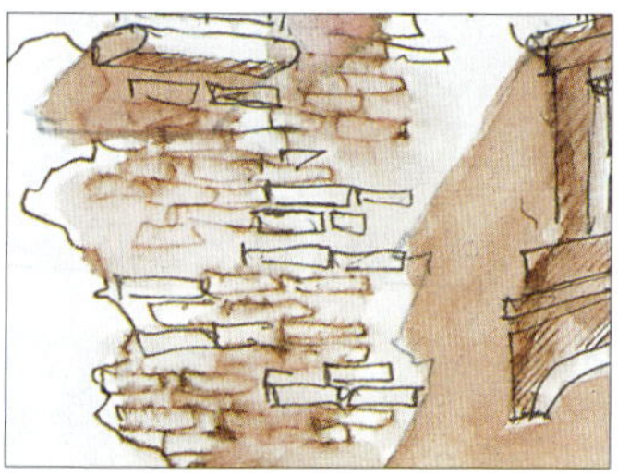

Both permanent and water-soluble ink have been used here, creating a combination of linear detail and soft tonal washes.

The linear detailing of the building, as in the balcony, has been drawn using permanent ink.

White gouache paint, which is opaque, is used to paint the light reflections on top of the dark patches of water.

Washing water over hatched lines produces an area of solid tone – the closer together the lines, the darker the tone.

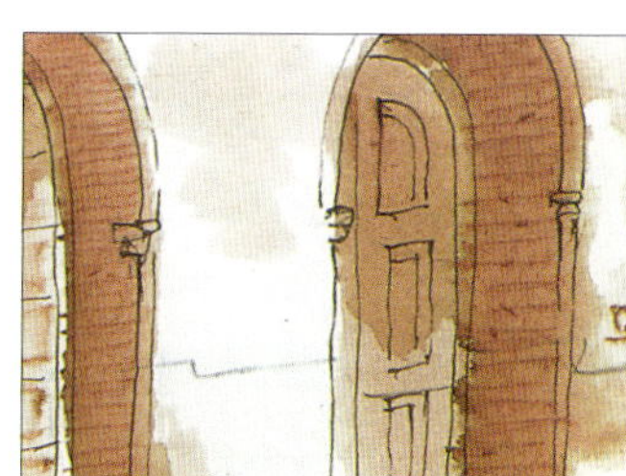

Cityscape in oil pastels

A construction site might not seem the most obvious subject for a drawing project but, if you choose your viewpoint carefully, the bold colours and graphic shapes can give you the chance to create a modern-looking, semi-abstract drawing. It will also test your ability to work with straight lines – always important when drawing buildings, whatever era they date from.

Scenes such as this can be found in towns and cities all over the world and recording a new building at all stages of its construction, from site clearance through to completion, makes an interesting long-term project. Moreover, many companies are waking up to the investment potential of buying original art – so who knows? If there is a prestigious building project going on near your home and your work is good enough, you might even be able to sell it to the owners to display in the reception area or to use in promotional literature.

Oil pastels are not renowned for their subtlety of colour, but for a subject such as this, which relies on the bold, primary colours of the building cranes for much of its impact, they are ideal. You need to press quite firmly on the oil pastels, so use a heavy drawing paper or an oil-painting paper for this project to avoid the risk of tearing the support.

Materials

- *Heavy drawing paper or oil-painting paper*
- *4B pencil*
- *Oil pastels: pale greys (warm- and cool-toned), bright blue, red, yellow, white, lilac, Naples yellow, black*
- *Scraperboard tool or craft (utility) knife*

The scene

The brightly coloured cranes stand out dramatically against the cloudless blue sky, while the straight lines of the cranes and the buildings under construction create a graphic, almost abstract composition. The diagonal lines of some of the cranes make the composition more dynamic.

1 Using a soft pencil, mark out the lines of the cranes and the buildings under construction. There is no need to put in any of the internal lines at this stage, but do make sure you measure all the angles and distances carefully.

2 Using pale grey oil pastels, block in the building on the right. Note that the shaded sides are cooler in tone than those in full sunlight, so alternate between warm- and cool-toned greys as required.

3 Block in the sky, using the side of a bright blue oil pastel and making sure you do not go over the lines of the cranes. Putting in the negative shapes of the background sky at this early stage makes it easier to see any thin lines of the cranes that you have not yet drawn.

Tip: It is easy to lose track of where you are in a complicated drawing such as this, so refer continually to your reference photo to make sure you don't apply the sky colour over any of the lines of the cranes.

4 Begin putting in the red lines of the cranes, using bold, confident strokes and pressing quite hard on the tip of the pastel. Lightly stroke the side of the pastel over the warm-toned shadow areas of the buildings.

5 Now put in the bright yellow of the cranes, filling in the spaces between the rungs with blue. Work white oil pastel over part of the sky and blend it with your fingers.

6 Using the side of a lilac oil pastel, roughly block in the shaded sides of the buildings on the right. (Note, in particular, the shadow cast on the building on the far right of the image.) Apply the same colour to some of the shaded interior floors of the building on the left. Work Naples yellow, which is a pale, warm yellow, over the warm-toned area of the building in the centre and add small dashes of red on the tall foreground building.

7 Using the tip of a black oil pastel to make strong, bold marks, draw the reinforced steel joists of the building in the background. Establish the different storeys of the building on the left, using a range of shadow colours (blue, lilac, black) as appropriate. Use the side of the pastels to make broad, lightly textured marks; you can then go over them with other pastels to blend the colours optically and create a more interesting shadow colour.

Assessment time

The drawing is nearing completion and only a few minor adjustments are needed. In places, the cranes are lost against the building or the sky and need to be more sharply defined. Some of the shadows need to be darkened slightly.

This crane merges into the building behind it and needs to be a little more clearly defined.

The lines of the white crane are quite delicate and will be hard to draw with a thick oil pastel.

8 Using a scraperboard tool or the tip of a craft knife, scratch off blue oil pastel to create the lines of the white crane in the centre of the image.

9 Scratch into the red crane on the left to create some highlight areas, and strengthen the red diagonal line so that the crane really stands out against the building.

The finished drawing

This artist has matched the medium to the subject beautifully. The bold, vibrant colours of oil pastels, which might be too brash and unsubtle for many subjects, are perfect for the bright, primary colours of the cranes and sky. Although it is difficult to draw fine details with oil pastels, they are the ideal drawing tool for the solid, graphic lines of this scene. Using the side of the pastels for the façades of the buildings brings another quality to the image and creates a lighter texture. Overlaying one colour on another, particularly in the shadow areas, has created interesting optical colour mixes that are much more lively and interesting than a flat application of a single colour could ever be.

Allowing colours to mix optically on the paper creates lively shadow effects.

The sgraffito technique allows you to scratch off the pastel and create fine lines.

Finger blending in the sky softens both the colour and the texture.

ROWNEY
Georgian
OIL COLOUR
FOR ARTISTS
COULEUR A L'HUILE
POUR ARTISTES
ÖLFARBE
FÜR KÜNSTLER
COLOR AL OLEO
PARA ARTISTAS

Water and Sky

The sky provides the source of light in a landscape painting and is thus a major factor in establishing the mood of a scene. No surprise, then, that it is a popular subject in its own right. Making studies of skies, in their many moods, is something that all budding landscape artists are well advised to do. This chapter looks at a whole range of skies and cloud conditions, from turbulent, fast-moving storm clouds to a tropical sunset that is saturated with vibrant reds, oranges and pinks. The way your strokes are applied to the paper or canvas is the key to producing different weather moods convincingly.

Another major element of landscapes is water – both naturally occurring features such as seas and rivers, and man-made structures like ponds and canals. As water provides a critical feeling of movement in scenes that might otherwise be static, it presents its own technical challenges and deserves special consideration.

This chapter begins with a gallery of drawings and paintings that you can study to see how other artists have tackled these subjects. It includes fifteen step-by-step projects in all the main drawing and painting media that you can use both as technical exercises and as a source of inspiration when devising your own sky- and seascapes.

Gallery

It is always interesting to see how other artists have approached the technical and creative challenges of portraying skies and water. This gallery section contains drawings and paintings by contemporary professional artists working in a range of media and styles, from loose, impressionistic studies in watercolour to bold, vigorous pastels and finely detailed oils. Study them carefully and see what lessons you can apply to your own work.

Unblended colour ►
Pastel need not be a soft and delicate medium; it is extremely versatile and responsive to the artist's visual interests and ways of working. In *Swans on the Thames*, Pip Carpenter has created energetic and exciting effects in the picture by laying heavy strokes of unblended colour, using the tip of the pastel stick.

Human interest ▲
You can often give additional interest to a landscape, or stress a centre of interest, by including one or two figures. In Ronald Jesty's *A Wild Day*, the men shielding their heads against the spray from the breaking wave and the woman pointing her hand introduce a narrative, and both these and the surrounding dark rocks provide contrasts of tone which draw attention to the picture's focal point.

Tinted ground ►
Using a tinted ground is a standard oil-painting practice that is just as applicable to acrylics. Here, the artist used a deep blue ground; the subsequent painting was done quite thinly, so that it modifies the blue without completely obscuring it and it contributes to the overall colour temperature. Note that the horizon line is placed in the centre of the image – something one is generally advised not to do, as it can make an image seem very static, but here it creates a mood of calm.

Sparkling sunlight ◄
8 a.m., Venice Lagoon, made by Ian Sidaway as the early-morning light highlighted the ripples on the water, uses carefully applied wet-on-dry washes. The dappled sunlight on the water surface was created by applying masking fluid prior to making any washes. Colours were kept crisp and clean by using no more than three overlapping washes. Note how the ripples conform to the laws of perspective by getting smaller as they get closer to the horizon.

►

Flat wash for sky ▲
In David Curtis's study *Sailing Boats*, the clear, pale sky behind the boats is achieved with a flat wash of watercolour. This has the effect of allowing the fine rigging on the boats to stand out from the background.

Light and shadow ◄
Timothy Easton is a master at capturing the subtle effects of light in oils. In this delightful painting entitled *Down to the Sea*, the highlights in the water are carefully touched in with white and white tinged with yellow, while the shadows on the sand are rendered in blues and blue-greys. The diagonal line that runs through the painting from top left to bottom right gives an otherwise tranquil scene a strong dynamic.

Soft, curving brushstrokes ▲

Paul Dyson's *Floating Leaf* is a simple little scene that many landscape artists might pass by in favour of a grander view. It is a study in contrasts – the softness of the water versus the solidity of the rocks; the vibrant colour of the leaf versus muted tones in the water. The brushwork is controlled, with the brushstrokes in the water following the direction of the water flow to create lifelike ripples. Note how the main centre of interest – the leaf – is positioned slightly off centre and at an angle to add interest to the composition.

Crisp edges ►

Ronald Jesty achieves his crisp effects and dense, glowing colours by working wet on dry, reserving highlights by painting carefully around them. You can see this effect on the background hills, the dark areas of rock and the water, where small patches of light-coloured paint have been left uncovered by later dark washes of colour. Note how his observation of the rocks beneath the water and the contrast of reflected light and shadow on the surface has helped produce a very realistic impression of a deep pool of clear water. Such elements of realism trick the eye into 'believing' a scene, even when other aspects are fairly abstract or stylized, such as the purple and red colours in the rock.

►

Colours of water ▲
Many different colours and tones can be discerned in water, particularly in reflections. They must be carefully controlled if the image is to appear convincing. In Jackie Simmond's lovely pastel painting, *Waterlilies and Reeds*, the strongest contrasts of tone are those between the lilies and the foreground water – a deep, rich blue reflected from the sky.

Using paint runs ◀
Watercolours are usually painted with the board held flat or at a slight angle, but in *St-Laurent-de-Cerdans*, Karen Raney has worked with the board upright on an easel, causing the paint to run down the paper at the bottom of the picture. She has left the foreground otherwise undefined – the runs of paint hint at reflections in water.

Textural techniques ►
This simple watercolour painting by Albany Wiseman, *Beached Boat at Low Tide*, is a study in texture, with masking fluid and paint both being spattered over the paper to create the shingle-covered beach. The spattering is subtle and does not detract from the boat, but it captures the pebbly beach very well.

Extracting the essentials ▼
Crooked Tree Against the Dazzle, by Timothy Easton, is, above all, a study of light and shade; any other elements have been so simplified that the painting is almost abstract. Easton has captured the effect of sunlight glancing on the water through his short, carefully blended strokes of white. The strong diagonal that runs upward through the painting gives it energy.

Quick sketches: Skies and clouds

The sky is such an integral part of most landscapes that any budding landscape artist would be well advised to spend time practising how to draw and paint it. Get into the habit of making quick sketches whenever you see an interesting sky. Landscape artists have always done this: the British artist John Constable (1776–1837) even described the practice in a letter to a friend as 'skying'. The light can change so quickly that a stunning skyscape can disappear within minutes – so the ability to work rapidly, even if it is just to make a reference sketch that you work on in more detail later, is invaluable.

Clouds almost always add visual interest and character to a sky, whether they be soft, fluffy white clouds in an azure-blue sky at the height of summer, broken cumulus clouds that allow shafts of light to break through and illuminate the landscape below, or heavy storm clouds that impart a brooding, sombre mood. Study the different types of clouds and the moods that they create.

The way that you treat skies and clouds, of course, depends on the medium in which you are working. With powdery mediums such as soft pastel or charcoal, you can blend the marks with your fingers or a torchon to create smooth areas of tone suitable for cloud-free sections of sky; alternatively, you can allow the texture of the paper to show through in the clouds themselves. In pencil and in pen and ink, you can create the different tones through simple hatching and crosshatching. In watercolour and acrylic paint, delicate washes and glazes allow you to build up the colour and tones layer by layer.

The scene
The glowing colours, both in the sky itself and in the reflections in the gently rippling sea below, were what attracted the artist to this scene. The heavy clouds are lit from above by the setting sun, and it is the contrast between the top-lit sections and the dark underbellies that gives the thick clouds a sense of volume and mass.

5-minute sketch: charcoal pencil ◄
Here, the artist created a range of tones by varying the amount of pressure she exerted on the pencil, with soft, diagonal hatching for the mid-tones and heavier scribbles for the darkest parts of the cloud masses. The white of the paper has been left to stand for the very brightest highlights. The rough texture of the paper also contributes to the overall effect.

5-minute sketch: watercolour wash ▶

By varying the dilution of the paint, you can create a wide range of tones. A light wash was initially applied for the mid tones, leaving the brightest areas untouched. For the darkest tones, a more concentrated mix of the paint was dropped in wet into wet. This creates layers of gradual of tone and soft edges.

30-minute sketch: soft pastels ▼

This sketch is a real explosion of colour! The pastels were applied vigorously, with some marks finger-blended to create smooth patches of blue sky, and other marks being left to pick up the texture of the paper and create texture in the clouds.

Quick sketches: Leading the eye

A riverside setting has lots of potential for interesting landscape sketches. If the river runs swiftly, there will be splashes and swirling eddies as the water breaks around rocks and other objects. Gentle ripples create a different mood, slightly distorting any reflections. Occasionally, you come across a hidden pool in which the water appears to be completely still, where the reflections are sharp and crisp. Each requires a different approach, from dynamic, energetic marks for rapidly flowing water to a more measured, controlled approach for very still water and reflections.

Whatever the mood of the river, it is often a good idea to use it as a compositional device to lead the viewer's eye through the picture. Bear this in mind when you position yourself on the bank to take a reference photo or make a sketch. A view along a river, where you can see how it meanders its way through the landscape, is usually more satisfying in compositional terms than one looking straight across from one bank to the other as, in the latter case, the river will form a broad horizontal band that cuts the composition in two and blocks the viewer's eye from moving any farther through the scene.

When you are drawing water, always remember that it takes its colour from the surroundings – although the colour is generally more muted in the reflection. In a riverside setting the greens and browns of nearby trees may be reflected in the water; alternatively, there may be patches of sky that are so bright that you need apply virtually no colour whatsoever to the support.

The scene

Here, the river forms a gentle curve that leads our eye through the scene to the buildings on the horizon. The sky is very bright and bland, with no dramatic cloud formations to add interest to the scene, so the reflections of the trees along the bank provide a feature in what would otherwise be a completely empty area.

5-minute sketch: sepia water-soluble pencil ▲

Five minutes is plenty of time for you to work out a composition for a larger drawing. Make a quick thumbnail sketch, roughly outlining the shapes of the main elements (including the reflections).

10-minute sketch: sepia water-soluble pencil ▲

A tonal study will require a little more time. Here, the artist lightly brushed a little clean water over some of the pencil marks to blend them to a tonal wash, leaving the brightest areas untouched.

15-minute sketch: sepia water-soluble pencil ►
In this sketch, more textural detail is evident. It is created by using the water-soluble pencil dry (on the grass on the near bank, for example) and on slightly damp paper, so that the marks spread a little (on the large tree on the far bank).

30-minute sketch: sepia water-soluble pencil ▼
In the longest sketch of the series, the scene is beginning to look more three-dimensional. Note how some elements, such as the large tree on the far bank and the grass in the foreground of the near bank, are given more textural marks, which helps to indicate that they are nearer the viewer and create a sense of recession in the scene.

Cloudscape in charcoal

Charcoal is a wonderful medium for drawing storm clouds, not least because of the intensity of tone that you can achieve with it.

Although clouds look random, your composition needs to be carefully planned. Start by selecting the area of sky that you feel is most dramatic, looking also at what is happening in the land or sea beneath as well as in the sky itself. Begin by establishing the general shape of the cloud mass, paying attention to the individual shapes that are contained within it.

If you find in the later stages that the light and mid tones are merging into the darks, do not be afraid to strengthen the darks still further so that the lighter marks stand out. Work on a heavy, good-quality drawing paper that can withstand quite rough treatment, so that there is no risk of the paper tearing, no matter how hard you scribble. A slightly rough paper is also a good choice, as the texture will show through in the finished drawing, adding another dimension to it.

Above all, do not be tempted to make your drawing too small. A subject like this, particularly in charcoal, demands bold, gestural drawing – and that is much harder to achieve on a small scale. Give yourself space to work and use your whole arm, not just your fingertips, so that your drawing has a feeling of energy and spontaneity.

Materials

- *Good-quality drawing paper with slightly rough texture*
- *Charcoal: thin and thick sticks*
- *Kneaded eraser*

The scene

This scene of dark, brooding storm clouds over the sea virtually demands a monochrome treatment. Charcoal seemed the obvious choice, as it allows you to combine smooth, finger-blended passages with more vigorous applications of the pigment. The texture of the paper plays a part, too.

1 Using a thin stick of charcoal, put in the horizon line, the dark undersides of the swelling waves and the edges of the main cloud mass. Do not try to put in all the clouds in one go: begin by simply locating different sections of the main cloud mass, so that you have something to use as a guide when you begin to apply some tone to the image.

2 Using the side of a thick stick of charcoal, scribble in the darkest bits of the clouds to help create a sense of their volume. Note how the charcoal picks out some of the paper texture.

3 Continue blocking in the darkest patches, working vigorously and energetically so that the drawing remains quite loose and spontaneous. Blend some of the marks with your fingers to create smooth areas of tone.

4 Apply tone to the sea in the same way and then drag the side of the charcoal down the paper to create the streaks of falling rain. From this point onward you will begin to refine the drawing.

5 Using your fingertips in a swirling, circular motion that echoes the shapes of the clouds, blend the charcoal pigment on the surface of the paper to soften the marks. You can use your fingers to work the pigment.

Assessment time

Only the very brightest patches of the sky have been left untouched, but the clouds themselves still look rather flat and one-dimensional. There is no real sense of volume, nor are the tonal contrasts strong enough – particularly in the sea, where the initial dark marks for the undersides of the waves are now virtually indistinguishable from the rest of the water. Getting the tones right in a drawing like this is always a gradual process of assessment and adjustment, so do not expect to complete this process in one go. Take your time and assess the relative tones carefully and continually.

The sea is almost all a uniform mid-tone.

The sharp band of light along the horizon is not sufficiently well defined; the sky and sea almost merge together.

The brightest patches of sky contain subtle tonal differences: at present, this area is too bright overall.

6 Using the tip of a thin charcoal stick, put in the dark shapes in the water – the undersides of the waves. Use short, scribbly marks that follow the direction in which the waves are flowing.

7 Go over the darkest bits of the clouds again, blending the marks with your fingertips as before to create more rounded, three-dimensional forms. Using the side of a thin stick, reinforce the lines of falling rain at the base of the clouds. You may need to darken the clouds more than you expect, so that the mid tones of the falling rain stand out.

8 Use the sharp edge of a kneaded eraser to wipe out pigment along the horizon line and create the band of light that separates the sea from the sky. Decide where you want to apply a little very pale tone to the very brightest patches of clouds, then dip your fingers in charcoal dust and lightly brush the pigment on to these areas.

Tip: Scribble some charcoal on to a piece of scrap paper, then gently rub your finger over the scribbles to transfer some of the powdery pigment to them.

9 Using a kneaded or a plastic eraser, carefully wipe off pigment in both the sky and the sea to create more mid tones. If you want to create fine lines to suggest the ripples in the water, use the sharp edge of the eraser, stroking it over the paper in the same way that you would make fine hatching lines with a pencil.

Tip: Re-assess the tones continually as you go: you may find that you need to darken some areas still further in order for the highlights to really stand out.

The finished drawing

This is a deceptively simple-looking drawing, but the tones have been carefully assessed and adjusted throughout to capture the dark, oppressive mood of the scene. Note the variety of the charcoal marks: the side of the charcoal has been dragged down the paper to create the bands of falling rain, the tip has been used to create fine, scribbly lines to denote the edges of the clouds, and the pigment has been finger-blended to create patches of soft tone. The white of the paper stands for the very lightest areas and tiny highlights have been created by wiping off pigment with an eraser.

In the sea, the dark undersides of the waves contrast with the tiny, bright patches of light reflected from the sky.

Note the different kinds of mark making – heavy, finger-blended scribbles for the darkest patches, vertical streaks for the falling rain, and a bright highlight created by wiping off pigment with an eraser.

Note the patches of pale tone, even in the very brightest parts of the clouds. These can be created by picking up a little pigment on your fingertips and very lightly stroking it on to the paper.

Stormy sky in acrylics

Although the small strip of land and the high-rise buildings at the base of this picture provide an essential calm, static point on which the viewer's eye can rest, the main interest undoubtedly lies in the dramatic and bleak, stormy sky, with its dark, billowing clouds and the warm glow of the setting sun shining through them.

When you are painting clouds, remember that you need to make them look like solid, three-dimensional forms, not mere wisps drifting across the sky – you know they are clouds of vapour but they look like solid objects. You should also follow the rules of perspective and make clouds that are far away smaller than those that are directly overhead.

For this project use acrylic paint thinly, flooding the paper with generous washes of dilute colour. The aim is to create an impressionistic scene, with no hard edges to the clouds and very little detail in the buildings. Let the paint do as much of the work for you as possible, such as puddling at the base of damp areas to form darker tones at the base of the clouds.

Materials

- *Watercolour board*
- *Acrylic paints: cerulean blue, alizarin crimson, burnt sienna, ultramarine blue, lemon yellow, titanium white*
- *Brushes: large round, medium flat*
- *Household plant sprayer*
- *Flow improver*
- *Absorbent paper towel*

The scene

The warm glow of an evening sunset contrasts dramatically with the glowering purple of the storm clouds in this scene. Note the complementary colours – purple and yellow – which almost always work well together. Although the silhouetted buildings along the skyline occupy only a small part of the picture area, they are critical in giving a sense of scale to the image.

1 Using a household plant sprayer, spray clean water on to the board over the areas that you want to remain predominantly blue. (You could brush on water – but the spray gives a more random, less controlled coverage.)

2 Mix a few drops of flow improver into cerulean blue paint. Using a large round brush, drop the paint into the areas that you dampened in Step 1; it will spread and blur to give a soft spread of colour.

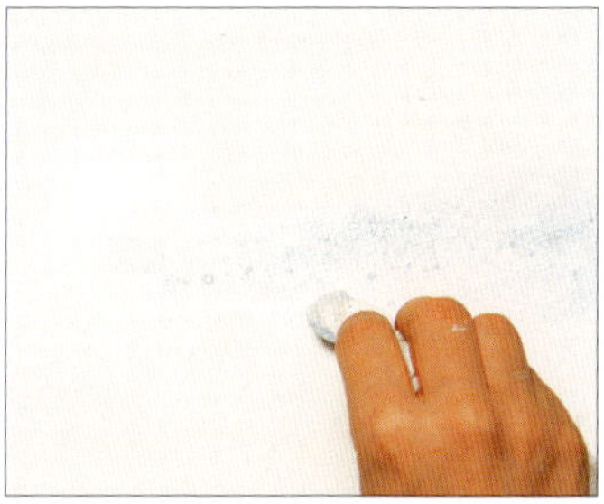

3 Scrunch up a piece of clean tissue or paper towel in your hand and carefully dab it on to the blue paint to soften the edges.

Tip: Keep turning the paper towel around in your hand so that you do not accidentally dab paint back on to an area from which you have just removed it.

4 Mix a warm purplish blue from cerulean blue and alizarin crimson and brush it over the land area at the base of the image with the large round brush. Mix a neutral purplish grey from burnt sienna and ultramarine blue. Spray clean water over the left-hand side of the painting and quickly drop in the neutral colour, allowing the paint to pool at the base of the damp area, as storm clouds are darker at their base.

5 Soften the edges of the clouds by dabbing them with a paper towel, as in Step 3. While the paint is still damp, dot in more of the dark mixture in the top right of the painting. The paint will spread wet into wet to form soft-edged patches of colour.

6 Using a watery version of the neutral purplish-grey mixture from Step 4, brush in a dark line above the purplish base, adding more burnt sienna nearer the horizon to warm up the tones. Allow the paint to dry. Mix a warm purple from burnt sienna and ultramarine blue and, using a medium flat brush, make broad, rectangular-shaped strokes for the high-rise buildings along the horizon line, varying the tones so that the nearer buildings are slightly darker than those that are farther away. Use strokes of different thicknesses to create a natural-looking variation in the shapes and sizes of the buildings.

Assessment time

You have now established the basic framework of the image and the main areas of colour – the blue of the open patches of sky, the dark storm clouds that dominate the scene, and the thin sliver of land with its high-rise buildings at the base. However, for the painting to look convincing, the clouds should be made more three-dimensional.

The clouds are soft-edged but do not appear to have volume.

Varying the tones of the buildings helps to create a sense of recession.

7 Mix a pale but warm, yellowy orange from lemon yellow, titanium white and a little burnt sienna. Brush this mixture into the breaks between the clouds, making horizontal brushstrokes that echo the direction in which the clouds are being blown in order to create a sense of movement in the sky. This adds warmth to the horizon and makes the dark storm clouds stand out all the more dramatically.

8 Continue adding this warm, yellowy orange, adding more burnt sienna to the mixture as you get nearer the horizon; the sun is sinking, so the colours are warmer nearer the horizon. Mix an opaque blue from cerulean blue and titanium white, and brush this mixture over the top of the sky, smudging the paint with your thumb to soften the edges and get rid of any obvious brushstrokes.

9 Dip a small piece of paper towel into the warm purple mixture that you used in Step 6 and squeeze out any excess moisture. Lightly stroke the paper towel over the yellow area just above the horizon to create streaks of storm cloud.

Tip: You could apply the paint with a rag or a sponge instead of a piece of paper towel. All these tools create a more random, spontaneous-looking effect than a brush and are very appropriate for a natural scene such as this.

10 Dab light opaque blue into the very dark area at the top of the picture, using your fingertips. Mix a purple from cerulean blue and burnt sienna and swirl it around the light area in the centre of the paper to darken it and give the clouds more of a feeling of depth. Mix a pale, warm yellow from burnt sienna, lemon yellow and titanium white and stroke on shafts of light coming down from the clouds with your fingertips. Using a flat brush, block in the shapes of the nearest buildings on the skyline; using warmer, darker tones in this area will make these buildings look closer to the viewer.

The finished painting

This is a convincing representation of a stormy sky at dusk. The colours are allowed to spread on damp paper and pool naturally, creating soft-edged shapes that are darker at their base and thus appear to have volume. Although the colour palette is limited and based mainly around the complementary colours of purple and yellow, the clever use of different tones of purple in the buildings at the base of the image creates a sense of recession.

The silhouettes of the buildings along the skyline are painted as simple rectangles of colour, exploiting the natural shape of the flat brush.

Purple and yellow are complementary colours and almost always work well together. Here, they create a warm-toned yet dramatic-looking composition.

There are no harsh-edged colours in the sky – dabbing the wet paint with a paper towel helps to remove any potentially distracting brushmarks.

Sunset in oils

This sunset was painted *alla prima* – that is, in one sitting. This is in stark contrast to the traditional method of oil painting, in which the paint is built up in successive layers, with each layer being allowed to dry (a process that may take many days) before the next is applied. In *alla prima* oil painting, the paints are applied in a single layer, often thickly.

One of the drawbacks of painting a sunset – or any fleeting effect of light – in the field is that the colours change incredibly quickly. By the time you have mixed the colour that you see in front of your eyes, it may already be disappearing from the sky. To get around this problem, mix your colours in advance and try to ensure that you have a separate clean brush for each one; this saves time and ensures that your colours stay fresh. Another option, of course, is to work from photographs.

It is also a good idea to have two whites on your palette – one to mix with warm tones and one to mix with cool – as this makes it easier to keep the warm and cool colours clean.

No matter how dramatic the sunset, it is generally best to include something other than the sky, simply to set the scene in context. Here, the palm trees in the foreground, with their beautifully curving branches, provide a foil for the sky behind. The gently rippling sea, too, adds visual interest and allows you to explore the effect of light reflected in moving water.

Note, however, that the trees are not solid black silhouettes. It is important to get some variation in tone even in areas that appear solid, otherwise everything will look very flat and one-dimensional. Here, they are painted in various dark, purply-brown mixes.

The artist began this painting by toning the canvas with warm pinks, violets, reds and oranges. The exact colours are not too important, as they will probably not show through in the finished work, but try to ensure they bear some relation to the final colours – so think about the colour temperature and use warm or cool colours as appropriate.

Materials

- *Primed canvas*
- *Oil paints: violet grey, permanent rose, cadmium scarlet, cadmium yellow orange, lemon yellow, titanium white, Mars violet deep, ultramarine blue, cadmium yellow deep, cobalt blue.*
- *Brushes: selection of filberts in different sizes*
- *Turpentine/white spirit (paint thinner)*
- *Old rag or absorbent paper towel*

The scene

It was, of course, the wonderfully vibrant colours of the sky that first attracted the artist's attention, but even the most dramatic sunset requires some kind of foreground interest in order to give it a context. Here, the artist included the two palm trees. The shapes form a bold shape at the base of the image, while the many fronds break up the silhouette and provide texture and additional visual interest.

1 Tone the ground with bands of warm colour, applied very thinly, leaving a space where the orb of the sun will go. Here, the artist used violet grey, permanent rose, cadmium scarlet and a mix of cadmium scarlet and cadmium yellow to create the orange.

2 Using lemon yellow, block in the sun. Mix a pinky red from cadmium scarlet and titanium white and scumble it loosely around the sun. Mix a warm dark from Mars violet deep, white and a touch of ultramarine blue and roughly mark in the larger palm tree.

3 Scumble cadmium scarlet, and a mix of cadmium scarlet and white, over the sky, varying the mixes as you see fit. Brush the same colour around the yellow of the sun to define its shape. Mix a vivid orange from cadmium yellow deep and cadmium scarlet and scumble it over the top of the sky, allowing some of the underlying permanent rose applied in Step 1 to show through.

4 Lightly mark out the main lines of the smaller palm tree, as in Step 2, using the very tip of a fine brush. Look at the reflection of the sun in the sea and put in some of the horizontal ripples, using the orange mixture from Step 3 and a mix of lemon yellow and white. You may find that half-closing your eyes makes it easier to see where different colours occur.

5 Mix a deep violet from permanent rose and violet grey and add some of it to the warm dark blue already on your palette. Hold your brush almost vertically, as you would when practising calligraphy, and put in some of the main fronds on the palm trees. To simulate the ripples on the water, dab on some deep violet, using short strokes and an almost dry brush, then repeat with the orange mix from Step 3. The colours blend optically on the canvas, helping to capture the interplay of many different colours as the light shifts.

6 Mix a dark, warm tone from Mars violet deep and ultramarine blue. Using a fine, almost dry, brush, put in more of the palm tree fronds, varying the amount of pressure you apply to create different marks and splaying out the bristles of the brush with your fingertips to create a fan shape reminiscent of the palm fronds. Brush the orange mix over the sea, using short, horizontal brushstrokes as before, then apply the same colour over the permanent rose that lies behind the palm tree.

Assessment time

Putting in the yellow of the sun and its reflection in the sea in the early stages has paid dividends, as the light, bright colour (which was applied very thinly) has a lovely luminosity. Both the sky and the sea lack the intensity of colour that they need and, although we have the beginnings of some broken colour in the ripples on the water, this needs to be taken much further. The shape of the palm trees has been drawn in, but they do not stand out enough against the background; they need to be darkened and more detail added.

Too much of the sky colour shows through behind the palm trees.

The sky needs to be more intense in colour, with a thicker coverage of paint.

The sea looks flat. More short, horizontal brushstrokes of colour are needed here to create the ripples in the water.

7 Apply more of the orange mix behind the palm tree, to cover up most of the initial wash of permanent rose. Using the same dark mixes as before, work on the palm trees. For the fronds, hold the brush almost vertically, about halfway along the shaft, and make a series of short dashes. For the branches, pull the brush over the canvas in sweeping, curving lines.

8 Add cobalt blue to the dark mix to cool it down and continue touching in the dark fronds of both trees. Cut in behind the fronds with the orange mix where necessary, and apply a thicker mix of orange, violet and yellow to the sea, using short horizontal brushstrokes, as before, to strengthen the intensity of the colours reflected in the water.

9 Stand back from your painting and assess the intensity of colour overall. Scumble the orange mix over the sky, allowing some of the earlier colours to show through in parts – particularly on the right-hand side, which is less orange and contains slightly darker, cooler tones than the area to the left of the sun. Skies are rarely, if ever, a flat, uniform colour, and allowing earlier colours to show through adds to the painting's liveliness.

The finished painting

This is a vibrant, colourful painting of a tropical sunset. Note how the horizon line is positioned above the centre of the painting: had it run right across the middle, the image would have had a much more static feel. The colours in the sea have been carefully observed and range from bright, warm yellows and oranges to darker, cooler violets, all of which helps to give the ripples in the water some form. The dark palm trees anchor the painting and provide strong shapes on which the eye can rest, while allowing some of the initial permanent rose wash to show through behind the palms and painting the trees in warm, dark purples rather than solid blacks has enhanced the impression of backlighting.

The thin wash of yellow used for the sun shines through subsequent glazes and gives the painting a lovely luminosity.

Dashes of broken colour capture the mosaic of reflections of the sun in the rippling sea beautifully.

Note the variety of brushstrokes used to paint the thick branches and delicate fronds of the palm trees.

Rainbow in acrylics

A rainbow is a spectrum of light that appears in the sky as a multi-coloured arc when the sun shines on droplets of moisture in the earth's atmosphere. But such a prosaic description does not capture the beauty of the spectacle – nor is it easy to capture it in paint.

One of the most important things to remember is not to make the rainbow too strong to begin with, otherwise it will completely dominate the painting. Start pale and build up the intensity of colour with subsequent layers – and alternate between the rainbow and the rest of the painting, so that you keep the whole painting moving along at the same pace and can continually assess each part in relation to the whole. Although we tend to think of a rainbow as having seven distinct colours – red, orange, yellow, green, blue, indigo and violet – it is, in fact, a spectrum, with no clear line between one colour and its neighbour. 'Feather' your brushstrokes to create smooth transitions.

You also need to think about how you are going to paint the surrounding area of sky. When the sky is very gloomy and overcast there is a temptation to view it as a flat expanse of colour, with little or no tonal variation. Look carefully, however, and you will see that there are many variations in tone. In the demonstration shown here, the artist has deliberately exaggerated this, and even introduced stronger contrasts of colour than are in the original scene for dramatic effect. Even so, he has taken care to blend the colours so there are no obvious brush marks.

When it came to painting the town in the foreground, our artist's approach was to look at things as blocks of colour and tone, rather than attempting to paint individual buildings in detail. The town is some distance away from the artist's viewpoint, but the contrasts of lights and darks, and warm and cool tones, supply enough information for us to be able to interpret the scene. However you could, if you prefer, opt for a more photo-realistic approach and put in lots of fine detail; it all depends on your individual style.

Materials

- *Canvas primed with acrylic gesso*
- *Acrylic paints: Turquoise, white, ultramarine blue, lemon yellow, vermilion, purple red, carmine, emerald green, yellow ochre, brown oxide, cadmium yellow*
- *Brushes: Selection of filberts in different sizes*
- *Absorbent kitchen paper*

The scene

On a murky, rainy day, a dazzling rainbow in the sky illuminates a patch of land in the distance. The curve of the bay draws the eye through the scene, while the town gives interesting foreground detail. There is a large expanse of empty sky, but the rainbow and headland are positioned 'on the third' – a strong compositional device.

1 Using a large filbert brush, wet the canvas with clean water. Brush a very dilute mix of turquoise and white acrylic paint over the sea and sky area, leaving space where the rainbow is going to go. Remember that the colour of the sky is paler near the horizon. The paint will blur and spread over the damp canvas, leaving just a pale wash of colour that you can build up to the desired shade and intensity with subsequent layers.

2 Using the tip of the brush and ultramarine blue, lightly draw in the line of the hill in the foreground that sweeps down to the sea and the distant headland. Brush lemon yellow over the rainbow area.

Tip: If you think you have made the initial wash too strong, dab off paint with a piece of paper towel.

3 Using a fine brush, apply vermilion over the left-hand edge of the rainbow and purple red to the edge of the vermilion, allowing the colours to blend on the canvas so that there are no harsh-edged transitions. Brush turquoise over the sea in the foreground, and then touch in the sandy patches of land on the distant headland in yellow ochre.

Tip: Do not worry if the yellow ochre blurs into the turquoise, giving a greenish tinge, as you can apply stronger, thicker colour later on. The purpose of these early marks is primarily to help you locate where things are in the painting.

4 Using the tip of the brush and purple red, put in the darker patches of land on the distant headland. Keep the paint thin at this stage and use short, tentative marks to search out the shapes. Scrub the same colour into the sky, keeping the coverage quite thin and uneven so that some of the underlying turquoise shows through.

5 Apply a faint line of carmine to the left-hand edge of the rainbow, followed by ultramarine to create a dark purple, and use light, gentle brushstrokes to blend the colours. Mix a bright but relatively dark green from emerald green and yellow ochre and dot in the greens of the headland. Dot in some brown oxide for the darker tones in the town buildings.

Tip: Make tentative marks with the brush to establish lines and shapes.

6 Now apply colour to the sandy beach in the foreground, using a mix of lemon yellow, white and a little vermilion, then add a slightly redder version of the same mix to the part of the sea where the colours of the rainbow are reflected. Begin to define the jetties and the shaded sides of the buildings with yellow ochre, various tones of dark purple mixed from carmine and cobalt blue, and brown oxide. Add white to the purple red on your palette and lightly brush it over the sea, allowing it to blend wet into wet with the colours that are already there.

7 To define the headland, block in light and dark tones as appropriate with mixes of lemon white and yellow in varying proportions for the sunlit patches, vermilion and white for the mid tones and more greens and purples for the darkest areas. Add definition to the foreground buildings by dotting in browns and reds for the roofs, and add cobalt blue as the base colour for the foreground grass. Mix ultramarine blue, white and a little purple red and brush it over the pale part of the sky to the right of the rainbow, 'feathering' your marks to get rid of hard edges.

Assessment time

With the light and dark tones giving some indication of the way the land undulates, the distant headland is beginning to have some sense of form – even though this area of the scene is fairly misty and indistinct. The position of the jetties in the foreground has been put in and the buildings of the town are beginning to take shape. However, both the sea and the sky require several more layers of colour.

More detail is required in the foreground.

The sky needs to look darker and more brooding.

There is no sense of movement in the sea and the colours are too pale.

8 Using a fine brush, touch in a mix of emerald green and white on the right-hand edge of the rainbow. Strengthen the light and dark tones on the headland; you may need to use a stronger, deeper yellow such as cadmium yellow, for the most brightly lit parts. Brush more colour into the sea, using relatively short, horizontal brushstrokes that echo the motion of the waves. Scumble more of the purple red and white mix into the sky, to create some tonal variation, blending the colours on the canvas as before to get rid of any obvious brushstrokes and allowing some of the underlying turquoise colour to show through.

Tip: Look at the lights and darks within the sea: even though the sea is relatively calm, these tonal contrasts reveal the shapes, structure and direction of the waves.

9 Using various mixes and tones of purple red overlaid with ultramarine, yellow ochre, brown oxide, and vermilion, add more definition to the buildings.

10 Apply more colour to the sea, building up thin glazes of turquoise; turquoise and white; purple red and white; white and vermilion as appropriate.

11 Using a fine brush, continue with the buildings in the foreground, alternating between warm and cool tones and lights and darks in order to suggest three-dimensional forms.

The finished painting

This is a lively painting in which the artist has created the effects of a fleeting moment, when colours vibrate and light glistens during a passing storm. The actual colours have been exaggerated for dramatic effect while still retaining the sombre, brooding atmosphere of the stormy sky. The gentle arc of the rainbow draws the eye down to the headland and foreground town, which is painted in just enough detail for it to be clear what is represented. There is a feeling of energy in both the sea and sky, due in part to the way the colours have blended wet into wet on the canvas but also to the way the artist has used horizontal brushstrokes in the sea to capture the direction of the waves.

Even though little detail is present the viewer's eye nonetheless interprets these simple blocks of colour as buildings.

Scumbling the paint on vigorously allows some of the underlying colour to show through, creating interesting mottling.

Applying several layers of thin, semi-opaque colour creates a variety of tones in the water.

Seascape in soft pastels

The range of marks that you can make with soft pastels – from soft blends and sweeping strokes made with the side of the stick to sharp, linear marks – is great for matching virtually any effect seen in nature. They are quick to use, allowing you to build up areas of colour rapidly, and are perfect for capturing fleeting effects of weather and light.

This project gives you the opportunity to practise different kinds of blending. A subject such as skies and clouds is perfect for relative newcomers to pastels; because the shapes are not critical, you can practise moving the pigment around on the paper without having to worry about getting the detail exactly right.

Materials

- *Pastel paper*
- *Grey pastel pencil*
- *Soft pastels: mid-grey, dark grey, black, reddish brown, mid-green, pale grey, mid-blue, dark brown, fawn, pale yellow*

The scene

This is a moody and atmospheric seascape, with storm clouds billowing overhead and sunlight glinting on the water. Although the colour palette appears limited at first glance, there are a number of different tones within the clouds and rocks and these need to be blended smoothly. The artist used two reference photos for this exercise – one for the detail of the foreground rocks and one for the stormy sky and sunlight sparkling on the water.

1 Using a grey pastel pencil, outline the headland and foreground rocks. The artist has changed the composition to make it more dynamic: in the photo, the horizon line is in the centre – but here it is positioned lower down.

2 Using the side of a mid-grey soft pastel, block in the darkest tones in the sky and blend with your finger. Allow some areas to remain darker than others, as there is a lot of tonal variation in the clouds.

3 Apply a darker grey pastel for the clouds immediately overhead. (The difference in tone helps to convey a sense of distance, as colours tend to look paler toward the horizon.) Build up the very darkest areas of cloud with more dark grey and black, blending the marks with your fingers as before. Remember to leave some gaps for the white of the paper to show through, to create the impression of sunlight peeping out from behind the clouds.

4 Block in the headland with a dark, reddish brown and smooth out the pastel marks with your fingers. Use the same reddish brown for the foreground rocks, then overlay the brown in both areas with a mid-green, blending the colours partially with your fingers so both colours remain visible.

5 Gently stroke the side of a pale grey pastel across the water area, leaving the central, most brightly lit section untouched.

6 Darken the water by overlaying touches of a dusky mid-blue, green and black. Do not overblend the marks or apply them too heavily: it is important to see some differences in colour within the water and to allow some of the white of the paper to show through to create the impression of light sparkling on the water.

7 Now build up more of the texture on the foreground rocks. Loosely block in the darkest areas (the shaded sides of the rocks) in reddish brown, then overlay dark brown and green and blend the colours slightly with your fingers. For the lighter sides of the rocks, use greys and fawns. Immediately the rocks will begin to look more three-dimensional.

Tip: The differences in tone within the rocks are subtle; you may find it easier to assess them if you half close your eyes, as you will then see the blocks of tone and not get distracted by detail.

Assessment time

Stand back from the image to assess what final small adjustments may be needed. Here, for example, the sky requires just a little more work as there are some small patches of cloud even in the very brightest part. The artist also judged that the sea on the far right of the image, which has the dark, brooding storm cloud directly overhead, was slightly too light in tone. In addition, the golden glow of the setting sun on the horizon still needs to be put in.

Without the glow of the setting sun along the horizon, we have no clues as to the time of day.

The addition of a few tiny patches of cloud to this area will add visual interest and prevent this area from looking completely burnt out and featureless.

8 Lightly draw a pale yellow line along the horizon and add touches of yellow in the sky to warm it up, blending the marks with your fingertips or a clean rag.

9 Using the tip of mid-grey pastel, put tiny dashes and dots of colour into the sea on the far right of the image to darken the area slightly and create the impression of wavelets and a sense of movement in the water.

The finished drawing

This drawing uses a number of blending techniques. In the sky, softly blended marks create the impression of swirling clouds. The texture and form of the rocks in the foreground are achieved by overlaying several colours, allowing each one to retain its integrity, and adding a few linear marks as the finishing touch. Our overall impression of the water is that it is a dark blue-grey, but on closer inspection we can see a number of different colours and tones within it – optical mixes that enliven the scene and also imply the movement of the waves in the sea.

The yellow along the horizon contrasts with the cool blues and greys used elsewhere and adds a touch of warmth to the image.

Note how effectively the white of the paper stands for the very brightest areas in both the sky and the sea.

Although little detail is discernible in the distant headland, some tonal variation is essential to prevent it from appearing as a solid silhouette.

Sunlit beach in oils

This simple-looking scene of an almost deserted beach on a bright summer's day gives you the chance to paint two of nature's most fascinating subjects – moving water and sparkling sunlight.

Painting the sea is interesting: how can you capture the constant ebb and flow of the water? The more time you spend in observation the better. Although the movement of the waves may seem random, if you stand still and watch for a while you will soon see a pattern. Look at the shapes that the waves make as they roll in toward the shore and try to fix them in your mind.

One of the risks of painting in bright sunshine is that you can be dazzled by the intensity of the light, with the result that you tend to make the scene too high key. Instead of capturing the brightness of the scene, as you intended, you will find that your work simply looks bleached out. Look for tonal contrasts within the scene and balance bright areas with dark, cooler shadows. The dark passages will make the light areas look even brighter.

When painting highlights, do not try to put in every single one or your work will look fussy. Half-close your eyes: this reduces the glare, enabling you to break down the pattern of light more easily and put in just the key highlight areas.

Finally there is the question of how to paint the sky. If you are painting *en plein air* and the clouds are fleeting, you may want to put them down quickly to capture the effects, whereas with a relatively static scene, you might concentrate on the land first. But remember that clouds have volume: look for the lights and darks within them that make them look voluminous.

Materials

- *Stretched and primed canvas*
- *Oil paints: olive green, cobalt blue, titanium white, alizarin crimson, cerulean blue, burnt umber, Indian yellow, cadmium red, black, lemon yellow*
- *Turpentine*
- *Brushes: small filbert brush, selection of small hogshair and sables*

The scene

The tide has receded, leaving shallow inlets illuminated by bright sunlight and large areas of exposed sand – an interesting contrast of colours and textures.

1 Using a thin mix of olive green, 'draw' the cliffs on the horizon, the lines of the waves and the little channels. At the outset the artist decided to add a small dog to the scene to focus the viewer's attention. Add its outline and shadow now.

2 Mix a bright, light blue from cobalt blue and titanium white. Using a small filbert brush, loosely scumble the mixture over the shallow areas of water in the foreground of the scene. Add a little alizarin crimson to the mixture to make it slightly more purple in tone, and brush in the line of cliffs along the horizon in the background. Mix a paler blue from cerulean blue and titanium white and use this mixture for the most distant area of sea.

3 Add a tiny amount of burnt umber to the purplish-blue mixture from Step 2 and blend this colour, wet into wet, into the darkest parts of the sea – the undersides of the waves that roll in toward the shore. Mix a rich, dark sand colour from burnt umber and Indian yellow and scumble this mixture over the sand, blending in a few strokes of cadmium red here and there, and adding purple for the very darkest lines along the edges of the water channels.

4 Add a little burnt umber to the bright blue mixture from Step 2, and scumble it over the deepest areas of the foreground water. Using short, vertical brushstrokes, loosely scumble various sand colours over the shallowest parts of the water, where the underlying sand is clearly visible.

5 Continue putting in the sand areas in the middle distance. Note that some areas are pinker and warmer than others; adjust the mixtures on your palette as appropriate. Block in the dog and its reflection in a dark mixture of olive green, black and a little burnt umber.

6 Continue to build up the tones in the water, using the same purplish blues as before to emphasize the darker areas. Overlay pale blue paint over the water-covered sand in the foreground, blending the vertical brushstrokes that you put down in the earlier stages to create the impression of sand seen hazily through shallow water.

7 Now start to work on the sky. Put in the clouds first, using light- and mid-toned greys mixed from burnt umber, cobalt blue and titanium white in varying proportions. Warm or cool the mixtures as necessary by adding a touch of pink or blue. Put in the bright blue of the sky using a mixture of cobalt blue and titanium white.

8 Use a darker version of the olive green, black and burnt umber mixture that you used in Step 5 to reinforce the shape of the dog and its reflection in the wet sand.

9 Now start to put in some of the reflected highlights on the crests of the waves, dotting in little specks of white tinged with yellow to give the impression of sunlight glancing off the surface of the water.

Assessment time

Now that the main elements and colours are in place, take time to assess the tonal balance of the painting as a whole. Although the orange of the sand and the blue of the sea are complementary colours and give the scene a lot of energy, they are both predominantly mid-tones. You need to reinforce the sense of sunlight within the scene – and, paradoxically, the way to do this is to make the dark areas darker, so that they form an effective contrast to the brightly lit parts.

Much of the picture space is empty, and the dog alone is insufficient to hold the viewer's interest More figures paddling in the sea would balance the composition.

You need to create a sense of sunlight sparkling on the water.

The sand is little more than a block of colour at this stage; it needs more texture.

10 Darken the water channels in the foreground, using the same purples and blues as before.

11 Touch some very pale yellow (made by mixing lemon yellow, a little Indian yellow and titanium white) into the top of the clouds to create the effect of warm sunlight.

12 Look at the colours within the sea: it is by no means a uniform blue. Add a little purple to your blue mixes to put in the darkest parts of the small waves as they break on the shore. Loosely block in the figures, using a purplish blue-black. As they are silhouetted, with the sun behind them, little detail is discernible. Add a hint of yellow to titanium white and put in fine lines to create highlights on the foam-tipped wave crests.

Tip: Do not add any solvent to the paint for this process: using the paint straight from the tube means that it is relatively dry, so the colours do not turn muddy even though you are overlaying paint on a layer that it still wet.

13 Continue putting lights and darks into the sea area, using small strokes and dotting in the highlights. In the deeper channels in the foreground water, use loose vertical strokes of a mid-toned blue to create the sense of light shimmering in the water. The brushstrokes will soon be blended out, but their direction is important as it helps to give the effect of sunlight glancing off the water.

14 Continue working on the foreground area, using the sand colour and blue mixes tinged with purple as appropriate. Gently and gradually blend the wet paint on the canvas and smooth out the brushstrokes.

15 Create more variety and texture in the exposed sand area by dotting in other colours – a light yellow mixed from lemon yellow and white, and burnt umber lines and dots. Dot the pale yellow mixture that you used in Step 12 on the wave crests to create the effect of sunlight sparkling over the water.

16 Mix a bright blue from cobalt blue and titanium white and scumble it over the top of the sky to darken it and allow the clouds to stand out more dramatically. The use of a dark colour at the top of the picture holds the viewer's eye within the frame, while the loose brushstrokes help to give an impression of movement in the sky.

The finished painting

This is an attractive painting of an almost deserted beach in summer. Lively brushstrokes convey the dark clouds scudding across the sky, and loose scumbles of colour over the water also help to convey a sense of movement. The viewpoint has been carefully chosen so that the wedge-shaped areas of sand in the foreground balance the composition and lead our eye through the painting. Although the dog and the silhouetted figures in the middle distance occupy only a small part of the scene, their position (roughly on the thirds) means that our eye is drawn to them.

The use of complementary colours (blue and orange) imparts a sense of energy.

Specks of yellow create the effect of warm sunlight glancing off the water.

The dog occupies only a small area, but its position means that our eye is drawn to it.

Rocky foreshore in pencil

As this scene has a limited colour palette of predominantly blues, greys and browns, it suits a monochrome medium. Graphite pencil was chosen for its versatility: it can produce fine linear detail with the tip and broad areas of tone using the side, while hatching and smudging increase the range and type of marks that can be made.

If you have good-quality pencils, you will probably be able to get away with using just one or two different grades. A good 2B, for example, can produce a wide range of tones depending on how much pressure you apply, so there should be no need for you to resort to a 5B or 6B for the very blackest tones. The graphite in cheap pencils, however, tends to snap or crumble if you apply a lot of pressure. You may also find that the graphite is bound in poor-quality wood, which simply crumbles away when you try to sharpen the pencil, making it virtually impossible to achieve a fine point. Experiment with different brands until you find one you like.

When you look really closely at a scene such as this, you will see that there is an incredible amount of linear and textural detail. The amount of detail that you include in your drawing is up to you: if you favour a photo-realistic approach, then you may decide to try to capture every single nook and cranny. If you do this, however, you must try to establish some kind of hierarchy in your own mind. If all your lines are the same weight, you may get lost in a plethora of detail in which every line is as important as its neighbour and nothing stands out. Alternatively, you could opt for a looser, less detailed approach that concentrates on the general shapes and lines of the scene and emphasizes the powerful geological forces that shaped the rocks and the landscape. The route that you choose depends on your own emotional response to the scene in front of you.

Materials

- *Good-quality drawing paper*
- *Pencils: F, 2B*
- *Kneaded eraser*

The scene

The stones along the water's edge and the larger boulders on the right point inward on slight diagonal lines, directing the viewer's eye toward the centre of the image – the gently lapping sea and the silhouetted mountains in the distance. The dark, brooding sky holds in the image at the top. This is a classic composition, with the sky and mountains occupying roughly two-thirds of the picture space and the stones most of the remainder.

1 Using a hard pencil (grade F), map out the composition. First, establish the horizon line, the line of the larger boulders jutting in on the right, and the mountains in the background. As you work, look for correspondences between one part and another that you can use as reference points to check that you are locating everything accurately. Drop faint vertical lines down from the tip or base of individual hills to see what they align with on the foreshore. You can erase these construction lines later, once you have sketched out the whole composition and are sure that you've located all the main elements correctly.

2 Continue until you feel you have mapped out all the key elements of the scene and positioned them accurately. Do not try to put in every single stone, but look at the overall shapes of the mountains and the shapes of the largest of the foreground boulders – anything that will help you locate where you are in the drawing as you commence with the more detailed stages. Take plenty of time over this: it is the most critical part of the drawing, because once you have got these major elements right, everything else, such as the shading, textures and tones, will fall into place.

3 Once you have got the main forms, you can begin to put in some of the smaller stones. Keep the drawing very linear at this stage. You can begin to introduce tone and shading later on.

Tip: Remember the rules of perspective: the stones along the water's edge appear smaller as they are farther away. Less texture and detail is evident here, too.

4 Switch to a 2B pencil, which is much softer, and begin putting in some of the darker cracks and crevices in the large boulders on the right, using strong, linear marks for all the crevices and loose hatching marks for the mid tones on the stone. This area is close to the viewer, so texture and detail are more in evidence here than in the background.

5 Shade the rocks behind the main foreground boulder, which are a mid-tone. Sharpen your pencil to a fine point, then use the side of the graphite to lightly apply tone. Begin applying tone to the foreground rocks on the foreshore in the same way.

Tip: Keep referring back to your source material so that you do not lose track of where you are in the drawing. It is very easy to get so caught up in shading and applying tone to individual stones that you lose sight of the drawing as a whole.

6 Put in the very dark shadows under the rocks to help develop a sense of form. At the same time, look for darker tones on the rocks' surface, which are due partly to their natural coloration and partly to the way light hits different planes of the stone, creating shaded and more brightly lit areas.

7 Using the side of the pencil, lightly hatch the mountains in the distance. Some are farther away than others, so look for subtle tonal differences between them to create a sense of distance and recession. Build up the tones gradually. It is easy to darken things later, but if you make the mountains too dark at the start you will destroy the drawing's tonal balance.

8 Using the side of the pencil, lightly hatch the sea with long, horizontal strokes that echo the direction in which the water is flowing. Smudge the pencil marks by rubbing across them with your fingers to create a smoother tone. Mould a kneaded eraser to a peak and gently lift off tiny highlights on the water.

9 Strengthen the darkest tones and continue putting in the mid tones on the foreground rocks, using loose hatching as before. Put in the shadows beneath and within the rocks to establish the different planes of the rocks' surfaces.

10 Add bold linear marks where necessary to delineate the individual rocks and put in the shadows and lines of any deep crevices. These marks will bring the picture together.

Tips: • A 2B pencil is capable of producing a wide range of marks. Vary the amount of pressure you apply to create marks of different densities.
• Do not try to put in every single line. Limit yourself to those that contribute to our understanding of the rock's form and structure.

Assessment time

The drawing is nearing completion and all the main elements except the sky have been put in. All that remains now is to increase the tonal contrast in certain areas and to decide how much textural detail you want to include in the immediate foreground. At this stage, you can decide on the details that will give the drawing atmosphere.

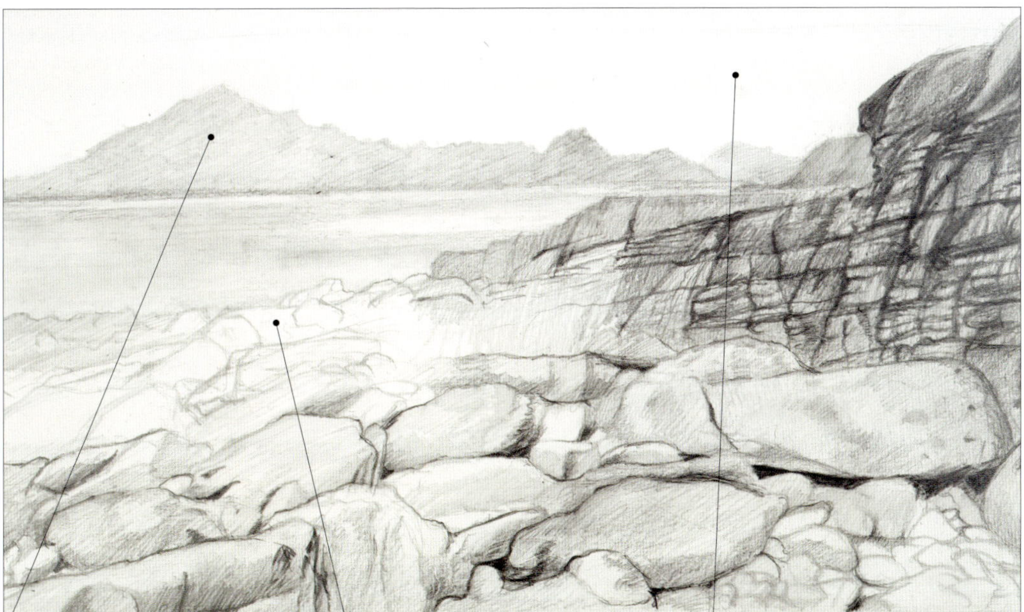

The mountains are similar in tone to the sea and need to be darkened considerably so that they can readily be distinguished from each other.

Virtually no tone or linear detail has been applied to the rocks along the foreshore. Although less detail is required here than in the foreground, at present the viewer's eye is drawn to this area because it is so much brighter than the rest of the drawing.

The sky is bland and featureless: dark, glowering clouds need to be added to complete the drawing and create mood.

11 Using the tip of the pencil, darken the background mountains so that they stand out more. Remember to look for differences in tone between different mountains to imply their spatial relationship to one another.

12 Apply light shading and any linear detail that you feel is necessary to the rocks along the foreshore. Remember that the detail in this area needs to be less evident than in the foreground.

13 Block in the darkest tones of the sky and blend the marks with your fingers to create smooth areas of tone. Use a charcoal-covered kneaded eraser to 'draw' any light-toned wisps of clouds within the very brightest patches.

14 Make light strokes using the side of the pencil to create the mid tones in the sky.

The finished drawing

The versatility of graphite pencil as a medium is well demonstrated in this drawing, with the marks ranging from strong linear strokes to subtle hatching and finger-blending. Although one could choose to add much more texture and detail to the stones than the artist has done here, there is more than enough to convey the three-dimensional nature of the subject. Note, in particular, how careful shading on the foreground rocks captures the undulations on the rocks' surface. Although the mountains in the background are virtually in silhouette, subtle tonal differences reveal that some peaks are farther away than others. The sea and the sky have been put in with light hatching, but again the tones have been carefully assessed in relation to the rest of the image. The light line of the horizon is made with an eraser.

Wispy areas of mid-tone are visible within the clouds, preventing the brightest patches of sky from looking completely empty and bland.

The side of the stone is in shadow, and hence darker than the top. Careful analysis of the tones is essential if you are to make the stones look three-dimensional.

Bold, confident linear marks made with the tip of the pencil are used to convey the deep, angular crevices in the foreground boulders.

Mediterranean seascape in soft pastels

This tranquil scene of waves lapping a Mediterranean shore is full of sunshine and light. Although the composition is simple there is plenty to hold the viewer's attention, from the partially submerged rocks in the foreground through to the town in the distance.

The main interest, of course, is the rippling sea itself, with its myriad tones of blue, green and even violet – and soft pastels are a wonderful medium in which to portray this. It is surprising how many colours you can see in the water. Water takes its colour from objects in and around it – the sky, rocks, seaweed and algae, and so on – so look at the surroundings, as well as at the water, as this will help you assess which colours are required. Half-close your eyes when you look at the scene, as this makes it easier to assess the different colours and tones. It is hard to be precise about which colours to use in this project, as soft pastels are available in such a huge range of colours, but put together a selection of blues, greens, violets and browns, from very pale to very dark.

Remember that the rules of both linear and aerial perspective apply to sea and sky just as much as they do to objects on land. Distant waves, for example, appear smaller than those close at hand. Colours also appear lighter with distance and texture is less pronounced – so smooth out your pastel marks on the sky and the most distant part of the sea by blending them lightly with your fingers or a rag.

Observe your seascape carefully before you draw. You will see that the waves follow a regular pattern, with incoming waves building to a peak and then falling back. Note how high they go and how far back they fall when they break around a rock or crash on the shore.

Materials

- *Cream pastel paper*
- *Neutral brown or grey pastel pencil*
- *Soft pastels: a selection of blues, greens, blue-greens, turquoises, violets, browns, oranges, ochres and white*
- *Soft rag*

The scene

The dark wall on the left forms a diagonal line at its base which directs the viewer's attention towards the town in the distance. The town itself is positioned roughly 'on the third' – a strong position in any composition.

1 Using a neutral-coloured pastel pencil, put in the lines of the headland and horizon and the dark, submerged rocks in the water. Note that the artist decided to make the headland and rocks more prominent in the scene and omitted the light-coloured concrete walkway in the bottom left of the reference photo.

2 Roughly block in the sky using the side of a mid-blue pastel and blend with a clean rag or your fingertips to smooth out the marks.

Tips: • Keep the coverage slightly uneven, to give some texture to the sky. If the colour is completely flat and uniform, it will look rather boring.
• If you use your fingers to blend the marks, wash your hands regularly so that you do not apply the wrong colour accidentally or create messy smudges. Using a torchon may help you to keep the paper clean.

3 Block in the wall on the left with a mid-brown pastel and smooth out the marks with a rag or your fingers. Scribble in the partially submerged rocks using the same colour.

4 Block in the sea using a turquoise pastel, leaving some spaces for the breaking wavelets. Note that the sea has some areas that are lighter than others, so apply less pressure here.

5 Apply a few light touches of a darker turquoise to the darkest parts of the sea in the background. Loosely scribble jade green over the foreground water to pick up the green tones, varying the amount of pressure you apply to get some variety of tone.

6 Looking carefully at their rough, uneven shapes, apply burnt orange over the tops of the exposed rocks in the sea near the base of the wall, switching to a reddish brown for their bases. Blend the marks gently with clean fingertips.

7 Look at the colours in the water. The underside of breaking wavelets contains some surprisingly dark greens and blues. Stroke these in lightly, making sure your strokes follow the direction in which the waves are moving. Gently smooth the marks a little with your fingertips – but do not overdo the blending, as allowing some of the underlying paper colour to show through helps to create a sense of movement in the water.

8 Continue building up different colours in the water, using dark greens and blues and dots of light spring green.

Tip: Remember to keep referring to your reference photo. It is easy to get carried away with building up the colours and forget to look at the shades that are actually there.

Assessment time

There is a lovely sense of movement in the sea and a good range of different tones and colours. However, the rocks themselves are nothing more than flat blocks of colour and need to be made to look three-dimensional.

The sky is too pale and uniform in colour and needs to be darkened in some areas.

The shape of the town is clear, but there is no detail on the buildings, so it looks flat.

The wall is a flat expanse of brown – it needs to look rough in texture and three-dimensional.

The rocks are little more than patches of colour and lack form.

9 Start to build up some tone and texture on the wall by scribbling on dark greens and browns, making horizontal strokes that suggest the blocks that it is built from. Smudge the colours with your fingers, allowing some of the underlying mid-brown that you put down in Step 3 to remain visible.

10 Repeat the process on the rocks surrounding the partially enclosed still pool, scribbling a reddish brown over the orange to build up the form. On the distant headland, put in the darkest colours of the buildings – the browns and terracottas of the roofs. Apply pale yellow ochre to the white of the headland so the paper does not look so stark.

11 Dot some light and mid-toned olive greens into the headland for the distant trees. Apply pale blue and mid-tone turquoise over the sky to darken it toward the top (because of the effect of aerial perspective, skies generally look paler close to the horizon). Blend with your finger as necessary to soften the effect.

12 Although little detail is visible in the distant town, you need to give some indication of the buildings. Look for the dark tones under the eaves of the roofs. Making small horizontal strokes, apply pale blues and greens over the most distant part of the sea and smooth them out with your fingers. Apply thin lines of dark brown around the bases of the partially exposed rocks.

13 Having now given the rocks some solidity, return to working on the foreground seascape again, and put in the white of the wavelets as they break around the partially exposed rocks. Use the tip of the pastel and dot in white here and there around this area. The softly lapping sea has only a gentle swell, so take care that you do not make the wavelets too big.

14 Continue adding texture to the foreground sea, making sure that the dark greens, blues and purples in this area are dark enough. Do not smooth out your marks too much: it is important to have more texture in the foreground of a scene than in the background, as this is one way of creating a sense of recession.

15 Continue building up form on the exposed rocks, using a range of dark oranges and browns as before. It is now time to put in the final touches – more tiny strokes of white for the breaking wavelets and horizontal strokes of dark greens and blues in the foreground sea, wherever you judge it to be necessary.

The finished drawing

There is a lively sense of movement in the sea: one can almost feel the ebb and flow of the waves and hear them lapping around the rocks. Note how allowing some of the paper to show through the pastel marks creates the effect of sunlight sparkling on the water. There is just enough detail in the distant headland for us to know that there is a town there; more detail, however, would draw the viewer's attention away from the sea in the foreground and destroy the illusion that we are looking almost directly into the sun, our eyes dazzled by its brilliance.

The wall provides solidity at the edge of the picture area and helps to direct the viewer's eye through the scene.

Small horizontal strokes of blues, greens and purples are used to convey the many different shades in the water.

Detail diminishes with distance, and so the pastel marks in this area of the sea are smoothed out to give less texture.

Crashing waves in watercolour

This project depicts a massive sea wave just as it is about to break over craggy rocks. Your challenge is to capture the energy and power of the scene.

Few people would go as far in their search for realism as the great landscape artist J.M.W. Turner, who is reputed to have tied himself to a ship's mast in order to experience the full force of a storm at sea. Fortunately, there are easier and less perilous ways of adding drama to your seascapes.

Construct your painting as if you are viewing the scene from a low viewpoint, so that the waves seem to tower above you. For maximum drama, capture the waves while they are building or when they are at their peak, just before they break and come crashing down. You can gauge the height of the waves by comparing them with rocks or clifftops, while including such features in your painting will provide you with both a focal point and a sense of scale.

Try to attune yourself to the sea's natural rhythms. Watch the ebb and flow of the waves and concentrate on holding the memory of this movement in your mind as you are painting. This will help you to capture the energy.

Finally, remember that water reflects all the colours around it. You may be surprised at how many different colours there are in a scene like this.

Materials

- *4B pencil*
- *140lb (300gsm) NOT watercolour paper, pre-stretched*
- *Watercolour paints: Payne's grey, phthalocyanine blue, cadmium yellow, lemon yellow, Hooker's green, cerulean blue, yellow ochre, raw sienna, sepia, violet, burnt sienna, cobalt blue*
- *Gouache paints: permanent white*
- *Brushes: medium round, fine round*
- *Mixing or palette knife*
- *Fine texture paste*
- *Ruling drawing pen*
- *Masking fluid*
- *Sponge*

The original scene

It is notoriously difficult to photograph a breaking wave at exactly the right moment, and so the artist used this photograph merely to remind herself of the energy of the scene and the shapes and colours.

Reference sketches

Tonal sketches are a very good way of working out the light and dark areas of the scene. You will find that it helps to think of the waves as solid, three-dimensional objects, with a light and a shaded side. Try several versions so that you get used to the way the waves break over the rocks.

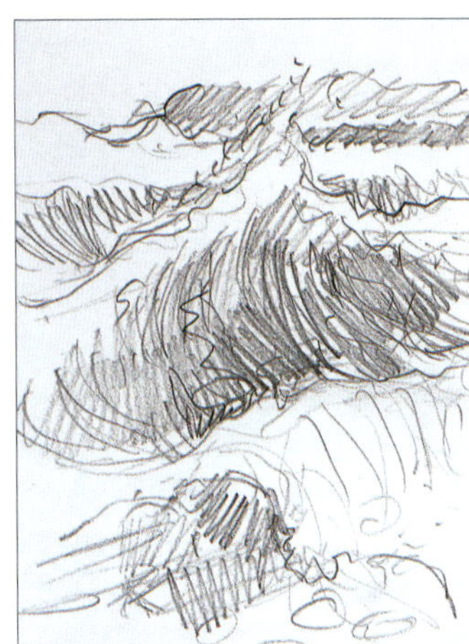

1 Using a 4B pencil, lightly sketch the scene, putting in the foreground rocks and the main waves. Take time to get the angles of the waves right: it is vital that they look as if they are travelling at speed and are just about to come crashing down.

2 Using a palette knife, apply fine texture paste over the rocks. Leave to dry. (Texture paste is available in several grades; the coarser it is, the more pronounced the effect. Here, the wave is more important than the rocks, so fine texture paste is sufficient).

3 Using a ruling drawing pen, apply masking fluid over the crest of the main wave and dot in flecks and swirls of foam in the water. Using a small sponge, dab masking fluid on to selected areas of the sea to create softer foamy areas. Leave to dry.

4 Mix a mid-toned wash of Payne's grey and another of phthalocyanine blue. Dampen the sky area with clean water and brush Payne's grey on to the right-hand side and phthalocyanine blue on to the left-hand side. Leave to dry.

5 Mix a strong wash of cadmium yellow with a touch of lemon yellow. Dampen the waves with clean water and lightly brush the bright yellow paint mixture over the tops of the waves.

6 While the first wash is still wet, brush Hooker's green into the yellow so that the colours merge together. Mix a darker green from Hooker's green, phthalocyanine blue and a little cadmium yellow and brush this mixture into the lower part of the waves, feathering the mixture up into the yellow so that the colours blend imperceptibly on the paper. Brush over this darker green several times to build up the necessary density of tone.

7 Mix a dark blue from phthalocyanine blue and cerulean blue and brush this mixture into the lower part of the large wave, feathering the colour upward. Because the previous washes are still wet the colours spread and merge together on the paper, building up darker tones without completely blocking out the underlying colours. Use loose, swift brushstrokes and try to capture the energy and power of the sea.

8 Mix a mid-toned wash of yellow ochre and brush it over the texture paste on the rocks, adding raw sienna and sepia for the dark foreground.

Tip: Allow the colour to 'drift' into the sea so that it looks as if the sea is washing over the rocks. Unless you do this the rocks will simply look as if they are floating on the water.

9 Mix a greyish blue from violet and Hooker's green. Brush little touches of this colour into the waves and into the pools at the base of the rocks, making swirling brushstrokes to help convey the movement of the water.

10 Using the dark green mixture from Step 6 and the brown used on the rocks, put a few dark accents into the waves. Soften the brushstrokes by brushing them with clean water to blend them into the other wave colours.

11 When you are sure that the paint is completely dry, gently rub off the masking fluid with your fingertips to reveal the foaming crests of the waves and the spattered highlights on the water.

Assessment time

Now that all the masking fluid has been removed, you can see how effectively the white of the paper has been reserved for the swirls and flecks of foam in the sea. However, these areas now look glaringly white and stark: they need to be toned down so that they become an integral part of the scene. However, you will need to take great care not to lose the very free, spontaneous nature of the swirling lines or the water will start to look too static and overworked. The contrast between the light and the very dark areas also needs to be strengthened a little in order to give a better feeling of the volume of the waves.

The exposed areas are much too bright.

The colours work well in this area, but there is not enough of a sense of the direction in which the water is moving.

12 Mix an opaque mauve from permanent white gouache, violet and a tiny touch of burnt sienna. Brush this mixture under the crest of the main wave, so that it looks like shadows under the very bright, white foam.

13 The exposed white areas look too stark against the dark colours of the water and rocks. Mix a very pale opaque blue from cobalt blue and permanent white gouache and cover up the exposed swirls of white in the water.

14 Soften the harsh markings by brushing over more of the cobalt blue and gouache mixture. Paint some swirls of white gouache at the base of the main wave. Putting a little opaque colour into the water helps to give it some solidity.

15 Spatter a few specks of white gouache above the crest of the wave for the flecks of foam that fly into the air. Do not overdo it: too much gouache could easily overpower the light, translucent watercolour washes that you have worked so hard to create.

16 Spatter a few specks of the cobalt blue and white gouache mixture above the rocks. (This area is very dark and pure white gouache would look too stark.)

17 Stand back from the painting and assess the tonal values. You may find that you need to darken some of the colours in the centre of the painting.

18 Using the same dark brown mixture as before, build up the tones on the rocks. They need to stand out from the water that surrounds them.

The finished painting

This is a dramatic and carefully observed painting that captures the energy of the scene to perfection. Note the many different tones in the water and the way the brushstrokes echo the motion of the waves. Masking fluid has been used to reserve the white of the paper for the foam of the waves – a simple yet very effective technique for painting moving water. The rocks provide solidity and a sense of scale, but do not detract from the large wave that is hurtling forwards.

Spattering is the perfect technique for depicting foam-flecked waves.

Dark tones in this area contrast with the light edge of the breaking wave and help to give the water volume.

The rocks provide a necessary point of solidity in the scene.

Loose, swirling brushstrokes capture the motion of the sea.

Twilight river in mixed media

This demonstration combines watercolour and soft pastels – lovely for portraying the fleeting effects of light. Start by applying a light watercolour wash for the underlying colour. You can then put either broad strokes of pastel on top and smudge them with your fingertips (creating smooth areas such as the heavy cloud bases in this scene) or apply short dashes of different colours for areas such as the rippling water, allowing the colours to mix optically on the support.

At a glance, you might think that the cityscape along the horizon line is all the same tone. However, look out for those subtle differences in tone that reveal the spatial relationships of the buildings. These tonal differences tell us, for example, that the buildings are behind the bridge (because they are slightly lighter in tone) or that we are looking at the side of a building rather than its façade. If necessary, exaggerate them slightly so that the viewer can 'read' the scene accurately.

As watercolour is the basis for the early stages of this painting, remember the basic principle of watercolour painting, which is to work from light to dark, and put down the very lightest colours (here, the pale, warm yellow of the setting sun) first.

Materials

- *Heavy watercolour paper*
- *Watercolour paints: ultramarine blue, cadmium yellow, Venetian red, alizarin crimson, phthalocyanine blue*
- *Brushes: Selection of round brushes in different sizes*
- *HB pencil*
- *Soft pastels: blue-grey, mid-lilac, warm cream, peachy yellow, blue-violet*
- *Sponge*
- *Cotton bud (cotton swab)*

The scene

Here, the setting sun casts a wonderful golden glow over the river, while the gentle ripples in the water impart a sense of movement. It is a study of a moment in time. The heavy clouds, lit from behind, add drama to the scene. It is generally not advisable to position your main subject in the very centre of the picture space, but here the silhouettes provide bold, graphic shapes that, along with their reflections, link the sky and water together.

1 Dampen the top third of the paper with a sponge dipped in clean water. Using a large, round brush, lay a wash of dilute ultramarine blue over the sky. Leave to dry. Dampen the lower two thirds of the paper. Mix a very pale yellowy orange from cadmium yellow and a little Venetian red and apply it over this area. Leave to dry.

2 Using an HB pencil, lightly sketch in the shapes of the silhouetted buildings and bridge.

Tip: Shade the undersides of the arches on the bridges to remind yourself that these areas are darker.

3 Mix a dark purple-blue from alizarin crimson and phthalo blue. Using a fine brush, block in the silhouettes and their reflections, adding more water to the mix for the lighter tones.

Assessment time

The watercolour stage is now complete. Although the painting of the buildings is almost monochromatic, by carefully judging the tones, the artist has managed to convey the spatial relationships and give the scene surprising depth and texture. The next stage is to build up the colour and texture in the sky and water.

Paler tones indicate that the buildings are farther away than the bridge.

Pale washes provide the undercolour for both the sky and water.

4 Splay out the bristles on your brush to resemble a fan shape (or use a fan brush) and dry brush on the ripples emanating from the piers of the bridge.

5 Dip a cotton bud in clean water and gently wipe off some small streaks of blue to create lighter cloud patches in the sky. The benefit of using a cotton bud for this, rather than a brush, is that you have more control and can lift off very precise shapes. Dab off any excess water with paper towel or a dry cotton bud if necessary.

6 Block in the heavy clouds with a blue-grey soft pastel, blending it with a mid-lilac for the lighter parts.

7 Put in the golden colour of the sky, using a warm cream for the lighter patches and a peachy yellow for the darker tones, cutting in around the edges of the cloud.

8 Using the blue-grey pastel, lightly put in the dark ripples in the water, making sure you allow both the underlying wash and the texture of the paper to show through.

9 Use the same blue-grey to strengthen the dark reflection of the arch of the bridge.

10 Using a fine brush and the deep purple-blue from Step 3, paint in the boats and their reflections. At the same time, tidy up the silhouetted buildings and their reflections.

11 Using the warm cream and peachy yellow pastels, strengthen the golden tones on the water.

12 Make any final adjustments that are necessary in the sky, darkening the top of the image by just stroking the side of a blue-violet pastel over the paper.

The finished painting

This delicate study exploits the unique characteristics of both watercolour and soft pastels to perfection. The subtle, translucent watercolour washes provide the basic undercolour for the whole painting and give it a wonderful feeling of luminosity, while the broken colour of the pastels captures the effect of light sparkling on gently rippling water beautifully. The slightly rough texture of the paper, too, plays a part in giving the scene vitality.

The bridge is warmer and darker in tone than the background buildings, so it appears closer to the viewer.

There is a lovely interplay of colours on the water, which seems to shimmer in the reflected light of the setting sun.

The pastel marks are softly blended to create the dark, heavy clouds.

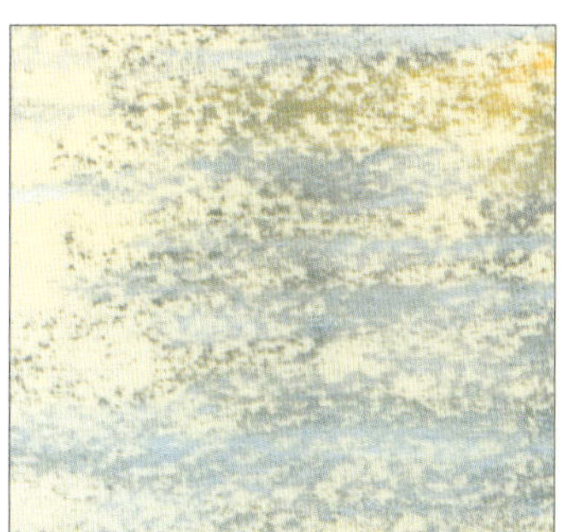

Lake with reflections in watercolour

Any artist would be happy to while away a few hours in these tranquil surroundings, sketching the bright, sunny colours of this lakeside scene in the heat of the summer, with the reflections of hillsides covered in trees.

However, straightforward symmetrical reflections can sometimes seem a little boring and predictable, so look out for other things that will add interest to your paintings. Sweeping curves, such as the foreshore on the right in this scene, help to lead the viewer's eye through the picture, while interesting textures such as the stones in the foreground are always a bonus.

This project also provides you with the challenge of painting submerged objects. Here you need to think about the rules of perspective: remember that things look paler and smaller the farther away they are. As an added complication, the way that water refracts lights also distorts the shape of submerged objects. Trust your eyes and paint what you see, rather than assuming that you know what shape things are. Remember to think of light and shade for the submerged stones, too.

Materials

- *B pencil*
- *Tracing paper*
- *140lb (300gsm) NOT watercolour paper, pre-stretched*
- *Watercolour paints: alizarin crimson, Naples yellow, phthalocyanine blue, phthalocyanine green, burnt sienna, French ultramarine, Payne's grey, quinacridone magenta*
- *Brushes: medium round, fine round, old brush for masking fluid*
- *Masking fluid*
- *Gum arabic*
- *Paper towel*

Tip: Leave the tracing paper attached to one side of the watercolour paper, so that you can flip it back over if necessary during the painting process and reaffirm any lines and shapes that have been covered by paint.

The scene

You can almost feel the heat of the sun when you look at this photograph of a lake in southern Spain. The foreshore and hillside are dry and dusty, while the lake itself appears to be slowly evaporating, exposing rocks in the shallows. Because of the angle at which the photograph was taken, the colours are actually less intense than they were in real life. The artist decided to exaggerate the colours slightly to emphasize the feeling of heat.

The distant mountains are muted in colour and will benefit from being made more intense in the painting.

Much of the foreground is made up of submerged stones. You could put some exposed stones in this area to add interest.

1 Using a B pencil, make an initial sketch on tracing paper to establish the main lines of your subject. When you are happy with the result, trace your sketch on to pre-stretched watercolour paper. Using an old brush, apply masking fluid to some of the large foreground stones. Leave to dry.

2 Mix alizarin crimson with a little Naples yellow and, using a medium round brush, brush the mixture over the mountains and up into the sky. Leave to dry. Mix a bright blue from phthalocyanine blue and a little phthalocyanine green. Dampen the sky with clear water and, while the paper is still wet, brush on the blue mixture, stopping along the ridge and drawing the colour down into the mountains. Leave to dry.

3 Mix a mid-toned orangey brown from Naples yellow and burnt sienna, and paint the dry and dusty foreshore of the lake, dropping in more burnt sienna for the darker areas. Leave to dry.

4 Mix a purplish grey from burnt sienna, French ultramarine and alizarin crimson. Using a fine round brush, brush clean water across the mountains and then brush on vertical marks of the grey mixture for the cooler, darker recesses. The paint will blur wet into wet on the damp paper, and spread, leaving no hard edges. Leave to dry.

5 Using the burnt sienna and Naples yellow mix and a medium round brush, paint the arid, sandy background on the top right of the painting. While this area is still wet, mix an olive green from phthalocyanine green, burnt sienna and a little Naples yellow and, using a medium round brush, paint in the loose shapes of trees and bushes. Paint the shadow areas in the trees in the same purplish-grey mix used in Step 4. Leave to dry.

6 Paint more trees on the left-hand side of the painting in the same way. Brush clean water across the sky. Mix Payne's grey with a little phthalocyanine green and, using the tip of the brush, dot this mixture into the damp sky area to denote the trees that stand out above the skyline. The colour will blur slightly. Leave to dry.

7 Using a B pencil, map out a few more stones on the shoreline. Mix a warm brown from burnt sienna and French ultramarine and brush in on to the foreground, working around the stones. Add more French ultramarine to the mixture and paint shadows around the edges of the stones to establish a three-dimensional effect. Leave to dry.

8 Brush clean water over the lake area. Mix burnt sienna with a little quinacridone magenta and, using a medium round brush, wash this mixture loosely over the shallow foreground of the lake, where partially submerged stones are clearly visible.

9 Brush phthalocyanine blue over the lake's centre. Wet the blank area at the top of the lake and brush on gum arabic. Add fine vertical strokes of Naples yellow, burnt sienna, quinacridone magenta mixed with French ultramarine, and the olive mixture used in Step 5. Leave to dry.

Assessment time
With the reflections in place, the painting is nearing its final stages. All that remains to be done is to put in some of the fine detail. Step back and think carefully about how you are going to do this. Far from making the painting look more realistic, too much detail would actually detract from the fresh, spontaneous quality of the overall scene.

This area lacks visual interest. Adding submerged stones here will indicate both the clarity of the water and how shallow it is at this point.

These stones look as if they are floating on the surface of the water.

10 Dip a medium round brush in clean water and gently lift off the flattened, elongated shapes of underwater stones, varying the sizes. You may need to stroke the brush backward and forward several times on the paper in order to loosen the paint.

11 As you lift off each shape, dab the area firmly with clean paper towel to remove any excess water. Turn and re-fold the paper towel each time you use it, to prevent the risk of dabbing paint back on.

12 The submerged stones in the foreground of the lake add visual interest to what would otherwise be a dull, blank area of the scene, but as yet they do not look three-dimensional. The large stones above the surface of the water and on the shoreline also need more texture if they are to look convincing.

13 Mix a dark brown shadow colour from burnt sienna and French ultramarine and, using a medium round brush, use this mixture to loosely paint the shadows underneath the submerged stones. This makes the stones look three-dimensional and allows them to stand out more clearly from the base of the lake. It also adds texture to the base of the lake. Leave to dry.

14 Using a fine brush, wet the area at the base of the reflection and touch in a mixture of French ultramarine and alizarin crimson to soften the edges. Mix burnt sienna with a little French ultramarine and use it to touch in the shadows under the largest rocks on the shoreline. Leave to dry. Using your fingertips, gently rub off the masking fluid.

15 Using a fine, almost dry brush, brush water over the exposed rocks and then drop in a very pale burnt sienna wash. Leave to dry. Dry brush a darker mixture of burnt sienna on to the rocks in places, for dark accents. To make the rocks look more three-dimensional, stroke on a little French ultramarine for the shadow areas.

The finished painting

This is a truly inviting image. The lake looks so realistic that you want to dabble your toes in it, while the feeling of heat is almost tangible.The artist's skilful use of complementary colours (the bright blue of the sky set against the rich orangey brown of the stones and earth) has helped to create a really vibrant piece of art.

Textural details, such as the dry brushwork on the rocks and the distant trees painted wet into wet, are subtle but effective, while the careful blending of colours in the reflections conveys the stillness of the water perfectly. The composition is simple, but the foreshore leads the eye in a sweeping curve right through the painting.

The lake is not a uniform blue throughout, but takes its colour from the objects that are reflected in it, as well as from the visible shallow areas.

A judiciously placed shadow under one edge of the stones helps to make them look three-dimensional.

The easiest way to paint the reflection of the small rocks in the distance is simply to paint a thin line of burnt sienna right through the middle.

Pond reflections in acrylics

Reflections in water are fascinating – but completely still and perfect mirror images of the nearby landforms or sky do not necessarily make for the most interesting drawing or painting. When the water is moving slightly, reflections are distorted and there is immediately more visual interest. Your challenge is then not only to capture the reflections convincingly, but also to create a gentle sense of movement.

Before you begin drawing or painting, take the time to look at both the shape and size of the ripples in the water. Are the ripples horizontal, caused by a slight breeze blowing over the water? Or are they circular, emanating from a subject moving through the water such as a small boat or water bird? Watch out for these shapes and form your brushstrokes accordingly.

Another useful tip if you are painting in watercolour or acrylics is to brush clean water over the paper before you apply any colour. Then, when you paint in the rippling lines of the reflections, the paint will spread and blur on the surface, wet into wet, creating soft-edged shapes that seem to have a movement of their very own.

Remember, too, the laws of perspective: in order to create a sense of distance, foreground ripples need to be larger and farther apart than those in the background.

Materials

- *Heavy watercolour paper*
- *HB pencil*
- *Acrylic paints: alizarin crimson, ultramarine blue, brilliant green, phthalo blue, yellow ochre, titanium white, lemon yellow*
- *Brushes: Selection of rounds and filberts in different sizes*

The scene

Unusually, the composition is split horizontally into thirds – the bankside area, the dark reflections of the foliage, and all the light, rippling reflections of the bare trees. Although the fisherman crouched on the bank is only a tiny part of this scene, he provides the focal point of the image. The ripples in the foreground water distort the reflections, adding interest.

1 Using an HB pencil, lightly sketch the main elements of the scene, putting in nothing more than generalized outline shapes for the bankside bushes. Take care to get the angles of the fisherman's shoulders and knees right – correctly observing details such as these is the key to the getting the pose right. Put in the main lines of the reflected trees as a guide for when you come to paint.

2 Apply a very dilute purple wash mixed from alizarin crimson and ultramarine blue over the reflection of the sky. Strengthen the mix for the tree trunk on the bank and the stonework along the bank edge. Mix a bright, mid-green from brilliant green and phthalo green and loosely wash it over the bushes on the left. Add more phthalo green and a little ultramarine for the dark green reflection in the centre of the image.

3 For the trees on the right-hand side, which are both darker and cooler in tone, add more ultramarine to the dark green mix from Step 2. Put in the fisherman's blue jacket in ultramarine. Wet the water area with clean water. Mix a dark brown from yellow ochre, ultramarine and alizarin crimson and, using a fine brush, put in the reflection of the main tree trunk and branches. The paint will spread on the damp paper, keeping the edges of the reflection soft.

4 Now start to build up some form in the bankside foliage, using mixes of yellow ochre, ultramarine and white in varying proportions. Half close your eyes so that you see the foliage as blocks of colour, rather than as individual branches of leaves.

5 Continue building up the foliage, adding lemon yellow for the lighter areas on the left. Paint the stonework of the banksides in a purple-pink mix of alizarin crimson, ultramarine and white. Begin putting in the dark blue-green reflection in the water with varying mixes of ultramarine and yellow ochre.

6 Work on the reflections, using the blue-green and purple-pink mixes from the previous step in varying proportions. Add white to some of the mixes to make them both lighter in colour and more opaque. Note how the reflections near the bank are broken by small ripples in the water: use short, horizontal brushstrokes to convey this.

7 Add more white to the blue-green mix and dot in the lightest patches in the foliage, varying the proportions of the colours in the mix as necessary. It is through these tonal variations that you will begin to give the foliage a realistic sense of form.

8 Now that the basic colours and shapes are in place, you can begin to refine the detail. Put in the branches and trunks within the foliage mass using the same purple-pink mix as before. Dry brush the grasses on the left-hand bank in a mix of brilliant green, white and yellow ochre. Paint the fisherman's jacket in a mix of ultramarine and white, and his jeans in ultramarine with a tiny amount of alizarin crimson. His skin tones are a mix of lemon yellow and alizarin.

Tip: Note how the fisherman's reflection is slightly distorted by the ripples in the water. It is only in completely still water that a reflection will be a perfect mirror image of the subject.

9 Put in the dark tones of the exposed patches of earth on the left bank in reddy browns mixed from alizarin crimson, yellow ochre and a touch of phthalo blue. Dot in the flowers using tiny dots of lemon yellow and lemon yellow mixed with white.

Tip: For really tiny dots such as these, try experimenting with using the tip of the brush handle, rather than the bristles, to apply the paint.

Assessment time

The foliage masses have been put in as generalized blocks of tone, but as they are quite a long way away it would be a mistake to attempt to render them in great detail. Note how the use of brighter, warmer tones in the foreground and cooler, bluer tones in the background helps to create a sense of distance. The painting is virtually complete and only a few finishing touches are needed – mostly in the bottom third of the image, where only the largest of the reflected branches have been painted.

Warm yellows and greens help to bring this area of the painting forward and imply that it is closer to the viewer than the bluer areas.

Cool, blue tones in the background indicate that this area is farther away.

Painting dark tones right up to the edge of the seated figure allows him to stand out more clearly from the background.

The reflections of many of the smaller branches are missing; as a result, this area of the painting is distractingly empty.

The viewer's eye is drawn to this area of the water, as it is so bright and featureless.

10 Wash over the water area with clean water. Using a fine brush and the same olivey, muted green mixes as before, strengthen the reflections of the large tree and put in more of the rippling, reflected lines of branches on the left-hand side. Hold the brush almost vertically, to create flowing, calligraphic marks.

11 Check the shapes and colours of the reflections, and touch in more muted greens on the left-hand side.

12 The reflections of the tower blocks on the right-hand side are very pale, but without the application of a little more colour this area will look very stark and white in relation to the rest of the image. Wash clean water over the area, then, using a neutral grey-brown and a fine brush, put in the rippled lines of the buildings and the lampposts on the bank.

13 Draw in the line of the fishing rod in pencil, then go over it with a dark purple-blue mixed from ultramarine and alizarin. When this is dry, very carefully brush a pale green highlight along the top edge.

The finished painting

This is a fairly loose, impressionistic sketch that is, nonetheless, full of atmosphere. The mood is one of quiet contemplation: the fisherman is positioned centrally on the width of the picture space, which generally creates a sense of calm in a picture, and, although he takes up only a small part of the image, it is to him that the viewer's eye is drawn. The limited palette of (predominantly) blues and greens enhances the feeling of tranquillity. The reflections take up about two-thirds of the image: were it not for the ripples in the water, which add a sense of movement, the painting might well look unbalanced.

The strong curve line of the bank helps to direct our eyes toward the fisherman.

The crouched figure of the fisherman is the focal point, even though he takes up only a small part of the picture space.

The foliage is painted as blocks of different tones of blue-green, creating a sense of depth within the foliage masses.

Note how the reflections blur, wet into wet, creating a sense of gentle movement in the water.

Woodland waterfall in watercolour

Waterfalls offer particular challenges to watercolour artists. Not only do you have to paint a liquid that lacks any real colour of its own, but you also need to make that liquid look wet and convey a sense of how quickly it is moving.

As always, the key is to try to convey an overall impression, rather than get caught up in attempting to recreate life, and paint every single water droplet and leaf. Before you start painting, and even before you make your first preliminary sketch, stop and think about what it is that appeals to you in the scene. Is it the intensity of the rushing water or the sunlight sparkling on the water surface? Is the waterfall itself the most important feature or are the surroundings just as interesting? This will help you to decide on the main focus of interest in your painting – and armed with this knowledge, you can decide how best to tackle the painting as a whole.

In real life, all your senses come into play: you can hear the water cascading down and feel the dappled sunlight on your face. In a painting, however, you have to convey these qualities through visual means alone. Sometimes this means you need to exaggerate certain aspects in order to get the message across – making the spray more dramatic, perhaps, or altering the composition to remove distracting features or make interesting ones more prominent.

Materials

- *B pencil*
- *Tracing paper*
- *140lb (300gsm) NOT watercolour paper, pre-stretched*
- *Watercolour paints: cadmium lemon, phthalocyanine green, Payne's grey, burnt sienna, phthalocyanine blue, alizarin crimson*
- *Brushes: large round, fine round, medium wash, old brush for masking fluid*
- *Masking fluid*
- *Low-tack masking tape*
- *Drawing paper to make mask*
- *Household candle*
- *Gum arabic*

The original scene

Although the scene is attractive, the lighting is flat and the colours dull. Here, the artist decided he needed to increase the contrast between light and shade. To do this, you need to carefully work out which areas will be hit by light from above and which will be in shadow. He also increased the size of the pool below the waterfall: paradoxically, the waterfall itself has more impact if it is surrounded by calmer areas.

The waterfall ends too near the bottom of the frame.

The colours are very subdued. Increasing the contrast between light and shade will make the painting more interesting.

1 Using a B pencil, make a sketch on tracing paper to establish the main lines of your subject and work out the size and shape of your painting. When you are happy with the result, transfer your tracing on to pre-stretched watercolour paper.

2 Place a sheet of white drawing paper between the watercolour paper and the tracing paper and draw around the waterfall area. Cut out the shape of the waterfall and place it in position on the watercolour paper as a mask, fixing it in place with low-tack masking tape. Gently rub a household candle over the area of water below the waterfall, keeping the strokes very loose. This will preserve some of the white of the paper and add an interesting texture.

3 Using an old brush, apply masking fluid over the white lines of the waterfall. Leave to dry.

4 Apply masking fluid to the bright highlight area of sky at the top of the picture area and leave to dry. Using a large round brush, brush clean water over the trees. Mix a strong wash of cadmium lemon and brush it over all the damp areas. Leave to dry.

5 Mask off the water area with paper. Mix a mid-toned green from cadmium lemon and a little phthalocyanine green. Holding a fine round brush at the same angle at which the branches grow, spatter water across the top of the picture. Spatter the damp area with green paint. Leave to dry.

6 Continue spattering first with water and then with the green mixture of phthalocyanine green and cadmium lemon, as in Step 5, until you achieve the right density of tone in the trees. Leave each application of spattering to dry completely before you apply the next one.

Tip: Spattering clean water on to the paper first, before you spatter on the paint mixture, means that the paint will spread and blur on the wet paper. If you spatter the paint on to dry paper, you will create crisply defined blobs of colour – a very different effect.

7 Add Payne's grey to the phthalocyanine green and cadmium lemon mixture and, using a fine brush, put in very dark tones along the water's edge in order to define the edge of the river bank.

8 Using a fine brush, brush burnt sienna between the leaves adjoining the dark spattered areas. Mix a rich brown from burnt sienna and Payne's grey and paint the tree trunks and branches. Leave to dry.

9 Using your fingertips, gently rub and peel the masking fluid off the sky area. The sky area is very bright in comparison with the rest of the scene, and so it is important to reserve these light areas in the early part of the painting – even though they will be toned down very slightly in the later stages.

Assessment time

The surrounding woodland is now almost complete. Before you go any further, make sure you have put in as much detail as you want here. The water takes its colour from what is reflected in it. Because of this it is essential that you establish the scenery around the waterfall before you begin to put in any of the water detail.

The line of the riverbank is crisply painted, establishing the course of the river.

The rocks in the waterfall have been marked in pencil, providing an underlying structure for the scene.

10 Using masking fluid, mask the long strokes of white that cascade down from the waterfall into the pool below. Leave to dry. Using a medium wash brush, brush clean water horizontally across the top of the water above the waterfall. Brush a little gum arabic on to the damp area. Keeping the brush fairly dry in order to control the colour, brush vertical strokes of phthalocyanine blue mixed with a little alizarin crimson and burnt sienna on to the damp area.

11 Brush straight lines of Payne's grey across the top of the waterfall to denote the edge over which the water topples. Mix Payne's grey with phthalocyanine blue and brush on to the waterfall itself, using a dry brush technique. On the lower part of the fall, make the marks longer and rougher to indicate the increased speed of the water. Leave to dry.

12 Re-wet the pool above the fall. Using a fine, round brush, touch cadmium lemon into the damp area. Dab on vertical strokes of cadmium lemon, burnt sienna, and phthalocyanine green for the tree trunk reflections. The colours will merge together and the fact that they are blurred helps to convey the wetness of the water.

13 Brush burnt sienna mixed with Payne's grey on to the cascade of water that runs into the pool.

Tip: By applying clean water to the surface before you paint, the strokes diffuse and blur, giving soft blends rather than hard-edged streaks of colour.

14 Working from the bottom of the waterfall upward, brush a mixture of Payne's grey and phthalocyanine blue into the waterfall. Note how the texture of the candle wax shows through. Keep the brush quite dry, dabbing off excess paint on paper towel, if necessary. Add a little alizarin crimson to the mixture for the darker water at the base of the fall.

15 Paint the rocks under the waterfall in a mixture of Payne's grey, phthalocyanine blue and a little alizarin crimson. Use the same mixture to paint more rocks poking up through the foam of the water. Dry brush water along the left and right edges of the painting and apply the rock colour – again with an almost dry brush. The paint will spread down into the damp area.

16 Stipple little dots of masking fluid on to the base of the pool below the waterfall for the white bubbles of foam. Leave to dry. Apply a light wash of phthalocyanine blue mixed with a little Payne's grey over the pool below the waterfall, brushing the paint on with loose, horizontal strokes. While the paint is still damp, run in a few darker vertical lines of the same mixture. Leave to dry.

17 Using a large brush and a darker version of the phthalocyanine blue and Payne's grey mixture, paint the dark area at the base of the pool with bold, zigzag-shaped brushstrokes. Leave to dry.

18 Using your fingertips, gently rub off the masking fluid on the lower half of the painting. Stand back and assess the tonal values of the painting as a whole. If the exposed area looks too white and stark, you may need to touch in some colour in the water areas to redress the overall balance of the scene.

The finished painting

This is a very lively rendition of a waterfall in full spate, which conveys the mood and atmosphere of the scene rather than capturing every leaf and twig in painstaking detail. Much of the paper is left white, in order to convey the full force of the rushing water. The painting has a stronger feeling of light and shade than the original photo, and hence more impact.

The white of the paper conveys the cascading, foaming water.

Skilful use of the wet-into-wet technique has allowed colours to merge on the paper, creating realistic-looking reflections.

Longer brushstrokes in the lower part of the waterfall help to create an impression of movement in the water.

Rock pools in mixed media

Working in mixed media can be an exciting process, as it offers you the chance to combine different kinds of marks and textural effects in the same painting. Before you start, however, think about the character of the landscape and decide which media will best suit your purpose. You can combine as many media as you wish, but think about how they will work together and try to exploit the unique properties of each.

In the rocky seashore scene demonstrated here, the artist used thin, translucent watercolour washes for the sky and background sea, soft pastel for subtle colour blends on the rocks, charcoal for strong, linear detailing, and acrylic paints mixed with modelling paste for the heavier impasto work on the foreground rocks. When you use modelling paste or texture paste, it is better to apply several thin layers rather than one thick one, allowing each layer to dry before you add the next.

It is generally a good idea to start by mapping out the main lines of a relatively complex scene such as this in pencil. Here, the artist used a water-soluble pencil, but you could use ordinary graphite if you prefer. These initial pencil marks may well be covered over by paint in the later stages, but the very act of making them will give you a better understanding of the natural rhythm of the landscape.

Materials

- *Heavy rough watercolour paper*
- *Watercolour paints: ultramarine blue, alizarin crimson*
- *Black water-soluble sketching pencil*
- *Acrylic paints: alizarin crimson, ultramarine blue, titanium white, yellow ochre*
- *High-viscosity acrylic modelling paste*
- *Soft pastels: orange-brown, pink-brown, blue, browns, ochres, bright olive green, bright green*
- *Charcoal: thin stick*
- *Brushes: Selection of rounds in various sizes*
- *Small painting knife*
- *Sponge*

The scene

The rocks lead the viewer's eye through the picture space in a series of diagonal lines to the sea and mountains in the background. The foreground is full of texture and the muted palette of soft blues, browns and ochres provides overall harmony.

1 Wet the paper all over with clean water. Mix a very dilute wash of ultramarine blue watercolour paint with a tiny bit of alizarin crimson and wash it over the support, leaving a few white patches in the sky for the cloud shapes. Dampening the paper first means that the paint will spread wet into wet over the support, leaving no hard-edged brush marks.

2 Using a black water-soluble sketching pencil, put in the main shapes of the rocks in the foreground and middle distance. Keep your marks very loose: do not try to include every crack or crevice, but simply pick out the main directional lines to help you establish the composition of the scene.

3 Mix a thick purple-pink from alizarin crimson, ultramarine blue and titanium white acrylic paints and blend in some acrylic modelling paste. Using a small painting knife, smear the mix over the foreground rocks, adding yellow ochre to the mix for the larger patches of lichen. Vary the texture: keep some areas very smooth and others highly textured.

4 Using orange-brown and pink-brown soft pastels, block in the seaweed-covered rocks in the middle distance. Delineate the darker patches within this area with a thin stick of charcoal.

Tips: • Do not overblend pastel colours – it is important that they retain their individuality, otherwise you will end up with very flat, muddy colours.

• Allow the texture of the paper to show through on the rocks.

5 Mix a cool blue from ultramarine and white acrylic paints with a tiny amount of alizarin crimson. Using a medium round brush, block in the shapes on the mountains in the background, varying the proportions of the colours to get some variation in tone and create a sense of recession.

6 Thin the paint mix by adding lots more water, then brush it over the sea in the background. Continue applying acrylic paint to the rocks, using the same mixes as before. Lightly stroke pink-brown or blue pastels over the foreground rock pools, then blend the marks with your fingers.

Assessment time

The main shapes and structures have been blocked in and we can see the beginnings of some texture and modelling on the rocks. However, many of the rocks still look rather flat and one-dimensional and it is hard to determine exactly which areas in the immediate foreground are water and which are rocks.

The sky looks bleached out, but this is easy to remedy. An initial pale wash often looks too pale once the painting has developed, but it is far better to build up the colour to the required density gradually, by adding more layers, than to make it too dark to start with. The sea in the background is also too pale and flat in relation to the rest of the image.

7 Overlay various browns, ochres and olive green soft pastels on the seaweed-covered rocks in the background, smoothing the marks with your fingers. To give the rocks more of a sense of form, put in the very darkest patches with strong charcoal marks.

8 Continue using the charcoal to block in the dark, shaded sides of the rocks, as well as for bold, linear marks for the cracks and crevices.

9 Using the small painting knife and the same purple-pink and acrylic modelling paste mixes as before, build up more texture on the foreground rocks. Then, using the tip of the knife, dot in the white foam of the wavelets in the sea so that you begin to create some sense of movement in the water.

10 Add more textural detail to the foreground rocks by dotting and stroking in some bright green pastels, for the lichen.

11 Mix a dilute, pale purple-grey from alizarin crimson, ultramarine and white acrylic paints and, using a fine brush, lightly touch more colour into the sky. Refine the shapes and tones of the mountains, too, using paler tones for the more distant mountains.

Tip: Use thick paint for solid land masses so that they stand out.

12 Apply a thin line of white acrylic paint along the base of the mountains, where they come down to the sea. Use the black water-soluble pencil to put in smaller stones on the spit of land in the middle distance.

13 Dab a small sponge in a blue-grey mix of ultramarine, alizarin crimson and white with a tiny bit of yellow ochre and lightly press it on to the foreground rocks to create a more lichen-like texture.

The finished painting

This is a lively, energetic painting that combines several media without ever allowing the unique qualities of each one to be overpowered by the others. Delicate watercolour washes capture the translucency of the sea and sky, while the solid land masses are conveyed in thicker, opaque acrylics. Soft pastels are applied lightly in the middle distance, allowing the texture of the paper to show through. The addition of modelling paste allows for heavier, impasto applications that perfectly convey the rough texture of the rocks. The colour palette is muted, consisting mostly of soft blues and pink-browns, with sharper touches of yellow ochre and bright olive greens in the lichen and seaweed.

The deep shadows under the rocks, drawn in charcoal, are an important part of the scene as they reinforce the point where the land ends and the water begins.

The solidity of the opaque acrylic paint contrasts well with the translucent watercolour used for the sky.

Combining acrylic paint with modelling paste creates a thick mix that is ideal for capturing the rough texture of these rocks.

Harbour moorings in watercolour

Ports and harbours are a never-ending source of inspiration for artists. The scene is constantly moving with the tide, and the changing seasons bring different conditions. Reflections in the water, patterns in the sand, and countless details from boat masts to barnacles: there are thousands of things to stir the imagination. The sound of lapping water and squawking gulls, and the smell of seaweed combine to make this one of the most enjoyable of all scenes to paint.

The key is to plan ahead and think about what you want to convey. Harbours are busy places, with lots of things going on and a host of details to distract the eye, and you will almost invariably need to simplify things when you are painting. Decide on your main focus of interest and construct your painting around it. You may find that you need to alter the position of certain elements within the picture space, or to subdue some details that draw attention away from the main subject and place more emphasis on others.

This particular project uses a wide range of classic watercolour techniques to create a timeless scene of a working harbour at low tide. Pay attention to the reflections and the way the light catches the water: these are what will make the painted scene come to life, and there is no better medium for these transient effects of the light than watercolour.

Materials

- *4B graphite pencil*
- *140lb (300gsm) NOT watercolour paper, pre-stretched*
- *Watercolour paints: cadmium orange, Naples yellow, phthalocyanine blue, cerulean blue, permanent rose, raw sienna, ultramarine blue, burnt umber, cadmium red, burnt sienna, light red*
- *Gouache paints: permanent white*
- *Brushes: old brush for masking, 2.5cm (1in) hake, small round, medium filbert, fine filbert, fine rigger*
- *Masking fluid*
- *Masking tape*
- *Plastic ruler or straightedge*

The scene

The tilted boats, wet sand and textures on the harbour wall all have the potential to make an interesting painting, but the sky and water are a little bland and there is no real focus of interest.

The town on the far side of the estuary is a little distracting.

The boats form a straight line across the image; it is unclear where the main focus of interest lies.

Preliminary sketch

The artist decided to make more of the water in his painting, introducing reflections that were not there in real life. He made this preliminary charcoal sketch to work out the tonal values of the scene. He then decided that the boats were too close together and that the scene was too cramped. In his final version, therefore, he widened the image so that the right-hand boat was farther away; he also introduced two figures walking across the sand to provide a sense of scale.

1 Using a 4B graphite pencil, sketch the scene, putting in the outlines of the harbour wall, distant hill, boats and figures. Look for the natural lines of balance of the figures and at how their weight is distributed: this is the key to getting the composition right. Indicate the different bands of sand and water in the foreground.

2 Using an old brush, apply masking fluid over the foreground water and the brightly lit right-hand side of the main boat to protect the highlight areas that you want to remain white in the finished painting. To get fine, straight lines, place a plastic ruler or straightedge on its side, rest the ferrule of the brush on top and gently glide the brush along.

3 Spatter a little masking fluid over the foreground of the scene to suggest some random texture and highlights in the sand and water. Be careful not to overdo it as you need no more than a hint of the sun glinting on these areas.

4 Mix a pale orange from cadmium orange and Naples yellow. Wet the sky in places with clean water. Using a hake brush, wash the orange mixture over the left-hand side of the sky and phthalocyanine blue over the right-hand side, leaving some gaps for clouds.

5 Using the same mixtures, carry the sky colours down into the water and sand, paying careful attention to the colours of the reflections in these areas. The warm colours used in the sky and sand set the mood for the rest of the painting.

6 Mix a dilute wash of pale greyish purple from cerulean blue and a little permanent rose. Wet selected areas of the sky with clean water so that the colours will merge on the paper. Using the hake brush, wash the mixture over the darkest areas of cloud on the left-hand side of the sky and bring the colour down into the background hills and water. Darken this greyish-purple mixture by adding more pigment to it and start putting a little colour on the shaded side of the largest boat in the scene.

7 Using the same mixture of cerulean blue and permanent rose, continue building up washes on the sides of the largest boat. It is better to start light and build up the colour to the correct density by applying several layers than to attempt to get the right shade of blue straight away.

8 Darken the harbour wall with a wash of cadmium orange mixed with Naples yellow. While still wet, drop in a mixture of phthalocyanine blue and a little raw sienna. Paint the reflections of the harbour wall in the wet sand. Apply a little cerulean blue to the main boat and the one behind it.

Tip: Do not make the wall too dark at this stage: assess how strong it should be in relation to the background.

9 Using a small round brush, apply a dark mixture of ultramarine blue, burnt umber and a little cadmium red to the main boat. Mix a purplish grey from cerulean blue and permanent rose and, using a ruler or straightedge as in Step 2, paint the shadow under the main boat. Leave to dry.

10 Using your fingertips, gently rub off the masking fluid to reveal the highlights on the water and sand.

11 Apply further washes, wet into wet, over the hill in the background of the scene so that the colours fuse together on the paper, using ultramarine blue and light red, with a touch of raw sienna for the dark areas in the middle distance. Continue building up the tones of the reflections and intensify the colour of the water by adding a little cerulean blue with a touch of Naples yellow.

12 To add more texture to the ridges of sand in the foreground, apply strokes of burnt sienna straight from the tube, lightly stroking an almost dry medium filbert brush over the dry painting surface. This allows the paint to catch on the raised tooth of the paper, creating expressive broken marks that are equally suitable for depicting the sparkle of light on the water.

Assessment time

The basic structure of the painting is now in place. There are four principal planes – the sky, the landscape on the far side of the river which has put some solidity into the centre of the picture, the boat and harbour wall (the principal centre of interest in the painting), and the immediate foreground, which is structured to lead the eye up to the boat. Now you need to tie everything together in terms of tones and colours.

All the boats need to be strengthened, as they are the main interest in the painting.

The land is not sufficiently well separated from the estuary area.

More texture and depth of tone are needed on the harbour wall to hold the viewer's eye within the picture area.

13 Now you can begin gradually to build up the washes to achieve the correct tonal values. Darken the harbour wall, using the original mixture of cadmium orange and a touch of raw sienna and build up the sandy area immediately in front of the main boat with the same mixture.

14 Using a small round brush and a dark mixture of ultramarine blue and light red, put in some of the detail on the boats. Note that, although the difference is quite subtle, one side of the boat is in shade and therefore darker than the other.

15 Now concentrate on the reflections of the boats, using colours similar to those used in the original washes. Do not make the reflections too opaque. Keep these washes watery and as simple as possible. Use vertical brushstrokes so that they look more like reflections.

16 Mix a warm blue from cerulean blue, permanent rose and a touch of burnt umber and put in the two figures and their reflections.

17 Using a fine rigger brush and resting the ferrule on a plastic ruler or straightedge, as in Step 2, put in the masts on the main boat in a mixture of ultramarine blue and light red and the rigging in a paler mixture of cerulean blue and permanent rose.

18 Using a filbert brush and the original mixture of cadmium orange and a little permanent rose, darken the stonework on the harbour wall. These uneven applications of colour give the wall texture and make it look more realistic.

The finished painting

This project brings together a range of classic watercolour techniques – wet into wet, building up layers of colour, using masking fluid to preserve the highlights, dry brush work – to create a lively painting that captures the atmosphere of the scene beautifully. The background is deliberately subdued in order to focus attention on the moorings. The main subject (the largest boat) is positioned at the intersection of the thirds, with the diagonal line of the sand directing the viewer's eye toward it. The different elements of the scene are perfectly balanced in terms of tone and composition.

The harbour wall is painted wet into wet to create muted but interesting colours and textures.

The town in the original scene has been replaced by an atmospheric blend of colours that suggests wooded hills.

The two walking figures introduce human interest to the scene and provide a sense of scale.

Glossary

Additive A substance added to paint to alter characteristics such as the paint's drying time and viscosity.
Alla prima A term used to describe a work (traditionally an oil painting) that is completed in a single session. *Alla prima* means 'at the first' in Italian.
Blending Merging adjacent colours or tones so that they merge into one another.
Body colour Opaque paint, such as gouache, which can obliterate underlying paint colour on the paper.
Charcoal Charcoal is made by charring willow, beech or vine twigs at very high temperatures in an airtight kiln. It is available in powder form and as sticks. It can also be mixed with a binder and pressed into sticks ('compressed' charcoal).
Colour
Complementary: colours opposite one another on the colour wheel.
Primary: a colour that cannot be produced by mixing other colours, but can only be manufactured. Red, yellow and blue are the three primary colours.
Secondary: a colour made by mixing equal amounts of two primary colours.
Tertiary: a colour produced by mixing equal amounts of a primary colour and the secondary colour next to it on the colour wheel.
Colour mixing
Optical colour mixing: applying one colour on top of another in such a way that both remain visible, although the appearance of each one is modified by the other. Also known as broken colour.
Physical colour mixing: blending two or more colours together to create another colour.
Cool colours Colours that contain blue and lie in the green-violet half of the colour wheel.
Composition The way in which the elements of a drawing are arranged within the picture space.

Closed composition: one in which the eye is held deliberately within the picture area.
Open composition: one that implies that the subject or scene continues beyond the confines of the picture area.
Conté crayon A drawing medium made from pigment and graphite bound with gum. Conté crayons are available as sticks and as pencils.
Dry brush The technique of dragging an almost dry brush, loaded with very little paint, across the surface of the support to make textured marks.
Eye level Your eye level in relation to the subject that you are drawing can make a considerable difference to the composition and mood of the drawing. Viewing things from a high eye level (looking down on them) separates elements in a scene; when viewed from a low eye level (looking up at them), elements tend to overlap.
Fat over lean A fundamental principle of oil painting. In order to minimize the risk of cracking, oil paints containing a lot of oil ('fat' paints) should never be applied over those that contain less oil ('lean' paints) – although the total oil content of any paint mixture should never exceed 50 per cent.
Fixative A substance sprayed on to drawings made in soft media such as charcoal, chalk and soft pastels to prevent them from smudging.
Foreshortening The illusion that objects are compressed in length as they recede from your view.
Form *See* Modelling.
Format The shape of a drawing or painting. The most usual formats are landscape (a drawing that is wider than it is tall) and portrait (a drawing that is taller than it is wide), but panoramic (long and thin) and square formats are also common.
Glaze A transparent layer of paint that is applied over a layer of dry paint. Light passes through the transparent glaze and is reflected back by the support or any underpainting. Glazing is a form of optical colour mixing as each glaze colour is separate from the next, with the mixing taking place within the eye.

Gouache *See* Body colour.
Graphite Graphite is a naturally occurring form of crystallized carbon. To make a drawing tool, it is mixed with ground clay and a binder and then moulded or extruded into strips or sticks. The sticks are used as they are; the strips are encased in wood to make graphite pencils. The proportion of clay in the mix determines how hard or soft the graphite stick or pencil is; the more clay, the harder it is.
Ground The prepared surface on which an artist works. Also a coating such as acrylic gesso or primer, which is applied to a drawing surface.
Hatching Drawing a series of parallel lines, at any angle, to indicate shadow areas. You can make the shading appear more dense by making the lines thicker or closer together.
Crosshatching: a series of lines that criss-cross each other at angles.
Highlight The point on an object where light strikes a reflective surface. Highlights can be drawn by leaving areas of the paper white or by removing colour or tone with an eraser.
Hue A colour in its pure state, unmixed with any other.
Impasto Impasto techniques involve applying and building oil or acrylic paint into a thick layer. Impasto work retains the mark of any brush or implement used to apply it.
Line and wash The technique of combining pen-and-ink work with a thin layer, or wash, of transparent paint (usually watercolour) or ink.
Manikin A jointed wooden figure that can be moved into almost any pose, enabling the artist to study proportions and angles. Also known as a lay figure.
Mask A material used to cover areas of

a drawing, either to prevent marks from touching the paper underneath or to allow the artist to work right up to the mask to create a crisp edge. There are three materials used for masking – masking tape, masking fluid and masking film (frisket paper).
Medium
(1) The material in which an artist chooses to work – pencil, pen, pastel and so on. (The plural is 'media'.)
(2) In painting, 'medium' is also a substance added to paint to alter the way in which it behaves – to make it thinner, for example. (The plural in this context is 'mediums'.)
Modelling Emphasizing the light and shadow areas of a subject through the use of tone or colour, in order to create a three-dimensional impression.
Negative shapes The spaces between objects in a drawing, often (but not always) the background to the subject.
Overlaying The technique of applying layers of watercolour paint over washes that have already dried in order to build up colour to the desired strength.
Palette
(1) The container or surface on which paint colours are mixed.
(2) The range of colours used by an artist.
Perspective A system whereby artists can create the illusion of three-dimensional space on the two-dimensional surface of the paper.
Aerial perspective: the way the atmosphere, combined with distance, influences the appearance of things. Also known as atmospheric perspective.
Linear perspective: this system exploits the fact that objects appear to be smaller the farther away they are from the viewer. The system is based on the fact that all parallel lines, when extended from a receding surface, meet at a point in space known as the vanishing point. When such lines are plotted accurately on the paper, the relative sizes of objects will appear correct in the drawing.
Single-point perspective: this occurs when objects are parallel to the picture plane. Lines parallel to the picture plane remain parallel, while parallel lines at 90 degrees to the picture plane converge.

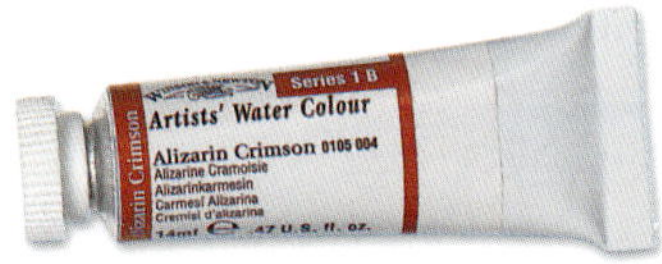

Two-point perspective: this must be used when you can see two sides of an object. Each side is at a different angle to the viewer and therefore each side has its own vanishing point.
Picture plane A imaginary vertical plane that defines the front of the picture area and corresponds with the surface of the drawing.
Positive shapes The tangible features (figures, trees, buildings, still-life objects etc.) that are being drawn.
Primer A substance that acts as a barrier between the support and the paints. Priming provides a smooth, clean surface on which to work.
Recession The effect of making objects appear to recede into the distance, achieved by using aerial perspective and tone. Distant objects appear paler.
Resist A substance that prevents one medium from touching the paper beneath it. Wax (in the form of candle wax or wax crayons) is the resist most commonly used in watercolour.
Sgraffito The technique of scratching off pigment to reveal either an underlying colour or the white of the paper. The word comes from the Italian verb *graffiare*, which means 'to scratch'.
Shade A colour that has been darkened by the addition of black or a little of its complementary colour.
Sketch A rough drawing or a preliminary attempt at working out a composition.
Support The surface on which a drawing is made – usually paper, but board and surfaces prepared with acrylic gesso are also widely used.
Solvent *See* Thinner.
Spattering The technique of flicking paint on to the support.
Thinner A liquid such as turpentine which is used to dilute oil paint. Also known as solvent.
Tint A colour that has been lightened. In pure watercolour a colour is lightened by adding water to the paint.
Tone The relative lightness or darkness of a colour.
Tooth The texture of a support. Some papers are very smooth and have little tooth, while others have a very pronounced texture.
Torchon A stump of tightly rolled paper with a pointed end, using for blending powdery mediums such as soft pastel, charcoal and graphite. Also known as a paper stump or tortillon.
Underdrawing A preliminary sketch on the canvas or paper, over which a picture is painted. It allows the artist to set down the lines of the subject, and erase and change them if necessary, before committing irrevocably to paint.
Underpainting A painting made to work out the composition and tonal structure before applying colour.
Value *See* Tone.
Vanishing point In linear perspective, the vanishing point is the point on the horizon at which parallel lines appear to converge.
Viewpoint The angle or position from which the artist chooses to draw his or her subject.
Warm colours Colours in which yellow or red are dominant. They lie in the red-yellow half of the colour wheel and appear to advance.
Wash A thin layer of transparent paint.
Flat wash: an evenly laid wash that exhibits no variation in tone.
Gradated wash: a wash that gradually changes in intensity from dark to light, or vice versa.
Variegated wash: a wash that changes from one colour to another.
Wet into wet The technique of applying paint to a wet surface or on top of an earlier wash that is still damp.
Wet on dry The technique of applying paint to dry paper or on top of an earlier wash that has dried completely.

Suppliers

Manufacturers

Daler-Rowney UK Ltd
PO Box 10
Bracknell
Berkshire RG12 8ST
United Kingdom
Tel: (01344) 461000
Website: www.daler-rowney.com

Derwent Cumberland Pencil Co.
Greta Bridge
Keswick
Cumbria CA12 5NG
United Kingdom
Tel: (017687) 73626
Website: www.pencils.co.uk

Sennelier
Max Sauer S.A.
Z.I. 2, rue Lamarck BP 204
22002 St-Brieuc Cedex
France
Tel: 02 96 68 20 00
Fax: 02 96 61 77 19
Website: www.sennelier.fr

Winsor & Newton
Whitefriars Avenue
Wealdstone
Harrow
Middlesex HA3 5RH
United Kingdom
Tel: (020) 8427 4343
Website: www.winsornewton.com

Stockists

United Kingdom

Art Express
Design House
Sizers Court
Yeadon LS19 6DP
Tel: (0113) 250 0077
Website: www.artexpress.co.uk

Atlantis Art Materials
7–9 Plumbers Row
London E1 1EQ
Tel: (020) 7377 8855
Website: www.atlantisart.co.uk

Ken Bromley Art Supplies
Curzon House, Curzon Road
Bolton BL1 4RW
Tel: (01204) 381900
Fax: (01204) 381123
E-mail: sales@artsupplies.co.uk
Website: www.artsupplies.co.uk

Dominoes
66 High Street, Leicester
Tel: (0116) 2533363
Fax: (0116) 2628066
E-mail: info@dominoestoys.co.uk
Website: www.dominoestoys.co.uk

Hobbycraft
Hobbycraft specialize in arts and crafts materials and own 20 stores around the UK.
Freephone (0800) 027 2387
Website: www.hobbycraft.co.uk

Jackson's Art Supplies Ltd
1 Farleigh Place
London N16 7SX
Tel: 0870 241 1849
Website: www.jacksonsart.co.uk

Paintworks
99–101 Kingsland Road
London E2 8AG
Tel: (020) 7729 7451
E-mail: shop@paintworks.biz
Website: www.paintworks.biz

Stuart R Stevenson
68 Clerkenwell Road
London EC1M 5QA
Tel: (020) 7253 1693
E-mail: info@stuartstevenson.co.uk
Website: www.stuartstevenson.co.uk

The Studio Art Shop
13 Crawford Arcade
King Street, Stirling FK8 1AX
Tel: (01786) 446454
E-mail: info@thestudioartshop.com
Website: www.thestudioartshop.com

Turnham Arts & Crafts
2 Bedford Park Corner
Turnham Green Terrace
London W4 1LS
Tel: (020) 8995 2872
Fax: (020) 8995 2873

United States

Many of the following companies operate retail outlets across the USA. For details of stores in your area, phone the contact number below or check out the relevant website.

Art Store
Website: www.artstore.com
(15 stores nationwide)

The Art Supply Warehouse
5325 Departure Drive
Raleigh
NC 27616-1835
Tel: (919) 878-5077
Fax: (919) 878-5075
Website: www.aswexpress.com

Dick Blick Art Materials
PO Box 1267
Galesburg
IL 61402-1267
Tel: (800) 828-4548
Website: www.dickblick.com
(More than 30 stores in 12 states)

Hobby Lobby
Website: www.hobbylobby.com
(More than 300 stores in 27 states)

Madison Art Shop
17 Engleberg Terrace
Lakewood
New Jersey 08701
Tel: (732) 961-2211
Fax: (732) 961-1511
E-mail: mail@madisonartshop.com
Website: www.madisonartshop.com

Michaels Stores
8000 Bent Branch Drive
Irving
Texas 75063
Tel: 1-800-6432-4235
Website: www.michaels.com
(More than 750 stores in 48 states)

New York Central Art Supply
62 Third Avenue/11th Street
New York
NY 10003
Tel: (212) 473-7705
Fax: (212) 475-2513
E-mail: sales@nycentralart.com
Website: www.nycentralart.com

Rex Art
2263 SW 37 Avenue
Miami
FL 33145
Tel: (305) 445-1413
Fax: (305) 445-1412
Website: www.rexart.com

Canada

Colours Artist Suppliers
10660-105 Street
Edmonton
Alberta
Canada T5H 2W9
Tel: 1-800-661-9945
E-mail: info@artistsupplies.com
Website: www.artistsupplies.com

Curry's Art Store
490 Yonge Street
Toronto
Ontario
Tel: 416 967-6666
E-mail: info@currys.com
Website: www.currys.com

Island Blue Print
905 Fort Street
Victoria
British Columbia V8V 3K3
Tel: 250-385-9786
Fax: 250-385-1377
E-mail: info@islandblue.com
Website: www.islandblue.com

Kensington Art Supply
132 10th Street NW
Calgary
Alberta T2N 1V3
Tel: 403-283-2288
Fax: 403-206-7095
E-mail: info@kensingtonartsupply.com
Website: www.kensingtonartsupply.com

The Paint Spot
10516 Whyte Avenue
Edmonton
Alberta T6E 2A4
Tel: 780-432-0240
Fax: 780-439-5447
E-mail: info@paintspot.ca
Website: www.paintspot.ca

Australia

Art Materials
Website: www.artmaterials.com.au

The Artists Warehouse
65 Sheridan Street
Cairns
QLD 4870
Tel: (0740) 316-947
E-mail: sales@artistswarehouse.com.au
Website: www.artistswarehouse.com.au

Oxford Art Supplies Pty Ltd
221–225 Oxford Street
Darlinghurst
NSW 2010
Tel: (02) 9360 4066
Fax: (02) 9360 3461
Website: www.oxfordart.com.au

Oxford Art Supplies Pty Ltd
145 Victoria Avenue
Chatswood
NSW 2067
Tel: (02) 9417 8572
Fax: (02) 9417 7617
Website: www.oxfordart.com.au

Premier Art Supplies
43 Gilles Street
Adelaide
SA 5000
Tel: (618) 8212 5922
Fax: (618) 8231 0441
Website: www.premierart.com.au

New Zealand

Draw Art Supplies Ltd
PO Box 24022
5 Mahunga Drive
Mangere Bridge
Auckland
Tel: (09) 636 4989
Fax: (09) 636 5162
Website: www.draw-art.co.nz

Fine Art Supplies
PO Box 58018
18 Neil Park Drive
Greenmount
Auckland
Tel: (09) 274 8896
Website: www.fineartsupplies.co.nz

Art Supplies.co.nz
312 Ti Rakau Drive,
Botany, Auckland
Tel: (09) 273 9450
Website: www.artsupplies.co.nz

Index

Notes

Notes

Notes

Notes

Notes

Notes

NOTES

Notes